Understanding Women's Empowerment in South Asia

Asok Kumar Sarkar · Satyajit Das Gupta
Editors

Understanding Women's Empowerment in South Asia

Perspectives on Entitlements and Violations

Editors
Asok Kumar Sarkar
Department of Social Work
Visva-Bharati University
Santiniketan, West Bengal, India

Satyajit Das Gupta
Legal Aid Services, West Bengal
Kolkata, India

ISBN 978-981-16-7540-9   ISBN 978-981-16-7538-6 (eBook)
https://doi.org/10.1007/978-981-16-7538-6

© The Editor(s) (if applicable) and The Author(s) under exclusive license to Springer Nature Singapore Pte Ltd. 2024

This work is subject to copyright. All rights are solely and exclusively licensed by the Publisher, whether the whole or part of the material is concerned, specifically the rights of translation, reprinting, reuse of illustrations, recitation, broadcasting, reproduction on microfilms or in any other physical way, and transmission or information storage and retrieval, electronic adaptation, computer software, or by similar or dissimilar methodology now known or hereafter developed.
The use of general descriptive names, registered names, trademarks, service marks, etc. in this publication does not imply, even in the absence of a specific statement, that such names are exempt from the relevant protective laws and regulations and therefore free for general use.
The publisher, the authors and the editors are safe to assume that the advice and information in this book are believed to be true and accurate at the date of publication. Neither the publisher nor the authors or the editors give a warranty, expressed or implied, with respect to the material contained herein or for any errors or omissions that may have been made. The publisher remains neutral with regard to jurisdictional claims in published maps and institutional affiliations.

Cover illustration: Maram_shutterstock.com

This Palgrave Macmillan imprint is published by the registered company Springer Nature Singapore Pte Ltd.
The registered company address is: 152 Beach Road, #21-01/04 Gateway East, Singapore 189721, Singapore

If disposing of this product, please recycle the paper.

Preface

We shall begin with a brief statement on how the very idea of bringing together a select group of serving and retired academics with substantial experience of NGO-run and civil society-led service-oriented and capacity-building women's care and justice activities for contributions to this collection of articles germinated in the midst of what could be called "our progressive tryst" with the knowledge enterprise to unravel the juggernaut of women's empowerment. Initially, drawing upon our knowledge of the academic and civil society accomplishments of about a dozen women's studies experts from within and outside India, we had prepared a list of prospective contributors and subsequently, began a process of sustained discussions regarding our requirements and their preferences for specific contents of articles we thought they could write to cover different themes and issues from their proven areas of expertise in a multi-layered exposition of the problematic of women's empowerment. Finally, our dialogues with nine of these twelve experts could reach a point of fruition and they agreed to deal with topics we have chapterized in this collection, which are self-explanatory and self-sufficient in terms of their bearings on varied causes and consequences of women's empowerment in a variety of socio-historical and politico-cultural milieus.

In the specific context of our exploration of the problems of empowerment of severely dispossessed and discernibly excluded or marginalized women who remain trapped or get involved in process of trafficking as well as in the whirlwinds of forced prostitution and self-chosen sex work, some of our contributors have accorded special weightage to the "lived realities" of these women, the "life-story" data for which has been procured with help of unstructured conversations with this extremely mobile and unimaginably floating group of interviewees. We should also like to mention in this connection that all due care and caution has been taken to ensure that the "standard ethical practices and injunctions of human subject research" followed in varied contemporary social science and human service projects and programs remain in place in matters of all our data collection exercises. Interrelated considerations of consent, confidentiality/anonymity and safety of these interviewees have been our topmost priority in so far as procurement of the said "life-story" data was concerned.

We would expect that this collection of writings will generate substantial intellectual resources for yet another stimulating churning of interest and enthusiasm among policymakers, academics, social activists, development functionaries, students and inclined laypersons concerned with women's studies in general and women's empowerment endeavors in particular. In their bid to grapple with myriad issues of women's empowerment, our contributors have enmeshed academic insights with civil society wisdom and thereby have emplotted narratives of a rare interventionist quality that, we hope, would lead to an enriched panorama of women's empowerment issues.

Santiniketan, India   Asok Kumar Sarkar
Kolkata, India   Satyajit Das Gupta

Contents

1. Introduction: Overarching Women's Empowerment   1
   Asok Kumar Sarkar and Satyajit Das Gupta

2. Before NGOs: Women's Organizations in Colonial India   17
   Geraldine Forbes

3. Politics of Women's Empowerment and Non-Governmental Organisations   35
   Malini Bhattacharya

4. NGO Activism and Women's Empowerment in India   49
   Biswajit Ghosh

5. Women's Participation in Rural Local Governance of Bangladesh: Progress and Challenges   75
   Soma Roy Chowdhury
   and Mohammad Rejaul Karim Siddiquee

6. Reproductive Health of Women and Human Development in Nepal Practical Challenges and Policy Implications   97
   Ishara Mahat and Kamal Gautam

7. Role of Micro Finance in Empowering Women Entrepreneurs of Rural Sri Lanka   125
   Rathiranee Yogendrarajah

8	Lives in Neglect, Deceit and Violence: Voices and Agencies of Trafficked Women Satyajit Das Gupta	163
9	Multiplying Insecurity: Disempowerment of Women's Agency in the Logistics of Transnational Trafficking Networks of South Asia Paula Banerjee	185
10	Equalizing Gender Imbalance in a Globalized World—The Issue of Transnational Abandonment of Women Shamita Das Dasgupta	199
11	Understanding 'Consent' in Rape Laws Ruchira Goswami and Aratrika Choudhuri	225
Index		249

NOTES ON CONTRIBUTORS

Paula Banerjee is IDRC-Endowed Chair, Centre on Gender and Forced Displacement, Asian Institute of Technology, Bangkok, Thailand. She is former Professor, Department of South and Southeast Asian Studies, University of Calcutta, and Member, Mahanirban Calcutta Research Group. She is also former Vice Chancellor of the Sanskrit College and University, West Bengal, former Dean of Arts, University of Calcutta, and former President, International Association for Studies in Forced Migration. Her publications include Statelessness in South Asia (2016), Unstable Populations, Anxious States (edited 2013), Women in Indian Borderlands (edited, 2012), and Borders, Histories, Existences: Gender and Beyond (2010).

Malini Bhattacharya is a Retired Professor of English and former Director, School of Women's Studies, Jadavpur University. She was a member of the National Commission for Women (2005-2008) and Chairperson of the West Bengal Commission for Women (2008-2011) and in both capacities, had substantial involvement in an entire range of state and NGO-run women's rights and care programs and initiatives. Her publications include Globalization: Perspectives in Women's Studies (2004), Kaler Joyjatra (Translation of Percy Bysshe Shelley's Writings, 2015), and in Radha's Name—Widows and Other Women in Brindaban and Talking of Power (with Abhijit Sen et al., 2008).

Aratrika Choudhuri is a Delhi-based corporate lawyer working for AZB & Partners, one of the premier full-service law firms in India. She regularly advises and represents high-profile issuers and underwriters on securities offerings. She has contributed to several research papers and articles to leading publications, including the International Company & Commercial Law Review (2019), ELCOP Yearbook of Human Rights (2018), Oxford Indian Yearbook of Comparative Law (2016), and IUP Journal of Corporate Governance (2017).

Soma Roy Chowdhury is an independent consultant and enlisted as a practitioner and associate with the Governance & Justice Group, UK, which works with governments and development practitioners in applying the principles of the different UN Conventions to the practical context of a given country. Please visit http://www.governanceju stice.org for details. She has extensive experience in managing large-scale projects in the areas of Access to Justice, Justice Reform, Human Rights, Women's Rights, Workers Rights, Advocacy, Public Interest Litigation, Research, Organizational Capacity Building including Strategic Planning, Proposal Writing/Fund Raising, Project Management, Improved Case Management, Legal Data Tracking and Analysis, and Monitoring and Evaluation. Having worked with leading international development partners such as DFID, DANIDA, NORAD, NOVIB, GIZ, SDC, USAID, OSJI, and the UN, among others, she has over 20 years of expertise in the stated fields. Her publications include a Study on Violence against Women in Bangladesh 2008–2009 (2010), adapting the ILO Code of Practice: Workplace Violence in Service Sectors (2011), co-editing of Role of the Bangladesh National Human Rights Commission in Ending Corporal Punishment in Educational Settings (2016), besides serving on the panel of external reviewers during August 2022 for the review of articles assigned by Asian-Pacific Resource and Research Centre for Women (ARROW) Re: ARROW for Change (AFC) on Understanding the Intersections Between Sexual Reproductive and Heath Rights, Disability Rights and Gender in Ending All Forms of Violence and Discrimination.

Shamita Das Dasgupta is a co-founder of Manavi, a US-based organization that focuses on domestic and sexual violence against women in the South Asian community. She has taught Psychology and Women's Studies at Rutgers University and in the Clinical Law program of the New York University Law School. Her publications include Globalization and Transnational Surrogacy in India: Outsourcing Life (2014),

Mothers for Sale: Women in Kolkata's Sex Trade (2009), Body Evidence: Intimate Violence Against South Asian Women in America (2007), a Patchwork Shawl: Chronicles of South Asian Women in America (1998), and the Demon Slayers and Other Stories: Bengali Folktales (1995). In her retirement, she is enjoying writing mystery stories in Bangla.

Geraldine Forbes is a Distinguished Teaching Professor Emerita of History and Women's and Gender Studies, State University of New York Oswego. A pioneer in the field of women's history in Colonial India, her publications include Women in Modern India (1999); An Historian's Perspective: Indian Women and the Freedom Movement (1997); Women in Colonial India: Essays on Politics, Medicine and Historiography (2004); Lost Letters and Feminist History: the Political Friendship of Mohandas K. Gandhi and Sarala Devi Chaudhurani (2020); and the edited memoirs of Shudha Mazumdar (1989), Manmohini Zutshi Sahgal (1994), and Haimabati Sen (2000).

Kamal Gautam is a Professor in the Central Department of Education, Tribhuvan University, Nepal. He has contributed several articles to SciRJ (Scientific Research Journal).

Biswajit Ghosh was the former Vice Chancellor and Former Professor of Sociology at the University of Burdwan and was also a visiting member of the Faculties of the Jawaharlal Nehru University, Shivaji University, Tripura University, and Vidyasagar University. He has written three major policy documents for the UNICEF, Government of West Bengal, and Save the Children. Apart from 112 articles, he has authored three volumes: Interrogating Development: Discourses on Development in India Today (2012), Social Movement: Concepts, Issues and Experiences from India (2020), and Exploring Social Movements: Theories, Experiences, and Trends (2024). He is in the editorial board of many journals.

Ruchira Goswami teaches at the West Bengal National University of Juridical Sciences (NUJS), Kolkata, where she offers courses in Sociology, Film and Law, Gender and Law, and Child Rights Law. Her course on representation of law in films explores the portrayal of human rights and social justice issues of vulnerable groups in films of various genres. She was the Head of the Centre for Child Rights at NUJS, set up in partnership with UNICEF. Her areas of interests include feminist movements and legal reforms, children's rights, representation of law in films, and intellectual property and women's rights. She has coauthored a book: "The Violent Domestic: Law, its Practice and Strategies of Survival" (Zubaan 2022) and extensively worked on projects related to women's rights including a recent project on understanding survival and resilience of domestic violence survivors funded by the British Academy. Her publications are in International Human Rights Law and Women's Rights, Intellectual Property and Women's Rights, Right to Food, etc. She is closely associated with several human rights and women's rights organizations and conducts workshops and capacity building programs on human rights issues with various stakeholders.

Satyajit Das Gupta is Director, Post-Graduate Diploma Course in Counselling (Affiliated to the Calcutta University), Legal Aid Services, West Bengal, and Member, Ethics Committee, KolGO Trg, a conglomerate of several regional and national medical institutions and establishments. He has been associated with the Calcutta University's Women's Studies Research Centre, Netaji Subhas Open University, West Bengal, and the Women's Justice Initiative of the Human Rights Law Network, India. He also coordinated the Karachi-Calcutta-Dhaka Linkage Project on "Processes of Unprotected Work in South Asia for the International Institute of Social History," Amsterdam. His publications include Mukher Kathay Itihas [History by Words of Mouth, Edited, 1997 & 2019] and Final Report on the DFLF-LASWEB-DIHR Study Tour on Comparative Aspects of Public Interest Litigation in India and China (2012).

Ishara Mahat is a Lecturer in the Faculty of Social Science at the University of Ottawa and Carleton University, Canada. She has also worked as a consultant with different national and international organizations including McGill Food Security Institute, Canada, and CIDA, Nepal. She has co-edited Sustainable Livelihood Systems in Nepal: Principles, Practices and Prospects (2015).

Asok Kumar Sarkar is Professor of Social Work in Visva-Bharati, India, and Chairperson of the International Consortium for Social Development-Asia Pacific Branch (ICSDAP). His publications include NGOs-The New Lexicon of Health Care (2005), NGOs and Globalization (Edited, 2008), Human Development and Sustainability: Challenges and Strategies (Co-Edited, 2017), Welfare of Disadvantaged: Exploring Community Development Approach (Co-Edited, 2018), and Contextualizing Peace-Experiences of Contemporary India and Neighbouring

Countries (Co-Edited, 2021). He is the founding editor of "Journal of Social Work and Social Development," a UGC-CARE-listed Indian journal, and served from 2010 to 2017.

Mohammad Rejaul Karim Siddiquee is a socio-legal researcher, human rights activist, and a legal practitioner at the Supreme Court of Bangladesh. He worked for different national and international organizations including International Disability Alliance, BlueLaw International LLP, Maxwell Stamp PLC, IMC Worldwide, Bangladesh Legal Aid and Services Trust (BLAST), and Bangladesh National Women Lawyers' Association (BNWLA). His publications include Lawyer's Manual (2019) and DPO Advocacy Handbook (2019) on the Rights and Protection of Persons with Disabilities Act, 2013, Mobilizing Disabled Peoples' Organizations to Implement Bangladesh's Disability Law (2022), which was published in the Oxford Journal of Human Rights Practice. He is also the recipient of the Acumen Fellowship (2020).

Rathiranee Yogendrarajah is Department of Financial Management and Member, Faculty of Management Studies & Commerce, University of Jaffna, Sri Lanka. She has published more than hundred research papers on women's decision making, poverty alleviation, and empowerment through micro-credit endeavors in several international journals like International Journal of Business and Management Review, International Journal for Economics and Business Management, Pearl Journal of Management, Social Science and Humanities, International Journal in Management and Social Science, and European Journal of Business and Management.

List of Figures

Fig. 7.1 Minimalist and integrated approaches to micro finance 133
Fig. 7.2 Multiple regression between micro finance and women empowerment 145
Fig. 7.3 Multiple Regression between different variables of Micro finance and Women empowerment at HH level 147
Fig. 7.4 Multiple regression between different variables of microcredit and women's empowerment at the community level 150

LIST OF TABLES

Table 7.1	Sample population of the study	140
Table 7.2	Categories of self-employable jobs in Northern Province	141
Table 7.3	Regression analysis between micro finance and women's empowerment	144
Table 7.4	Regression analysis between the dimensions of micro finance and women empowerment at household level (model summary)	145
Table 7.5	Regression analysis between dimensions of micro finance and women empowerment at household level (ANOVA)	146
Table 7.6	Regression analysis between the dimensions of micro finance and women empowerment at household level (coefficients)	147
Table 7.7	Regression analysis between the dimensions of micro finance and women empowerment at community level (model summary)	149
Table 7.8	Regression analysis between the dimensions of micro finance and women empowerment at community level (ANOVA). ANOVA	149
Table 7.9	Regression analysis between the dimensions of micro finance and women empowerment at community level (coefficients)	149
Table 7.10	Hypotheses testing	153

CHAPTER 1

Introduction: Overarching Women's Empowerment

Asok Kumar Sarkar and Satyajit Das Gupta

I

Women's Empowerment: A Panoramic Conceptualization

The discernible multi-dimensionality of the concepts of "empowerment" in general and "women's empowerment" in particular has had inherently evolving historical and cultural connotations across several academic disciplines and varied geo-political domains of practical application. But for ensuring the clarity of the specific intellectual purpose of the overarching exercise we would like to carry out in this introduction, we will begin by referring to some crucial lessons derived from the history of the concept of empowerment in the contemporary development discourse. Writing

---

A. K. Sarkar
Department of Social Work, Visva-Bharati University, Santiniketan, India
e-mail: asok.sarkar@visva-bharati.ac.in

S. Das Gupta (✉)
Legal Aid Services, West Bengal, Kolkata, India
e-mail: satyadg085@gmail.com

© The Author(s), under exclusive license to Springer Nature Singapore Pte Ltd. 2024
A. K. Sarkar and S. Das Gupta (Eds.), *Understanding Women's Empowerment in South Asia*,
https://doi.org/10.1007/978-981-16-7538-6_1

1

about two decades back, Anne-Emmanuele Calves had emphasized how the feminists were then protesting and resisting, locally as well as globally, against the 'neutralization and throwing off track' of the concept of empowerment by the neoliberal, patriarchal and neocolonial development model that perpetuated and reinforced inequitable power relations, in the transformation of which lay the possibility of reconnecting with the original conception of empowerment and rejecting the individualist, de-politicized, vertical and "instrumental" definition of empowerment imposed by international development organizations.[1]

In another formulation that relates somewhat more structurally to a known world of women's activities, a three-dimensional model of women's empowerment has been proposed to gain a deeper understanding of women's empowerment in the field of microfinance services. This model proposes that women's empowerment can take place on three distinct dimensions: (1) the micro-level, referring to individuals' personal beliefs as well as actions, where personal empowerment can be observed; (2) the meso-level, referring to beliefs as well as actions in relation to relevant others, where relational empowerment can be observed; and (3) the macro-level, referring to outcomes in the broader, societal context where societal empowerment can be observed.[2]

It always remains instructive to note how in the midst of a densely positioned plethora of rather tendentiously positivist conceptual formulations of women's material well-being and mental entitlements male chauvinistic and patriarchal social policy practitioners have legitimized in the domain of mainstream discourses on globalized privatization of economic activities and structural adjustments wherein women's participation in these processes has led to an acutely burgeoning 'feminization of poverty'[3] in most developing and underdeveloped Third World countries; feminist critics have posed some very searching foundational questions regarding the role and fate of disadvantaged and underprivileged women in terms of the very purpose and impact of such paradigmatic developmental chnages.[4] Although women's lot in such social and cultural transformation processes has had regionally different features of deprivation, exploitative dealing and propensities for protest,[5] this plethora of particular regional variations in the extent and quality of women's well-being[6] relates closely to the following three key considerations of their 'lived realities' in family and workplace environments: (a) nature and extent of male involvement in domestic affairs[7]; (b) nature and extent of physical and mental abuse and violence at home and workplace[8] and

(c) nature and extent of 'unpaid' and 'gainful' work.[9] In the context of these substantive concerns and considerations of processes women's empowerment endeavors do have to be carried through, it should stand pretty much relevant to refer to what Ian Smillie considers "one of the best articulations of the 'empowerment approach' to women and development."[10]

Mentioning about Sara Longwe's recognition of the 'triple role' of women as 'reproducers,' as 'producers' and as 'community managers' and distinguishing between "issues like food production, which are the common concern of men and women everywhere, and the ways in which a particular food-related intervention may impinge on a woman's day, her role in the family, and her role in the community," Smillie goes on to point out how "Longwe breaks women's development into a hierarchy of five criteria": "The first and most basic has to do with welfare: the relative welfare between women and men. The second relates to access: do women have access, on an equal basis with men, to land, labour, credit, and so on. The third has to do with conscientization: an 'understanding of the difference between sex roles and gender roles, and that the latter are cultural and can be changed... a belief in sexual equality.' The fourth criterion is participation. 'Equality of participation means involving women ... in the same proportion in decision making bodies as their proportion in the community.' And the fifth criterion is control: 'equality of control over the distribution of benefits,' a balance of control between men and women so that neither side is in a position of dominance or subordination."[11]

One obvious logical corollary of this very widely prevalent development-welfare-empowerment continuum of women's individual and social existence may now take us into the varied realm of feminist writings for substantiation and validation of the same in terms of thoughts and insights coming from these empathetic observers of issues affecting women's lives across geo-political cultures and systems of governance. Hence, to that effect, we will now very briefly refer to a selective cross-section of writings by Western and Indian feminist academics and civil society functionaries,[12] all of whom have categorically focused on what we would call 'women's existential trials and trepidations in adversities of patriarchy.' The central tendency underlying their diverse analytical insights on and real-life knowledge of women's sufferance, exploitation, abuse and degradation builds on the following "five contexts of shifting gender regimes and power relations": (1) context of female well-being;

(2) context of social change and politics of accountable governance; (3) context of interpersonal and family violence; (4) context of intimate partner violence; and (5) context of neoliberal feminization of poverty and labor marginality.

Against the general backdrop of these ordeals women keep struggling perennially in a family-community-society continuum of negotiations, Dumpsey had constructed 'four accounts' of domestic violence on the basis of inputs coming from the criminal justice system, the legal and sociological/social science academia and the domestic violence advocacy community. These are: violence account, domestic account, structural inequality account and Johnson's account of the 'patriarchal terrorism' and 'situational couple violence.'[13] We do consider it quite instructive here to also refer to a select corpus of Naila Kabeer's critically acclaimed writings on the challenges and pitfalls of women's empowerment endeavors in Bangladesh wherein, in the context of probing the bottlenecks of such endeavors, she has shaded interesting light on the complicated enmeshing of the issues of citizenship, gender justice and paid work. Overwhelmingly rather, Kabeer thus emphasizes the crucial importance of women's struggle for both rights and entitlements in a male-dominated world of rugged and ubiquitous discriminatory encounters.[14]

These multifaceted existential encounters of women's lives have provided much of the thematic substance we have gone by in our selection of the contributors to this collection of writings on women's empowerment and the subjects and chapterization of their articles. In major part, we have wanted a broad narrative thread of violence against and violation of women's existence in the family-community-society continuum of happenings to run through all the chapters as an academic and civil society tour-de-force in historical and contemporary settings. One of our main objectives has been to move along the very highly contentious "path of women's lived experiences" in their depth and spread of such historical and contemporary settings and to do justice to the societal richness and eco-geographical adversities of the same, we have chosen to move from the local to the global ramifications of how women have had to brave and negotiate with all the ups and downs of these processes of change and transformation with a view to establishing their indomitably courageous and ever-improvising agencies as survivors and victims of forces that have always circumvented and/or hindered their empowerment.

II
Women's Engagements and Encounters in History, Theory and Society

In her richly documented article on women's organizations in colonial India, Geraldine Forbes artfully uses the narrative-building skill of a professional historian to establish the points of continuity shown by women-run non-governmental public actions of the past and contemporary times in 'defining goals, developing organisational structures, linking work to international agendas, and securing financial support from foreign sources.' Seeking to de-romanticize the past, which has been constructed as a time when women worked selflessly to improve the lives of women and also de-valorizing women's voluntary work in the colonial era, she ventures to argue that "women's organisations – in the past and the present – have to walk a thin line between advocacy for progressive agendas and losing the support of their base and society," arguing that "an organisation that gets its support from abroad is less beholden to the society within which it works" and that the paramount necessity is one of working for 'change and adaptation' through 'research and transparent practices.'

Before entering the very rugged terrain of women's responses and actions in a world of burgeoning violence, abuse and exploitative machinations perpetrated by incurably patriarchal forces, we have also deemed it important to set a macro-level theoretical agenda for understanding the underlying politico-economic forces of system movers and shakers that go a long way in hindering or advancing women's concerns for survival or emancipatory collective action. In the second chapter, Malini Bhattacharya has made an attempt to deal with some of these complex theoretical and ground-level issues by looking into what she has termed "politics of women's empowerment," maintaining that "when the term entered the discourse of women's movement, 'empowerment' could no longer remain a comfortably seamless term offering not only a panacea for gender-based discrimination, but it also acquired a distinct connotation of self-reflexivity by remaining amenable to critical questioning and analysis within the movement." Basing her narrative also on her own practical experiences of working with an entire range of women's care and rights NGOs, which she had earned in particular during her tenures at the National and West Bengal State Commissions for Women as well as from her active participation in various social and political movements of women, Bhattacharya charts out the merits and demerits of handling varied women's issues relating to service delivery and capacity-building by government-run agencies and NGOs.

She goes on to maintain that "gender inequality and gender injustice constitute an integrally connected set of perennial social problems, which arise from the socially embedded politics of patriarchy with its entangled considerations of class, caste and religion." She advances the argument that "empowerment of the disempowered sections of society, including that of women, cannot happen outside this extremely uneven playing field wherein inhospitable and/or hostile social and political forces conspire constantly against women. It can never be possible to invest women with power from above and it is only through a broadening of the democratic space and revitalization of the different institutions of civil society that we shall be able to proceed firmly in the direction of empowering women in the truest sense of the term."

In the context of the interchangeability and/or intermingling of the roles agencies of the state, NGOs and other civil society institutions play in ensuring women's rights and entitlements, the contentions and arguments made, in the next two chapters, by Biswajit Ghosh and Soma Roy Chowdhury would assume critical significance. Ghosh presents a detailed narrative exposition of how despite several well-known success stories of spirited and purposeful NGO-run development work on women's empowerment in India, these external interventions involving formation of self-help groups and microfinance activities fall far short of meeting the "myriad 'bread and butter' and other existential issues facing poor and disadvantaged women" owing to "multi-layered concerns and considerations arising out of caste, class, religion, culture and market-related pitfalls and dilemmas of development." Roy Chowdhury, on the other hand, while setting priorities for eliminating challenges to ensuring women's participation in rural local governance in Bangladesh, has opined against following a policy of quotas and reservations and very strongly established the need for "partnership between government and non-governmental organizations" to "eliminate gender discrimination and biases and barriers to effective participation of women in local politics" by creating effective 'institutional mechanisms through legislative reforms,' enhancing some administrative measures like 'increasing budgetary allocations,' 'strengthening the knowledge base on policy and strategy development,' 'addressing issues of violence and sexual harassment and abuse' and 'closing the gap between international human rights covenants and national laws, policies and practices.'

It thus stands pretty much warranted by the very logic of understanding women's welfare and entitlements that the essential 'micro-level' ground realities of programs and initiatives can indeed become genuine yardsticks of empowerment women acquire as a result of such NGO or state-run developmental endeavors. In this context, in Chapter 6, Ishara Mahat and Kamal Gautam have dealt with several practical challenges and policy implications relating to Nepalese women's reproductive health and human development to argue that "community-based organizations and local NGOs" can build effective mechanisms for mobilizing communities to develop "massive awareness for utilization of antenatal and postnatal services as well as delivery of integrated health services at local levels." Studying the impact of microfinance-based entrepreneurial activities on the empowerment of women in rural Northern Sri Lanka, Rothiranee Yogendrarajah has shown, in Chapter 7, that microfinance alone isn't sufficient for enhancing women's socio-economic status. She goes on to emphasize that along with monitoring and guidance for clients and stakeholders in matters of marketing, packaging and publicity, awareness of health care, nutrition, need for generation of savings and availabilities of insurance would also play crucial roles in maximizing the benefits of such microfinance activities.

Violating Women: Empowerment Against Abuse, Assaults and Abandonment

It stands axiomatically true that violence—physical, mental, economic and cultural—is an omnipotent and omnipresent reality of the lives of women of all classes and creeds and any meaningful attempt to empower women of any class or creed will have to negotiate perennially with the ways and means of all forms of violence as these keep spreading their tentacles into women's homes and social surroundings. One of the most conspicuous among these chronics is the very intricately interrelated phenomena of trafficking and sex work, two of the most prominent features of the oldest of flesh trades women have been the merchandise of since almost the inception of human civilization. Locating his exercise somewhere in between the discourses emanating from the two mutually antagonistic schools of thought represented by the liberal-feminist and other abolitionist mantle-bearers of anti-trafficking work, which have sustained the much-publicized "rescue-rehabilitation-re-integration" narrative of the government and NGO-run palliative anti-trafficking programs, and the radical feminist advocates of the "right to sex work" and also recognizing the crucial need to explore systemically viable ways of recovering the voices and agencies of the victims and survivors of trafficking, forced prostitution and variously chosen sex work, in Chapter 8, Satyajit Das Gupta has tried to draw a compact bunch of critical inferences on the family and community-based processes through which these activities have continued to thrive in a continuum of neglect, deprivation, exploitation, deceit and violent abuse of women and girls in areas where very poor and low-caste young Hindu and Muslim women get trafficked under the garb of offering domestic service and through the means of sham marriage mostly with north Indian men.

Drawing upon biographically structured narrative fragments of lived experience of a select group of victims and survivors of trafficking, many of whom get goaded into forced prostitution at some later stages or take up sex work thereafter, some macro-family and socio-economic background-related data collected through a purposefully conducted survey as well as some documentary information coming from court records and other administrative sources available with the families of the victims in connection with their complaints and cases against the traffickers, Das Gupta has uncovered interesting details of the involvement of victims' families and a section of panchayat functionaries and local police personnel in the multi-layered processes of trafficking and also pointed snippets of assertion on the part of those women and girls who come to acquire a certain economic stability on account of their earnings from sex work. He shows that trafficking and it's immediate and long-term aftermaths lead to a very "complicated enmeshing of personal, social, and political considerations in the intermingled and shifting spaces of material culture, systemic inequities, emotional or mental involvement, discernibly violent and exploitative power relationships, and individual motivations and ambitions." In Das Gupta's view, all these women and girls, whether victims or survivors of trafficking or prostitutes under compulsion or choosers of sex work, would feel empowered if their voices are heard and their agencies are recognized.

In the next chapter, Paula Banerjee has focused on "multiplying insecurity and disempowerment of women's agency in the logistics of transnational trafficking networks of South Asia." She, too, has critically looked into some of the established and received ways of dealing with the phenomenon of trafficking by maintaining that "evolution of the discourse on trafficking in the last few decades in the context of South

Asia is a muddled history of systematically equating notions of female vulnerability with that of victimhood by the media and migration with criminal activities by the state apparatus," contending that "in this age of sacred borders, by conflating trafficking with migration the states criminalize all those who are migrating. Also by conflating trafficking with sex work such criminalization is justified as these people are seen as sexually available and morally reprehensible." Referring to the huge number of women who migrate to India from Bangladesh and Nepal and also to the phenomenon of internal migration within several states of India and developing the crux of her argument on the basis of a couple of specific case studies and stories involving Bangladeshi Hindu, Muslim and Rohingya women migrants from Bangladesh and Myanmar, Banerjee succinctly makes the following observations: "xenophobia and misogynism symbolize a woman as alien and her body as polluting. It then becomes easy to criminalize her in the name of national security and punish her aberration. But women are not passive victims. They fight the situation and keep coming back so that they can survive and dream of a better future."

But this resilience and courage to confront adversities thrown up by societal processes and technologies of governance may not help women in ordeals of all shades, and in Chapter 10, Shamita Das Dasgupta has elaborated the sufferings of one such acutely perturbed group of Indian women who get deserted by their NRI spouses and the circumstances of their abandonment, emphasizing these male perpetrators' insensitivity to their wives' and children's hardships. She has attempted to discuss some of the issues that have arisen as community-based organizations (NGOs or CBOs), along with country governments, and have struggled to respond to the victims' needs, adroitly culling the experiences from her work at Manavi, the oldest South Asian culture and language-specific anti-violence against women organization in the U.S.

The phenomenon of wife desertion has indeed acquired much importance as a new transnational issue of women's empowerment endeavors of the current times of globalized marital culture and practices. Das Dasgupta maintains that the most pressing question the transnationally abandoned Indian women want answered is why they have been deserted by their husbands, which, she feels, may never be fully or satisfactorily resolved. Nevertheless, on the strength of the argument that a "community's culture, tradition of gender roles, and the intricacies of lived realities shape the types and substance of abuse against its womenfolk and that violence is not a static phenomenon, rather its contents and dynamics change according to current socio-political environments," Das Dasgupta has firmly "included abandonment of wives in the category of violence against women and has posited it against India's socio-cultural backdrop of marriage, tradition of patrilocality, role of natal family, divorce, and marital responsibilities." On top of all these factors, she holds, "the current issues of mass migration, economy, and the power differentials between the West and India have (also) to be taken into account."

In the end, then, it becomes rather obvious that prospects and pitfalls of women's empowerment struggles and initiatives get quite inextricably linked up with a range of ever-protruding and rather trickily intractable considerations of patriarchy and its conventions and conditionalities of power-wielding mechanisms that operate through the multi-prong apparatus of the state and community-society conglomerates. It is this wider discursivity of power relationships between the judicial arm of the state, civil society and sexual assaults upon women perpetrated through the instrumentality of rape that constitutes the core subject matter of the last chapter of this collection, Ruchira Goswami and Aratrika Choudhuri's 'Understanding 'Consent' in Rape Laws.' They have raised the argument that "public discourse on rape that emerged in the 1970s in India was marked by the dissonance between the conceptualization of rape in Indian legal discourses, on one hand and the emergent feminist movements on the other" and constructing quite a dense narrative of a good number of well-known landmark case laws dealing with varied rape-related issues, they have sought to show that "this dissonance has undergone far-reaching changes, in terms of content, structure and form" and "yet one aspect appears immutable: the indubitable existence of the gap and disconnect between these two discourses in spite of the passage of several decades since."

Moving up to the issues of sexual harassment and rape in workspaces from the time of the Vishaka Guidelines of the mid-1990s to those raised in the very recent #MeToo movement, they argue that "despite the shifting of onus of proving consent to the accused in custodial rape situations post the 1983 amendment, and the widespread public mobilization of Indian feminist discourses on women's sexuality and bodily autonomy, the change in the judicial discourse in regulating workplace sexuality and gradually moving away from emphasis on the complainant's character were very slow." Pointing at the judicial endorsement of an "inexplicably regressive patriarchal sexual mores of consent," they have emphasized the strategic significance of the 'sharing of experiences by survivors of sexual violence' and the need to "articulate their journeys of negotiating with the legal system." They also consider it very important to bring "to the forefront the stories of women from the underrepresented SC/ST categories, issues of caste-based commercial sexual exploitation, and victim-blaming in the Indian hinterland" and also "demonstrate the need for intersectionality of the #MeToo movement" as "the movement has been critiqued as operating among urban, middle class elite with digital access and also with little visibility or representation of women from disempowered communities who lack access to the internet, let alone the linguistic-technocratic skills/power to engage effectively in these spaces." Goswami and Choudhuri have concluded by exerting that "it becomes imperative that the feminist movement against sexual violence reach its critical mass in terms of intersectionality and participation of women from all sections of society."

Notes

1. Anne-Emannuele Calves, 'Empowerment: The History of a Key Concept in Development Discourse', Revue Tiers Monde, Vol. 200, No. 4, 2009, pp. 735–749 at (PDF) https://www.researchgate.net/publication/282978215_Empowerment_The_History_of_a_Key_Concept_in_Contemporary_Development_Discourse (Translated by Armand Colin from the original French version of the article "Anne-Emmanuèle Calvès, «Empowerment»: généalogie d'un concept clé du discours contemporain sur le développement").
2. Marloes A. Huis, Nina Hansen, Sabine Otten, and Robert Lensink, 'A Three-Dimensional Model of Women's Empowerment: Implications in the Field of Microfinance and Future Directions', Frontiers in Psychology, September 28, 2017, at https://doi.org/10.3389/fpsyg.2017.01678.
3. Sylvia H. Chant, Gender, Generation and Poverty: Exploring the 'Feminization of Poverty' in Africa, Asia and Latin America, Edward Elgar, Cheltenham, 2007.
4. Pamela Sparr, ed., Mortgaging Women's Lives: Feminist Critiques of Structural Adjustment, Zed Books, London, 1994; Haleh Afshar, ed., Women and Empowerment: Illustrations from the Third World, Palgrave Macmillan, London, 1998; Gita Sen,

'Gender Equality and Women's Empowerment: Feminist Mobilization for the SDGs', Special Issue: Knowledge and Politics in Setting and Measuring SDGs, Vol. 10, No. S1, 2019.
5. Valentine M. Mughadam, From Patriarchy to Empowerment: Women's Participation, Movements and Rights in the Middle East, North Africa and South Asia, Syracuse University Press, Syracuse, 2007.
6. Mary L. Connerley and Jiyun Wu, eds., Handbook on Well-Being of Working Women, Springer Netherlands, Dordrecht, 2016; Maria Sagrario Floro, 'Women's Well-Being, Poverty and Intensity', Feminist Economics, Vol. 1, No. 3, 1995; Jules Holroyd, Feminism and Well-Being—The Routledge Handbook of Philosophy of Well-Being (Routledge Handbooks Online), 2015 at https://www.routledgehandbooks.com/doi/10.4324/9781315682266.ch38.
7. Nalini Khurana and Ravi Verma, 'Men-Streaming' Women's Economic Empowerment', GENDER, December 13, 2018 in idr at https://idronline.org/men-streaming-womens-economic-empowerment/; Engaging Men in Women's Economic Empowerment and Entrepreneurship Development Interventions: An ILO-WED Issue Brief at https://www.ilo.org/wcmsp5/groups/public/---ed_emp/---emp_ent/---ifp_seed/documents/briefingnote/wcms_430936.pdf; Gender Equality and Women's Empowerment in India, National Family Health Survey (NFHS-3) India 2005–06, International Institute for Population Sciences, Deonar, Mumbai, Ministry of Health and Family Welfare, Government of India; 'Empowering Boys and Men to Achieve Gender Equality in India', Journal of Developing Societies, Vol. 26, No. 4, November 2010, pp. 455–471; Larissa Jennings, Muzi Na, Megan Cherewick, Michelle Hindin, Britta Mullany, and Saifuddin Ahmed, 'Women's Empowerment and Male Involvement in Antenatal Care: Analyses of Demographic and Health Surveys (DHS) in Selected African Countries', BMC Pregnancy and Childbirth, August 2014, Article No. 297 at https://bmcpregnancychildbirth.biomedcentral.com/articles/10.1186/1471-2393-14-297).
8. Women Empowerment, Social Norms and Domestic Violence: The Impact Initiative for Development Research, Principal Investigator: Paul Collier. Lead Organisation: University of Oxford

(Blavatnik School of Government) and Co-Investigators: Marije Leonie Groot Bruinderink (Amsterdam Institute for International Development, AIID); Ramadan Mohamed (American University in Cairo); Karlijn Morsink (University of Oxford); Wendy Janssens (Amsterdam Institute for Global Health & Development, AIGHD) at https://www.theimpactinitiative.net/project/women-empowerment-social-norms-and-domestic-violence; 'Exploring the Impacts of Women's Economic Empowerment Initiatives on Domestic Violence: A Summary Report for Oxfam's Knowledge Hub on Violence Against Women and Girls and Gender-Based Violence', Oxfarm Research Reports, March, 2019 at https://oxfamilibrary.openrepository.com/bitstream/handle/10546/620867/rr-womens-economic-empowement-domestic-violence-120919-en.pdf;jsessionid=C2CFD8A33B6B9817069DE478D9CFBADD?sequence=2; Leela Visaria, 'Violence Against Women in India: Is Empowerment a Protective Factor?', Economic and Political Weekly, Vol. 43, No. 48, November 29–December 5, 2008, pp. 60–66; Farwah Qasim and Varalakshmi Vemuru, 'Examining the Relationship Between Women's Empowerment and Gender-Based Violence: The Case of the Nigeria for Women Project', May 13, 2019 at https://blogs.worldbank.org/africacan/examining-relationship-between-women-empowerment-and-gender-based-violence-nigeria; Kavita Sethuraman, Richard Lansdown, and Keith Sullivan, 'Women's Empowerment and Domestic Violence: The Role of Sociocultural Determinants in Maternal and Child Undernutrition in Tribal and Rural Communities in South India', Food and Nutrition Bulletin, National Library of Medicine, National Centre for Biotechnology Information, Vol. 27, No. 2, June 2006 at https://pubmed.ncbi.nlm.nih.gov/16786979/.

9. Anweshaa Ghosh and Deepa Chopra, 'Paid Work, Unpaid Care Work and Women's Empowerment in Nepal', Taylor & Francis, Contemporary South Asia, Vol. 27, No. 4, November 2018, at https://www.tandfonline.com/doi/abs/10.1080/09584935.2019.1687646; Unpaid Work, 'Discussions at Empower Women, Empower Women—Unpaid Work; Unpaid Care Work: The Missing Link in the Analysis of Gender Gaps in Labour Outcomes', OECD Development Centre, December 2014 at

https://www.oecd.org/dev/development-gender/Unpaid_care_work.pdf; 'Women's Economic Empowerment—Alleviation of Unpaid Care Work', Bill & Melinda Gates Foundation at https://ww2.gatesfoundation.org/equal-is-greater/element/alleviation-of-unpaid-care-work/; 'Unpaid Care and Women's Empowerment: Lessons from Research and Practice', Policy Brief of the Growth and Economic Opportunities for Women (GrOW) Programme, International Development Research Centre (IDRC) at https://idl-bnc-idrc.dspacedirect.org/bitstream/handle/10625/56369/IDL-56369.pdf?sequence=2&isAllowed=y.

10. Ian Smillie, The Alms Bazaar: Altruism Under Fire—Nonprofit Organizations and International Development, Intermediate Technology Publications Ltd., London, 1995; See, in particular, Chapter-V entitled 'The Pink Elephant: Empowerment and the Status of Women'.

11. Ibid., p. 96 (of Chapter-V), Smillie refers to and quotes from Longwe's article entitled 'Gender Awareness: The Missing Element in the Third World Development Project', FINNIDA, 1989, a revised version of which was published in Changing Perceptions: Writings on Gender and Development, Oxfam, Oxford, 1991.

12. Gita Sen, Gender Equality and Women's Empowerment: Feminist Mobilization for the SDGs, Wiley Online Library, January, 2019, at https://onlinelibrary.wiley.com/doi/full/10.1111/1758-5899.12593; Cecilia M. B. Sadenberg, 'Liberal vs. Liberating Empowerment: A Latin American Feminist Perspective on Conceptualising Women's Empowerment' (Article first published December, 2008), in (eds.), Deepta Chopra and Catherine Müller, IDS Bulletin on 'Connecting Perspectives on Women's Empowerment', Vol. 47, No. 1A, March 2016 (Also at https://opendocs.ids.ac.uk/opendocs/bitstream/handle/20.500.12413/9698/IDSB_47_1A_10.190881968-2016.115.pdf?sequence=1); Sandra G. Turner and Tina M. Maschi, 'Feminist and Empowerment Theory and Social Work Practice', Journal of Social Work Practice, Vol. 29, No. 2, 2015, pp. 151–162 (Also see Taylor & Francis Online at https://www.tandfonline.com/doi/full/10.1080/02650533.2014.941282); Devendra Kothar, 'Empowering Women in India: Need for a Feminist Agenda', Journal of Health Management, Vol. 16, No. 2, June 2014, pp. 233–243 (Article first

published online: June 10, 2014 at https://doi.org/10.1177/ 0972063414526112); Michelle Madden Dempsey, 'What Counts as Domestic Violence? A Conceptual Analysis', William & Mary Journal of Race, Gender, and Social Justice, Vol. 12, No. 2, 2005–2006 (Online pdf version at https://scholarship.law.wm.edu/cgi/viewcontent.cgi?article=1106&context=wmjowl).
13. Dempsey, ibid., pp. 320–332.
14. Naila Kabeer, 'Empowerment, Citizenship and Gender Justice: A Contribution to Locally Grounded Theories of Change in Women's Lives', Ethics and Social Welfare, Vol. 6, No. 3: Gender Justice, 2012 (Taylor & Francis Online at https://www.tandfonline.com/doi/full/10.1080/17496535.2012.704055?scroll=top&needAccess=true); 'Economic Pathways to Women's Empowerment and Active Citizenship: What Does the Evidence From Bangladesh Tell Us?', The Journal of Development Studies, Vol. 53, No. 5, 2017: 'Microfinance and Gender: Issues, Challenges and the Road Ahead' guest edited by Supriya Garikipati at https://www.tandfonline.com/doi/full/10.1080/00220388.2016.1205730; 'Paid Work, Women's Empowerment and Gender Justice: Critical Pathways of Social Change', 2016 at http://s3-eu-west-1.amazonaws.com/pathwaysofempowerment-org-production/downloads/paid_work_women_s_empowerment_and_gender_justice_working_paper_original8b.

CHAPTER 2

Before NGOs: Women's Organizations in Colonial India

Geraldine Forbes

Srila Roy begins her article on contemporary Indian feminism with a quotation about the threat to "resistance" posed by NGOs. "Many," Srila Roy writes, "worry that institutionalisation and professionalisation in NGO activity undermine if not effectively erode the political edge of progressive social movements like women's movements"[1] (Roy 2011, p. 587). Other authors point to NGO reliance on funding streams, the professionalisation of their staffs, attention to the advice of experts, and careerism. The assumption behind these criticisms of contemporary NGOs is that women's organisations and movements in the past attracted women of passion who pursued social justice and egalitarian politics without any interest in remuneration. For example, Maitreyi Krishnaraj, who extolled the "activism and valiant mobilization" of the women's movement, wrote that the "liberal funding" of NGOs, which she characterised as providing careers for articulate women, casts "doubt on

G. Forbes (✉)
State University of New York Oswego, Oswego, NY, USA
e-mail: geraldine.forbes@oswego.edu

© The Author(s), under exclusive license to Springer Nature Singapore Pte Ltd. 2024
A. K. Sarkar and S. Das Gupta (Eds.), *Understanding Women's Empowerment in South Asia*,
https://doi.org/10.1007/978-981-16-7538-6_2

their role as the true spokespersons of peoples' interests"[2] (Krishnaraj 1998, p. 394). Vibhuti Patel concurred: NGOs have "taken away steam from the women's liberation movement"[3] (Patel 2012). These women and other feminists critical of the proliferation of NGOs connect the decline in autonomous women's organisations since the 1990s to what is disparagingly characterised as the "NGOisation" of feminist issues.

Agreeing with these critiques of NGOs requires a romanticised history of the autonomous women's movement of the 1970s and 1980s. While there was much that was exciting and productive about this period, historians are now discussing different aspects of this movement and what it accomplished[4] (Roy 2015). And while today's NGOs differ significantly from the autonomous organisations of the 1970s and 1980s, they can be compared to colonial-era women's organisations in terms of their models for associational structures; ties to foreign women; connections to international organisations, funding, and projects; and how participation affected the lives of the women who joined them. In this essay, I will discuss a variety of women's organisations in colonial India. This is not a history of women's organisations in the colonial period but rather an effort to draw out ways in which women's organisations in India have been connected to Western women, ideas, and institutions. These connections did not prevent political action or a progressive social agenda in the past and do not necessarily do so now.

In the present as in the past, the feminist movement has been international with women learning from one another, borrowing and adapting theory and strategies, and supporting each other in their efforts to gain rights for women. However, these exchanges occur within contexts of colonialism, imperialism, Western hegemony, nationalism, global capitalism, and economic liberalisation. Examining the history of women's organisations and the contexts in which they operated can free us from an idealised vision of the past and help us evaluate the contribution of contemporary NGOs to the women's movement.

MODELS FOR ASSOCIATIONAL STRUCTURES

When Saraladevi Chaudhurani began the *Bharat Stree Mahamandal* [Indian Women's Federation] in 1910, she was inspired by the model of the Young Women's Christian Association. She dreamed that what women had done in Christendom, women could do in Hindustan. ... form a great sisterhood of purely Indian women extending over the whole of the service of humanity ... – a sisterhood that would at once be an index to the energies of Indian womanhood as well as a story for everyone supplying energy to it.[5] (Sarala Devi 1911, p. 344)

The association began with a resolution passed at a meeting of the Ladies Section of the Indian National Social Conference in 1909. The next year, a group of women met in Lahore and elected Mrs. B. N. Sen president. Sarala Devi was elected General Secretary and charged with establishing the society, drawing up a constitution and set of rules, and making plans to set up branches around the country.

One could recount similar stories for many of the women's organisations that emerged between the first decade of the twentieth century and the 1930s. Saroj Nalini Dutt (1887–1925), the founder of the Women's Institute Movement in Bengal, began some of the earliest Mahila Samities in rural areas and played a major role in promoting interaction between Indian and British women. In the beginning, Saroj Nalini focused her attention on middle-class women since she defined the "woman problem" in much the same way as did members of her father's generation.

Seclusion, lack of formal education, and restrictions on movement were the main problems to be overcome; lectures, social organisations, and literature provided the method of attack. However, following trips to England and Japan, Saroj Nalini became more concerned with the economic problems of widows and lower-middle-class women. She subsequently shifted the focus of her work to economic uplift and embarked on a number of income-generating schemes.

Accompanying her husband to the districts of Bengal, Saroj Nalini organised village level *Mahila Samities* where women were encouraged to define their needs and present these to the proper authorities. These *Mahila Samities* also promoted formal and informal female education. Eager to establish their presence, the women imitated the organisations of the men they had married. Electing presidents and secretaries, they called meetings to order, required members to pay a membership fee, solicited resolutions, and kept minutes. Following the pattern established by the Raj, they presented their requests, for example for medical attention, to the appropriate civil servants.

In 1921, Saroj Nalini travelled to England and Japan with her husband and son. While abroad, she met and talked with a number of women leaders and visited innumerable women's organisations and institutions designed to improve women's situation. Greatly impressed by both the spirit of social service and the happiness and energy of young women, she returned to Bengal more committed to work in the villages. From 1921 until her death in 1925, she worked to establish rural women's village associations dedicated to the improvement of health and education[6] (Dutt 1941, pp. 101–109).

Whether in Lahore or Allahabad, or the districts of Bengal, these early women's organisations adopted the structure and trappings of associations in Europe. Presidents, secretaries, constitutions, rules of order, membership fees, stated goals, regular meetings and minutes, and plans of action were their hallmark. There was nothing organic or traditional about these organisations—they did not organise their meetings to coincide with traditional holidays, bind their members with women's rituals, or adopt names that reflected the everyday lives of their members. In this sense, they embraced the professionalism of colonial civil society, bringing the trappings of European organisations to the daily lives of women who, at least in some cases, were illiterate and had little knowledge of those they imitated.

Ties to Foreign Women

One does not have to look far to find close ties between foreign women and the Indian women who played prominent roles in the early women's organisations. Although the *Bharat Stree Mahamandal* did not have any British women on its organising committee, Sarala Devi wrote that women missionaries imparting home education to Indian women were her models. Rather than denouncing their work, she recognised that many Indian women had received education at their hands and the time had now come for Indian women to "take up the load" and spread female education to those families that feared Christian proselytising. In doing so, Indian women would be able to focus on the vernacular, influence elderly women, and help women of all religions and castes develop spiritually and morally[7] (Sarala Devi 1925, pp. 101–103).

The Women's Indian Association [WIA], one of the three major all-India organisations to emerge in the wake of World War I, had much closer ties with foreign women. Theosophists Margarat Cousins and Dorothy Jinarajadasa, both Irish feminists, met with members of the Tamil Madar Sangam [Tamil Ladies Association] formed to promote female education, particularly English language instruction, and the teaching of crafts. They founded a new organisation in 1917 and named it "the Women's Indian Association" because membership was open to both Indians and Europeans. Annie Besant became the first president with Margaret Cousins, Dorothy Jinarajadasa, Mrs. Malati Patwardhan, Mrs. Ammu Swaminathan, Mrs. Dadhabhoy, and Mrs. Ambujammal as Honorary Secretaries. By the end of the first year, there were 33 branches; within five years, 43 branches, 20 centres and 2,300 members.[8]

The other two major all-India women's organisations, the National Council of Women in India [NCWI] and the All-India Women's Conference [AIWC], begun in 1925 and 1927, respectively, were equally influenced by women from other countries. During World War I, Indian and British women who supported the war linked their various organisations in a Women's Council. After the war, Ishbel Maria Hamilton-Gordon, the Marchioness of Aberdeen and President of the International Council of Women from 1922 to 1936, invited the Indian Council to join the International Council in 1924.

Lady Mehribai Tata, the wife of Sir Dorab Tata and chair of the Executive Committee of the Bombay Council of the NCWI in its first year, adopted a philanthropic style modelled on that of upper-class English women. Because of their connections with British women and the wealth and status of the leading members, the NCWI remained aloof from politics in the early years. Socially, they opted for the status quo. As late as 1928, when the Bengal Council of the NCWI passed a resolution asking for a female probation officer for Calcutta, they recommended the appointment of a British woman. They argued proposals to have an Indian woman do this type of work were too "progressive" and should be avoided for some time[9] (Bengal Provincial Council Report, 1928–1929).

The more political and less conservative All-India Women's Conference [AIWC] was equally influenced by foreign women. When the Director of Public Instruction in Bengal asked Indian women to tell the government what kind of education they wanted for girls, Margaret Cousins sent letters to Indian women leaders throughout the country urging them to act. When the AIWC held its first meeting in Pune in 1927, there were 58 delegates from local conferences and over 2,000 observers (men and women). In her opening remarks, the Rani of Sangli made it clear that the AIWC was not imitating Western models. Indian girls, she insisted, needed a special type of education, not feminist in nature for that would imply antagonism between men and women, but an education to help them understand their position as "supplemental" to that of men. The first President, the Maharani Chimnabai Saheb Gaekwad of Baroda, focused on social customs—especially purdah and child marriage—that she argued hindered efforts to promote female literacy. This was a time of women's awakening, she said, noting women's new interest in politics but she too called for education compatible with "women's nature." Over the years, the AIWC enlarged its focus to include a wide range of social issues and became involved in the freedom struggle. By the mid-1930s, they no longer wanted British women in leadership positions.

While the role of foreign women diminished with time and the growth of the nationalist movement, there can be no doubt their views of women's roles in society, organisational models, and financial support played a role in the development of Indian women's organisations. The role of foreign women in the movement to gain the vote is especially significant. The first franchise delegation of Indian women, which met members of the Montagu-Chelmsford Committee, included Annie Besant, Margaret Cousins, and Dorothy Jinarajadasa. Margaret Cousins had applied for an audience for women and inserted

> a couple of extra sentences about political rights, or rather 'opportunities' in the draft of the memorandum. I know the women interested in the deputation believed in being citizens of their country and they wrote agreeing to the addition, so the vote was claimed.[10] (Cousins 1941, p. 33)

When Herabai Tata and her daughter Mithan went to London in 1919 to give evidence before the Joint Parliamentary Committee on the Government of India bill, they met and worked with members of two British organisations, the Women's Freedom League and Women's International League, who lobbied on their behalf[11] (Bombay Chronicle 1920, p. 12).

The appointment of the Simon Commission in 1927 led to the second stage of the "votes for women" movement with the major Indian women's organisations boycotting the Commission. To counter this move, British groups continued to lobby for the vote for Indian women and encouraged women without close ties to the nationalist movement to cooperate. For example, Member of Parliament and feminist Eleanor Rathbone, who had long been interested in India and the "problems" of Indian women, supported the extension of political rights to Indian women through a special franchise and the reservation of seats[12] (The

Hindu 1932, p. 7). Although she championed women's right to vote, Rathbone was a supporter of Katherine Mayo and like Mayo, dismissive of the Indian nationalist movement.

When the White Paper emerging from the Third Round Table Conference was published in 1933, it included voting rights for women with property and women who had passed the Matric exam as well as reservation of seats. The AIWC, WIA, and NCWI opposed these measures and supported, with Congress, universal adult franchise. When these organisations claimed to speak for all the women of India, they were challenged by individuals and women's organisations, many with close ties to Rathbone and other British feminists.

While the civic mindedness of foreign women, especially from Great Britain and the USA, and the organisations they formed provided a model for Indian women entering public life, Indian women came to resent the "maternal imperialism"[13] (Ramusack 1990, pp. 315–316) of their British mentors. Although the problems started much earlier, by the mid-1930s different political interests made it difficult for anyone to pretend that Indian and British women shared the same interests.

The Influence of International Organisations

Despite the fact that India was under colonial rule and not a "self-governing Colony, or Dominion or State," it became a founding member of the League of Nations at its inception. This anomaly, as Sundaram calls it,

> automatically meant her [India's] admission to the International Labour Organization, the permanent Court of International Justice, ... and several other League, semi-League and non-League organizations, which cropped up with such astounding rapidity and ingenuity during the inter-war period.[14] (Sundaram 2015)

One of the first gender topics tackled by the League was "White Slavery," a term coined in nineteenth-century England to draw a parallel between the lives of English girls in Europe's regulated brothels with the horrors of the Atlantic slave trade. Emerging from the movement to stop this traffic, the National Vigilance Association to Suppress Vice drafted the first International Agreement for the Suppression of the White Slave Traffic, enacted in 1904 and amended in 1910. Two years after the

League of Nations was created in 1919, it held an International Conference on White Slavery, which led to the 1921 International Convention that moved beyond "White Slavery" to condemn "Traffic in Women and Children."

The emerging Indian women's organisations in India, following the League of Nations, lobbied municipal governments and states in the 1920s and 1930s to pass legislation to suppress "Immoral Traffic." However, India's membership in the League presented thorny problems because of what Legg has called its "internal geography": British India and the princely states[15] (Legg 2014, p. 104). The League of Nations' Convention on trafficking could have regarded Indian princely states as "foreign states relative to India" and the procurement and transport of women and girls across borders to British India, international acts. But British officials viewed it as "impracticable" to follow the obligations imposed if the princely states were treated as foreign states. Instead, they considered the princely states and British India as signatories to the Convention[16] (Legg 2014, pp. 107–108). This meant that girls and women transported from Nepal to British India, for example, would not be considered "Trafficked."

The Convention required signatory countries to stop the White Slave Trade, prevent trafficking in women and girls, prosecute acts connected to trafficking, return trafficked women to their home countries, and deport traffickers. However, since officials tended to define "worthy trafficking victim[s]" as "young and virginal"[17] (Tambe 2009, p. 72), they seldom took action. In a Bombay police report to the League of Nations, it was made clear that a European woman "who had been seduced or been a prostitute" was not regarded as a victim of "white slavery." However, the League held that even prostitutes could be trafficked. More in sync with the League, missionary groups and vigilance associations, which included Indians, rescued women, housed them in shelters, and if foreigners, returned them to their own countries[18] (Tambe 2009, pp. 72–74).

Indian women entering public life in the 1920s and 1930s embraced the agenda of social purity activists from England. As I have discussed in another article, middle-class women new to public life were conscious of the criticism levelled at them and anxious to differentiate themselves from women of the streets[19] (Forbes 1988, pp. 54–97). Viewing this as a function of the "new patriarchy," which emerged under colonial rule, Indrani Chatterjee discussed how the "new Indian woman" had to be different in deportment and style from Western women and from the "indigenous common woman, who was characterised as quarrelsome, sexually promiscuous and vulgar"[20] (Chatterjee 1990, p. 27). When these middle-class women marched in demonstrations, they wore white or orange saris, underscoring their purity and setting themselves apart from other women who inhabited the streets. When they demanded the vote, they agonised over sharing polling places with propertied women who made their living from sex work. For example, Mrs. Kumudini Basu, secretary of the Bharat Stree Mahamandal, wanted to see the number of women voters increased but feared how voting might force respectable women to mix with and/or perhaps be confused with "undesirable women." Her solution: revive the Cantonment laws, register prostitutes with the police, and use these lists to force sex workers to use separate polling places[21] (Forbes 2002, pp. 221–239).

After the Montagu-Chelmsford Reforms, women and men pushed their legislatures to pass laws to suppress "Immoral Traffic." What becomes evident at this time is the shift—in India and worldwide—away from condemnation of the "fallen woman" to concern for rescue and prosecution of those who preyed on women and profited from their "immoral" labour. As Southard points out, we can clearly see the shift in views and the extent to which Indian women in these organisations took their clues from the League of Nations. The League opposed regulation—condemning licensing and government-run brothels as ineffective in controlling venereal disease or preventing exploitation[22] (Southard 1995, p. 229). Members of the All Bengal Women's Union [ABWU] regarded prostitutes as "victims of social and economic malaise," forced into sex work in their youth but interested in leaving the trade and becoming respectable[23] (Southard 1995, p. 229).

In supporting League initiatives, Indian women largely accepted League assumptions about prostitution and trafficking and saw social purity legislation as the best way to help women in the sex trade. Bombay was the first province to set up a Social Purity Committee (1920) and push for the Prevention of Prostitution law (1923). The same year, the municipality of Calcutta enacted legislation against brothels. In 1930, Madras passed the Suppression of Immoral Traffic Act and Bengal, in 1933, the Suppression of Immoral Traffic[24] (Southard 1995, pp. 219–220). Women and women's organisations played an important role in the passage of these laws and acts, which closed brothels and made it illegal to live off the earnings of a prostitute.

While there were few independent studies of women engaged in sex work, the League of Nations required its members to answer a questionnaire and the Indian government passed the task to its provincial governments. In Calcutta, the Commissioner of Police interviewed 50 prostitutes in 1935. Although there are significant gaps in the information presented (questions asked, circumstances, caste, amount of money earned, translation, editing, etc.), this survey is one of the few documents about Indian prostitutes in the first half of the twentieth century. Mining the report for details, Chatterjee maintains that the women's testimony refuted two common assumptions about prostitution: that marriage protected women, and that prostitutes were led to the trade after being raped or abducted. Of the women surveyed, all had been married, 17 had been widowed. Both married and widowed women suffered hardships of various kinds. The married women were driven out or ran away to escape abuse and ill treatment; destitute widows found employment as domestics but left this work to enter prostitution. Chatterjee writes,

> The larger common factor in all these women's backgrounds seems to be their emotional uprootedness before their entering "the life." Given that they had virtually no education and very little resources to make a living, being orphaned, widowed, oppressed within, and estranged from, the family might have pushed them into destitution.[25] (Chatterjee 1990, p. 34)

The women were not kidnapped/abducted/raped, but "recruited" from their villages—usually by local people—who provided protection for the journey to the city. While some of the women expressed regret for their decisions and testified they wanted to leave prostitution, others made it clear they were willing to remain in the trade, perhaps because they saw no alternative.

As Stephen Legg has pointed out, "as the internationalist movement to stamp out trafficking, and tolerated brothel zones, picked up pace, so did the codification of prostitutes and their treatment"[26] (Legg 2016, p. 8). Prostitutes were not excluded from the archive, Legg writes, but rather "over-written, interpreted and *represented*. They are spoken for, they do not speak"[27] (Legg 2016, p. 8). The women in organisations that wanted to eradicate prostitution and save women engaged in sex work must have been aware of the overlapping problems that affected these women: caste, poverty, gender discrimination, violence, and lack of options but this complexity seldom disturbed their stated goals.

The Bombay Hindu Women's Rescue Home Society [BHRHS] was similar to the ABWU in its views and goals. In 1928, the BHRHS admitted 29 women and 21 children to their rescue home; in 1929, they sheltered 70 women and 39 children. They described the majority of the women they accepted as "fallen," and others as "poor," "deserted by husbands," "sent by the courts," and "rescued."[28] Roughly half of the women were "fallen," one quarter had been "rescued [from brothels]" and one quarter were sent to the rescue home by the courts. The report included sketches of eight of the females with some details about age, region, and circumstances. Of the eight, two ran away with lovers and were deserted, three ran away following abuse, one had been sold into marriage, one had a spat with her husband, and one was sold to a brothel.[29]

What becomes obvious from even these brief biographies, which omit essential data about age, caste, social class, education, and families, is that all the women suffered from multiple problems. The women who ran away with lovers did so because they were abused, those who were abused often lacked family members, and some had run away after being threatened or attempting suicide. However, none of them were defined as "trafficked" since they had not been transported across international boundaries, even if they came from Nepal. What Indian women gained from the ILO was the focus on saving women from prostitution, which it was assumed could be done by closing brothels and enacting laws against living from the earnings of the sex trade. Assuming a particular route into sex work and the desire to be rescued and rehabilitated, women's organisations supported legislation and rescue homes, which provided shelter and often some training in handicrafts. Working on the basis of an international model, they did not study the women they wanted to rescue nor develop programmes that would address the intersectionality of the disadvantages these women faced.

Financial Support

From their inception, women's organisations struggled to support their activities. Interested in professionalism, they realised they needed space, a paid staff, and the means of communicating their work to the public. When the *Bharat Stree Mahamandal* was establishing its branches, Sarala

Devi visited each of the designated cities to meet with prominent women. To support the Mahamandal's educational work (payment for teachers, carriage fees for teachers, peon's salary, postage, and telegraphs), each member was required to pay an annual fee of Rs 1[30] (Sarala Devi 1911, p. 347). Since the fees were never sufficient to cover costs, the Mahamandal relied on special donations—in honour of a daughter's wedding or from wealthy women supporters.[31]

The National Council of Women in India set the annual membership fee at Rs 15 requiring Rs 500 to become a life member and Rs 1,000 to become a patron. When it was first organised, the National Council had three life patrons: the Dowager Begum Saheb of Bhopal, Maharani Saheb of Baroda, and Lady Dorab Tata. The president was H. H. Maharani of Baroda who continued to serve the organisation as president in 1928, 1930–1934, and 1936–1937. From 1938 to 1944, the Maharani Setu Parvati Bayi of Travancore was president. Other women who held important positions on the executive committee included Lady Dorab Tata; Miss Cornelia Sorabji, India's first lady barrister; Mrs. Tarabai Premchand, the wife of a wealthy banker; Mrs. Shaffi Tyabji, a member of one of Bombay's leading Muslim families; and Maharani Sucharu Devi of Mourbhanj, a daughter of Keshub Chunder Sen. These were women of wealth and position, capable of affording the expensive travel expected of the Council's leaders and with enough space to house the Council "office."

The ambitious programmes of the All Bengal Women's Union—legislation and setting up a rescue home—sent them in search of funds. In the early years, they relied on individuals but in later years they approached the Tata Iron and Steel works, the Royal Turf Club, and the Indian football Club. Other income-generating projects included raffles, performances, and the sale of handicraft items[32] (Southard 1995, p. 239).

Reading the records of rescue homes and other institutions, one becomes acutely aware of their need for adequate financial resources to support their plans, rent or buy space for projects and offices, and publish minutes and reports. The leaders of these organisations understood the importance of professionalism in handling organisational matters, including utilisation of funds. They also had to please their wealthy and socially conservative patrons and donors, which often meant avoiding feminist solutions. While some of the radical members of the AIWC addressed structural inequality by advocating equal education, divorce, women's right to inherit, and employment for women, those involved with "fallen women" focused on social purity legislation and "rescue."

How Women Were Affected?

It is easier to discuss the impact of these organisations on the women who ran them than on those they sought to help. Legislation such as the 1929 Child Marriage Restraint Act [Sarda Act] made little difference in the lives of girls but women's organisations hailed it as a great success, and as Sinha pointed out, it secured their place as full-fledged members of Indian society even though the act was not enforced.[33] In fact, the number of child marriages increased as people rushed to have their children married before the Act came into effect.[34]

Other efforts, for example to secure voting rights for women or to prohibit women from working in mines, signalled the commitment of women's organisations to the modernisation project but did not benefit the majority of women. The real beneficiaries were middle-class women who gained experience in organisational work. They learned first-hand the dynamics of the political world and how to make their influence felt in social and political spheres. Some became frustrated with the class and caste prejudices of their organisations and left to work with marginalised women who had remained largely untouched by the agendas of most major women's organisations.

Conclusions

Does this history of women's organisations in colonial India help us understand NGOs today? I began with the critique of contemporary NGOs as overly dependent on foreign expertise, agendas, and financial support. This critique valorises earlier women's organisations suggesting erosion of progressive agendas. This essay seeks to de-romanticise the past, which has been constructed as a time when women worked selflessly to improve the lives of women. The issues that contemporary NGOs face: defining their goals, developing organisational structures, linking their work to international agendas, and securing financial support, are not new. Whether we look at the National Council of Women in India or the All Bengal women's Union, the issues were similar. And, while we criticise today's NGOs for jumping to please a funding organisation in Japan, the USA, or the Netherlands, it is important to remember the fees paid by NCWI members and the ABWU's successful lobbying of Tata Iron and Steel Works for donations. Women's organisations—in the past and the present—have to walk a thin line between advocacy for progressive agendas and losing the support of their base and society. While one might argue that an organisation that gets all of its support from abroad is less beholden to the society within which it works, the Bombay Hindu Women's Rescue Home Society's dependence on patrons who believed in the sanctity of marriage led them to send most of their victims back to their husbands and seek grooms for unmarried women.

What is needed, I would argue, is the application of the same analytical tools we use as historians to look at the goals and work of present-day NGOs. Just as we can examine the caste and class prejudices of women's organisations in colonial India and ask who benefitted, we can look at how contemporary NGOs spend their funds and the extent to which they meet their goals. And, we can look for change and adaptation as NGOs grow in experience. Perhaps most important, we can call on NGOs to carry out research and be transparent in reporting their work. If NGOs are going to live up to their stated goals, they need to explore where they have been successful and where they have failed. This might, I realise, endanger their funding but it is essential for long-term success. Just as most Indian women's organisations in the colonial period adapted to the changing times and responded to the political situation, many NGOs have and are changing as they develop a deeper understanding of the needs of their clients.

Notes

1. Srila Roy, "Politics, Passion and Professionalization in Contemporary Indian Feminism," *Sociology* 45, no. 4 (August 2011): 587.
2. Maitreyi Krishnaraj, "Women and the Public Domain," *Economic and Political Weekly* 33, no. 8 (February 21–27, 1998): 394.
3. Vibuti Patel, "NGOisation of the Women's Movement: Survival vs Autonomy," FeministsIndia (March 12, 2012).
4. Srila Roy, "The Indian Women's Movement: Within and Beyond NGOization," *Journal of Asian Development* 10, no. 1 (2015): 96–117.
5. Sarala Devi, "A Women's Movement," *Modern Review* 10, no. 7–12 (October 1911): 344.

6. G.S. Dutt, *A Woman of India* (Calcutta, 1941); Padmini Sen Gupta, "Saroj Nalini Dutt," *Pioneer Women of India* (Bombay, 1944): 101–109; Geraldine Forbes, "Women's Movements in India," *Social Movements in India*, v. 2, Ed. M.S.A. Rao (New Delhi, 1979): 149–165.
7. Sarala Devi, "Bharar-Stri-Mahamandal: Antapur Strisiksa," *Bharati* 49, no. 1–3 (1925): 101–103. Trans. Hena Basu.
8. Kamala Bai L. Rau, *Smrutika: The Story of My Mother as Told by Herself* (Pune: Dr. Krishnabai Nimbkar, 1988): 26–32; "A New Society for Indian Ladies," *New India* (May 10, 1917): 9; Mrs. D. Jinarajadasa, "The Emancipation of Indian Women," *Transactions of the 8th Congress of the Federation of European National Societies of the Theosophical Society Held in Vienna* (July 21–16, 1923), ed. C.W. Dijkgraat (Amsterdam, 1923): 86; "Women's Indian Association," *Quinquennial Report, 1917–1922*, WIA Papers.
9. Bengal Provincial Council Report, NCWI Report, 1928–1929.
10. M. E. Cousins, *Indian Womanhood Today* (Allahabad, 1941): 33.
11. "Mrs. Besant and Indian Women's Franchise," *The Bombay Chronicle* (March 18, 1920): 12.
12. "Reservation of Seats for Women," *The Hindu* (February 19, 1932): 7.
13. Barbara Ramusack, "Cultural Missionaries, Maternal Imperialists, Feminist Allies: British Women Activists in India, 1865–1945," *Women's Studies International Forum* 13 (1990): 315–316.
14. Dr. Lanka Sundaram, "India in League of Nations," *Pragati* (May 24, 2015).
15. Stephen Legg, "An International Anomaly? Sovereignty, the League of Nations and India's Princely Geographies," *Journal of Historical Geography* 43 (2014): 104.
16. Ibid.: 107–108.
17. Ashwini Tambe, *Codes of Misconduct: Regulating Prostitution in Late Colonial Bombay* (University of Minneapolis Press, 2009): 72.
18. Tambe: 72–74.
19. Geraldine Forbes, "The Politics of Respectability: Indian Women and the Indian National Congress," *The Indian National Congress*, ed. D.A. Low (Delhi: Oxford University Press, 1988): 54–97.
20. Indrani Chatterjee, "Refracted Reality: The 1935 Calcutta Police Survey of Prostitutes," *Manushi* 57 (March–April 1990): 27.

21. Geraldine Forbes, "'Women of Character, Grit and Courage;' The Reservation Debate in Historical Perspective," *Between Tradition, Counter Tradition and Heresy*, ed. Kumud Sharma (New Delhi: Rainbow Publishers, 2002): 221–239.
22. Barbara Southard, *The Women's Movement and Colonial Politics in Bengal, 1921–1936* (New Delhi: Manohar, 1995): 229.
23. Southard: 229.
24. Southard: 219–220.
25. Chatterjee: 34.
26. Stephen Legg, "Anti-Vice Lives: Peopling the Archives of Interwar India," *Global Anti-Vice Activism, 1890–1950* (Cambridge: Cambridge University Press, 2016): 8.
27. Ibid.: 8.
28. *The Hindu Women's Rescue Home Society, Second Annual Report*, January 1, 1929 to December 31, 1929 (Bombay, 1929).
29. Ibid.: 21–23.
30. Sarala Devi, "A Women's Movement," 47.
31. Ibid.: 348–349.
32. Southard: 239.
33. Mrinalini Sinha, *Specters of Mother India: The Global Restructuring of an Empire* (Durham and London: Duke University Press, 2006), p. 153.
34. GOI, Home Dept. Judicial. File No. 818/33, 65/30.

Bibliography

A New Society for Indian Ladies. 1917. *New India*, May 10.
Bengal Provincial Council Report. *National Council of Women in India Report, 1928–1929*.
Chatterjee, Indrani. 1990. Refracted Reality: The 1935 Calcutta Police Survey of Prostitutes. *Manushi* 57 (March–April): 26–36.
Cousins, M.E. 1941. *Indian Womanhood Today*. Allahabad: Kitabistan.
Devi, Sarala. 1911. A Women's Movement. *Modern Review* 10 (7–12) (October): 344–350.
Devi, Sarala. 1925. Bharar-Stri-Mahamandal: Antapur Strisiksa [Indian Women's Federation: Women's Education Within the Home]. *Bharati* 49 (1–3): 101–103, trans. Hena Basu.

Dutt, G.S. 1941. *A Woman of India Being the Life of Saroj Nalini (Founder of the Women's Institute Movement in India)*. Calcutta.
Forbes, Geraldine. 1988. The Politics of Respectability: Indian Women and the Indian National Congress. In *The Indian National Congress: Centenary Hindsights*, ed. D.A. Low, 54–97. Delhi: Oxford University Press.
Forbes, Geraldine. 1979. Women's Movements in India: Traditional Symbols and New Roles. In *Social Movements in India*, vol. 2, ed. M.S.A. Rao, 149–165. New Delhi: Manohar.
Forbes, Geraldine. 2002. 'Women of Character, Grit and Courage;' The Reservation Debate in Historical Perspective. In *Between Tradition, Counter Tradition and Heresy: Contributions in Honour of Vina Mazumdar*, ed. Kumud Sharma, 221–239. New Delhi: Rainbow Publishers.
Government of India, Home Department. Judicial. File No. 818/33, 65/30.
Indian Franchise Committee. 1932. Oriental and India Office Library. Q/IFC/21-BengalEvidence File, E-Ben-132.
Jinarajadasa, D. 1923. The Emancipation of Indian Women. In *Transactions of the 8th Congress of the Federation of European National Societies of the Theosophical Society Held in Vienna*, July 21–16, ed. C.W. Dijkgraat. Amsterdam.
Krishnaraj, Maitreyi. 1998. Women and the Public Domain. *Economic and Political Weekly* 33 (8) (February 21–27): 391–395.
Legg, Stephen. 2014. An International Anomaly? Sovereignty, the League of Nations and India's Princely Geographies. *Journal of Historical Geography* 43: 96–110.
Legg, Stephen. 2016. Anti-Vice Lives: Peopling the Archives of Interwar India. In *Global Anti-Vice Activism, 1890–1950: Fighting Drinks, Drugs, and 'Immorality*. Cambridge: Cambridge University Press. Accessed from the University of Nottingham repository: http://eprints.nottingham.ac.uk/27895/1/ANTIVICE%20LIVES%20BLANK.pdf [November 26, 2016].
Mrs. Besant and Indian Women's Franchise. 1920. *The Bombay Chronicle*, March 18: 12.
Patel, Vibuti. 2012. NGOisation of the Women's Movement: Survival vs Autonomy. *FeministsIndia*, March 12 http://feministsindia.com/ngoisation-of-the-womens-movement-survival-vs-autonomy/ [Accessed December 23, 2016].
Ramusack, Barbara. 1990. Cultural Missionaries, Maternal Imperialists, Feminist Allies: British Women Activists in India, 1865–1945. *Women's Studies International Forum* 13: 309–321.
Rau, Kamala Bai. 1988. *Smrutika: The Story of My Mother as Told by Herself*, trans. Indirabai M. Rau. Pune: Dr. Krishnabai Nimbkar.
Reservation of Seats for Women. 1932. *The Hindu*, February 19: 7.

Roy, Srila. 2011. Politics, Passion and Professionalization in Contemporary Indian Feminism. *Sociology* 45 (4) (August): 587–602.
Roy, Srila. 2015. The Indian Women's Movement: Within and Beyond NGOization. *Journal of Asian Development* 10 (1): 96–117.
Sen Gupta, Padmini. 1944. Saroj Nalini Dutt. In *Pioneer Women of India*. Bombay: Thacker & Co.
Sinha, Mrinalini. 2006. *Specters of Mother India: The Global Restructuring of an Empire*. Durham and London: Duke University Press.
Southard, Barbara. 1995. *The Women's Movement and Colonial Politics in Bengal, 1921–1936*. New Delhi: Manohar.
Sundaram, Lanka. 2015. India in League of Nations. *Pragati*, May 24. http://pragati.nationalinterest.in/2015/05/india-in-league-of-nations/ [Accessed October 29, 2016].
Tambe, Ashwini. 2009. *Codes of Misconduct: Regulating Prostitution in Late Colonial Bombay*. Minneapolis: University of Minnesota Press.
The Hindu Women's Rescue Home Society, Second Annual Report, January 1, 1929 to December 31, 1929 (Bombay, 1929). Tara Premchand Papers.
Women's Indian Association. *Quinquennial Report, 1917–1922*. WIA Papers.

CHAPTER 3

Politics of Women's Empowerment and Non-Governmental Organisations

Malini Bhattacharya

I would like to begin by saying that this paper is largely of a general and impressionistic nature. I have been associated with the women's movement in India for a very long time now, and it seems to me that we have been witnessing a progressive thinning down of the links between academics and activists involved in this movement. So at this present juncture, it has become all the more important to put down in black and white, for posterity, the fragmented experiences of those who had remained involved in the movement since the time when these changes had not taken place. This urge has motivated me to do my little bit in this regard.

The term 'empowerment' itself entered the discourse of the women's movement in India sometime in the 1990s. The Country Paper presented by the Indian Government to the World Conference of Women in Beijing in 1995 read: 'The approach of the Eighth Plan (1992 - 1997), which

M. Bhattacharya (✉)
Kolkata, India
e-mail: malinibhattacharya43@gmail.com

© The Author(s), under exclusive license to Springer Nature Singapore Pte Ltd. 2024
A. K. Sarkar and S. Das Gupta (eds.), *Understanding Women's Empowerment in South Asia*,
https://doi.org/10.1007/978-981-16-7538-6_3

had regarded women as equal partners in development processes, marked a progress from the goal of development to that of empowerment of women'. International publicity and government approval have given the term a hegemonic edge that found expression subsequently in the declaration of a national women's empowerment policy or a government-sponsored 'Stree Shakti Varsh' (women's empowerment year) with a bevy of schemes for women. In fact, the evidence of the continuing potency of the term becomes apparent in the fact that in the year 2016 itself, the government came up with the second national policy on women's empowerment. But when the term entered the discourse of women's movement, 'empowerment' could no longer remain a comfortably seamless term offering not only a panacea for gender-based discrimination, but it also acquired a distinct connotation of self-reflexivity by remaining amenable to critical questioning and analysis within the movement.

The first Status Report on women in independent India had been entitled 'Towards Equality' (1974) and had been commissioned by the government as a document to be sent to the United Nations in preparation for the International Women's Year (1975). Its title bore reference to the basic promise made in the Indian Constitution to all citizens of India, including women, and the group of intrepid women researchers, who had worked on it, meant it to be a comprehensive and impartial critique of the extent to which that promise had been fulfilled after three decades since Independence (Mazumdar 2010, pp. 68–70). The clear-headed emphasis of the Report was on the importance of government intervention in providing impetus to such fulfilment. Two decades later, the rhetorical perspective had changed significantly both within and outside the sphere of government action on women's affairs.

Much greater emphasis is now being put on 'civil society' as a major stakeholder in the process of development. It is through the efforts of 'civil society', more than through the political establishment, that the recipients of benefits of governmental schemes and programmes are now to be given agency or 'decision-making power' in bringing about their own development. So 'empowerment' becomes a term signifying the transformation of the passive beneficiary into an active participant in developmental processes. This is the time when non-governmental organisations come to acquire overwhelming significance in government rhetoric as representatives of 'civil society' that's pre-eminently capable, by virtue of having an extra-political character, of mediating processes of empowerment of people in need of development.

Even from the mid-1970s, the emergence of autonomous groups/ platforms/voluntary organisations, which professed to be unattached ideologically or structurally to any political party, was noticed in our women's movement. Together with women's organisations, which functioned directly as wings of political parties in power or in opposition, or as their flexible mass-fronts of such parties, these autonomous groups and organisations had played a significant role, throughout the 1970s and 1980s, in mobilising women from different segments of society for struggles against gender injustice and inequality. At the same time various left-led women's organisations were developing some independent agenda on different women's issues through a great deal of critical internal deliberations. In spite of ideological differences and debates among themselves, which women's studies analysts have amply recorded (Armstrong 2013, pp. 58–69), these joint forces of the autonomous organisations and left-led women's organisations helped the women's movement of this period surge ahead powerfully in varied forms all over the country. The autonomous women's movements also made important contributions in combining research with activism, which became instrumental in laying the foundations of Women's Studies in India.

The two major issues of dowry and sexual violence had brought the different groups of the women's movement to the path of a united struggle. The Supreme Court's verdict in the Mathura Rape Case in 1979 exonerating the accused policemen involved in the crime had created opportunities for nationwide mobilisation and campaign in which both 'politically oriented' and 'autonomous' women's groups were active. The formation of the Dahej Virodhi Chetna Manch in 1982 was another example of joint action. As a result of the thrust of their united action, important amendments came to be enacted in the existing laws on dowry and rape. The retrograde Muslim Women's Act, which sought to subvert the Muslim woman's right to maintenance, and the shocking incident of the 'suttee' of Rup Kanwar in Rajasthan were other occasions in the 1980s when various participants in the women's movement were jointly able to expose the duplicity in the Indian state's approach to women's issues. But did it in any sense contribute to women's empowerment?

My argument here is that it did. Even autonomous women's groups highlighting the primacy of patriarchy over class did emphasise a politics of gender in which the existing bastions of social and political power were both found to be heavily weighed against women. The presence of these forces motivated the Left women's groups also to rethink the politics of patriarchy in a class-divided society. If politics signifies all kinds of organisation of power within a particular social formation (class-based, caste-based, gender-based) and if the different strands in the women's movement challenge that formation, whether at the social level or at the level of state power, then the initial burgeoning of the concept of 'empowerment' may be imagined situated here itself. In this instance, 'empowerment' comes through mobilisation of women, awareness-raising and agitation and the aim would remain one of decentralising and democratising the means and methods of governance so that there is a structural change towards a more even distribution of power in the entire social formation.

Mobilisation in the women's movement enhanced the capacity of the participants to actively facilitate this process, and this is what took the movement forward. The social message sent by the left and radical women's groups which developed through mobilisation and awareness-raising was so potent that organisations like Durga Vahini, the women's wing of the RSS, traditionally thriving on propagation of ideas of religion/caste-based authoritarian control, also had to revamp their public image by offering their own version of 'empowerment' to women mobilised by them. Anxiety to match what was happening in the secular women's movement was surely one of the reasons for what Tanika Sarkar called a 'flamboyant wave of a militant reclaiming of public spaces by Hindu women' (Sarkar 1998, p. 184).

In the mid-1990s, the Constitution was amended to facilitate local self-government through elected panchayats and municipalities and to decentralise economic and administrative governance. Women were given 33% reservation in these local bodies and this was another opening for foregrounding the issue of women's empowerment, which also led to their actual active engagement with developmental agenda at the grassroots levels. The amendments were passed in the Parliament at that time without any opposition, but the first batch of elected women, particularly in the rural local bodies, had a very tough time as their efforts to run these bodies were severely undermined by their families, by society and by administrative functionaries.

In particular, those women who were educationally backward and those who came from dalit or adivasi backgrounds were insulted and denigrated on account of being women and prevented from doing their work. Jokes about the 'panch-pati' ruling the roost in the name of his elected wife did the rounds and questions were raised as to who would make the 'rotis' at home if the woman attended the panchayat office. The erstwhile male 'pradhan' would refuse to vacate the 'pradhan's chair for his 'low-caste' female successor. In this power-struggle, the elected women members even had to face threats and violence. But a very large number of such elected women managed to learn their work in the face of varied adversities and to run the panchayats successfully even in states where women's movements were weak.

A very real empowerment of women, inhering in governance at the grassroots levels rather than in the agitational mode, was achieved here, and this was as much the locus of 'empowerment' as the agitations and campaigns on the streets because it brought a certain change in the balance of power. As disempowered women were able to handle different matters relating to decision-making, those on the other side, who had concentrated power in their hands for a long time, were able to have a feel of the new situation. These examples perhaps make it clear that I am looking at 'empowerment' as part of a democratic process in which, while the passive recipients had assumed a decisive role, others who had been all-powerful suffered a diminution of their status and influence. In the panchayati raj, these developments materialised at the level of utilisation of family land and at the social level where caste questions were pre-eminent and also at the administrative level where the government officer used to be looked upon as a minor god. This is what I would call the politics of empowerment. What might also be noted in this narrative is that in the examples of active participation, I have given, the term 'civil society' may be applied in a very comprehensive sense. In other words, for our purpose, the term may be taken to refer to agitating women's groups, whether they are affiliated to a political party or not as well as to elected women members of local bodies. According to the logic of this argument, the elitist nuance that the concept of 'civil society' sometimes acquires in the discourse of empowerment may be done away with.

In the term 'civil society', the word 'civil' is contrasted with the terms 'political', 'military', 'ecclesiastical' and 'criminal'. It is seen as a community of citizens who relate to one another in their secular life in different ways without the intervention of the polity and the administration. Quite often today, there is a shift from this broader definition so that the term comes to be used only for that restricted elitist segment of civil society which professes to be impartial and not swayed by political interests. In other words, to be 'above politics'. Governments are run by political parties and those who run the administration may flout the rule of law to serve their political masters of the moment, and even political parties in the opposition may have their own short-term electoral interests. In contrast to such vitiation of public cause, 'civil society' comes eventually to be highlighted in the discourse on empowerment in the above narrower sense, and it rests on the argument that it is privileged 'non-political' citizens alone who can keep a check on political bias to prevent partisan issues from undermining public interest.

The forward thrust in the women's movement in the 1980s and 1990s had also led to the recognition of another kind of 'semi-civil' institutions which did facilitate empowerment of women—the women's commissions functioning at the national and state levels. It was not without a long process of internal deliberations and active negotiations with the governmental authorities that the women's movement was able to ensure the creation of the National Commission for Women as a statutory body through enactment in Parliament in 1991. The first National Commission was set up the year after. The West Bengal Commission for Women, one of the first commissions to be set up at the state level, also came into being in 1992 and the majority of states followed suit. The women's commissions were nominated bodies and even their statutory quasi-judicial position could not always ensure sufficient autonomy and independence of status. At best, their power was only recommendatory.

The functioning of these institutions was an implicit recognition of the democratic norms of governance and the authority of civil society and in some states, where the commissions were able to maintain their vital ties with the women's movement, they succeeded in wresting a degree of functional autonomy and in making governments adopt some of their recommendations. They also got active support from many NGOs. Some effective steps could be taken following the implementation of laws against domestic violence and consequently, limited progress was achieved in sensitising the police, the administration and the judiciary regarding women's issues. This gave women more self-confidence to stand up against violence. But it is also true that in some states, if there were commissions at all, they were made to remain as a weak appendage to the state government and eventually in the course of the new millennium, their position was further compromised even as NGOs come to be recognised as the only true representatives of 'civil society', specifically for the reason that they had no obligation to any political party and could be impartial mediators in the agenda of empowerment.

So what is being emphasised here is the distinction between women's organisations with or without political affiliations, women's representatives elected through political processes of local self-government and half-way houses like the women's commissions, on the one hand, and the politically 'neutral' NGOs, on the other. Of course, it must be admitted that in spite of there being a real distinction between the mode of working of NGOs and that of the autonomous women's organisations of the 1970s and 1980s, their purposes often coincided and many autonomous women's organisations turned into NGOs. What basically changed in this transformation was the mode of functioning—the agitational mode took a backseat while interventions through administrative channels became more important. Many women's organisations, whether having political affiliations or not, used to have legal cells where women requiring legal counselling and litigational assistance would be given support. An NGO too may run a legal cell, but the difference is that the latter would have a professional set-up and would not be run mostly by volunteers. Sometimes to ensure justice to affected women or to raise general issues of gender justice, it would be absolutely necessary for non-NGOs to take to the mode of campaigning and agitation, while generally NGOs would go for mediation with the administration.

This professionalisation of social work is the most significant contribution of NGOs to the field of social and human service with funding coming to them in the form of projects from government or non-governmental sources, enabling them to become mediators between the government departments and agencies and their beneficiaries. Organisations affiliated with political parties obviously were not project-based and could not avail themselves of this opportunity. Nor were all the NGOs necessarily women's organisations, although many of them might pre-eminently be doing projects on gender issues. But with the increase in project-based schemes for women, the intervention of the NGOs into society through such projects proliferated so much that some people have said that there has been an 'NGO-isation' of the women's movement. There are of course still many organisations which have stood midway, retaining some characteristics of their voluntary set-up and at the same time being compelled to respond to a sort of pressure become accredited professionalised NGOs.

In course of the last two or three decades, it has been the policy of the central and state governments of India to assign the work that used to be done directly and exclusively by government officials through government departments to accredited NGOs working at the grassroots levels. This has led to the emergence of the notion that as representatives of civil society, NGOs can motivate the stakeholders and beneficiaries to active participation in processes of development much more effectively. This discourse is especially powerful because it does not come from the government agencies alone but it gets generated through various international funding agencies as well. There is evidence coming from authentic research and documentation to show that NGOs are often able to avoid bureaucratic hassles in functioning and to deliver social sector goods and services with less wastage. Their programmes of 'capacity-building' and their training schedules in 'management of social engineering' do indeed help women to understand their own rights within the ambit of concerned projects and to function with more self-confidence and alacrity. These projects also often generate some remunerative work which directly empowers people in an economic system where regular livelihood options are extremely scarce. With all these advantages in place, it is no wonder that the NGO sector has developed by leaps and bounds.

They have proliferated both in the developmental sector and in the sector of social and human services and have stamped the mark of their presence through manifold activities. They have engaged in energising people to participate in building up resources like water and electricity, running nutritional schemes and training Anganwadi workers, women in self-help groups and even women members of panchayats and have set up their infrastructures in remote areas where government presence is minimal. They also have helped people in running schools and primary health centres. There has been significant intervention by NGOs in rescuing and rehabilitating trafficked women and in providing shelter to survivors of domestic violence. As a matter of fact, there have been government directives to involve accredited NGOs to ensure that the police follow the correct procedures in rescuing trafficked women.

During my years in the West Bengal and National Commissions for Women a good number of programmes used to be carried out with the active involvement of NGOs. Some important cases may be recalled. Between 2006 and 2011, a scheme for 'safe migration' of women going for work from West Bengal to other states was implemented by the West Bengal Commission for Women in collaboration with an NGO and some block panchayats in the district of Murshidabad. There has been more than one incident also of the Commission rescuing girls from red-light areas with police intervention and with the help of NGOs, particularly in arranging for the rehabilitation of the rescued girls. In 2007–2008, two young girls who were trafficked from West Bengal and detained as domestic slaves near Delhi could only be rescued, sheltered and returned to their families by the National Commission for Women with the active help from several NGOs. Even after their restoration to families, one NGO took the responsibility of monitoring the situation to prevent re-trafficking. The West Bengal Commission for Women also conducted extensive surveys on the implementation of the Domestic Violence Act of 2005 or of the Visaka Guidelines on Sexual Harassment, (the law was not yet in place at that time) issued by the Supreme Court, with NGOs working in districts. There was no dearth of cooperation on either side.

But in spite of all this, partly due to larger political-economic changes in the country in the last three decades or so, all these positive interactions have failed to bear the expected fruit. What has happened in consequence is often referred to as 'empowerment of NGOs'. If this has not automatically led to greater involvement of civil society in the broadest sense of the term and also to greater empowerment of women, it is my conclusion that the principal reason for this has been the simultaneous disempowerment of other significant sections of civil society like the political and non-political women's organisations, the panchayats and the statutory commissions. The class base of civil society institutions and governmental bodies prevents an overcoming of do-gooding philanthropy and empowerment of the labouring women is still a distant dream.

In the long run, it has meant that the scope of work for the NGOs is becoming severely limited. Although all kinds of 'hot' money, black and white, are floating all over the system, the flow of funds from government schemes is drying up. In recent months, with FCRA regulations becoming highly selective and many well-known NGOs being prevented from getting foreign assistance, the scheme-based work that NGOs have been preoccupied with is also getting hampered. The fact of the matter is that the scheme-based professional NGOs have not been able to replace other democratic processes and institutions or to fill up the significant gaps left by the relative undermining of agitations and movements involving large numbers of women and make interventions at the level of local self-government.

Big NGOs, with substantial funding from government and non-government sources, sometimes with foreign financial assistance, had a role to play in this undermining, although this is not to say that they were solely responsible for it. As I have said, both government and non-government funders were eager to initiate the process and the NGOs were the instruments in implementing the over-all change in policy. Their area of developmental work sometimes coincided with work that came within the ambit of the panchayats. NGOs took over the work that the panchayats could not do immediately either due to paucity of funds or due to rules and regulations they were subjected to reach the targeted beneficiaries within a short time. The 'gram sabha', which is the platform of direct democracy within panchayats and requires the participation of all adult residents within the locality, couldn't be formed easily and was often given a go-by, while the tangible immediate benefits distributed by NGOs in the locality attracted people towards them and sometimes even resulted in a loss of confidence in the panchayat system.

In some states, one reason as to why the women's commissions failed to lift themselves from the ground was the fact that fund-rich NGOs were already doing a part of their work with the blessings of the governments of those areas. The rise of the big NGOs also affected the women's movement on the ground because they were able to demonstrate that even without mobilising and agitating, some of the immediate demands of women in a particular locality could be realised through the mediation of NGOs. Project-based work also generated some limited scopes for employment, mostly casual, which addressed the basic issue of livelihood and left no time for women to join movements on larger social issues. Fear of losing work loomed large.

In my opinion, this is not the real route to women's empowerment in the sense in which I have used the term in this paper. It brings us too close for comfort to the trap of perpetuating the relationship of dependency between benefactors and beneficiaries which gets reflected in the internal power politics of NGOs. How far can even internal democracy be maintained when a few professionals getting high emoluments have control over a large number of needy women? Even if the positive factor of benefits outweighs the negative effects of dependence, the possibility of abuse of power still cannot be excluded. At the worst, the relationship degenerates into exploitation with the NGO re-inventing itself as a micro-finance institution (MFI) offering financial assistance at high rates of interest to women who are unable to approach banks. Again, sometimes the NGO turns into an intermediary for the market, buying cheap and selling dear articles produced by the beneficiaries. Very often, rural women possessing traditional skills and without access to the market, are exploited in this manner.

I am not saying that this is how all NGOs function, but I do hold that there is little to prevent them from such indirect sabotage of their originally envisioned role. It is the inevitable result of the change in policy that also brought them into prominence. Now this has come full cycle with the Central Government getting into the mode of handing over to big NGOs the work that was being done under the ICDS and mid-day meal schemes, jeopardising the meagre livelihood of thousands of women who were engaged in these schemes. While creating some new jobs for their own professionals and functionaries, these NGOs will now be taking away the jobs that these needy women had been given by the government.

This is just the other side of the policy which initiates a surreptitious process of disempowerment of the panchayat system by denying funds and adopting other politically oriented means of disenfranchisement. In fact, the disempowerment of the panchayat system goes hand in hand with the failure of successive governments in fulfilling the electoral promises to carry out the agenda of reservation for women in the central and state legislatures. It is in tune with this that in Haryana, some other states are reportedly following suit, amendments have already been made in the Panchayat Act to bring in educational qualifications, etc. as criteria to restrict truly disempowered women from fighting panchayat elections. This would consign them to the role of passive beneficiaries once again.

The oppositional role that movements have in a democracy can hardly be sustained by NGOs on their own. Being dependent for resources on governmental and non-governmental funding agencies, they have to carry out the agenda decided and imposed by the latter. This means that even the much-touted idea of the political impartiality of NGOs does not hold water in so far as they have to work in tune with the political agenda of their funders and donors. Even in the parameters of surveys they sometimes conduct, the problematic is already limited by such agenda so that criticality of any kind has to be shunned or ruled out. When there is a strong movement and strong democratic institutions exist in a system of governance, even NGOs can push themselves beyond the margins of the prescribed agenda. But when these are being undermined, any questioning from within the NGOs can hardly find space to articulate itself.

Sometimes it is argued that if NGOs can 'deliver the goods' or access some of the benefits available within the system more efficiently for those who need it. Is it not important that they should be allowed and even encouraged to do so? However, it is not as if the efficiency of the NGO is self-evident and could be taken for granted. There are 'efficient' and 'not-so-efficient' NGOs just as there are 'efficient' and 'not-so-efficient' panchayats or women's commissions. What is important is that all of them have their own modes of operation and there are certain objectives which an elected panchayat may achieve but an NGO may not. Activating people to give leadership in the processes of achieving their own development and well-being takes a long time and cannot be effected simply by making some benefits available to them. This is the ultimate objective of the panchayat system, and it remains beyond the purview of NGOs. Similarly, the objective of systemic change, which lies ingrained in the oppositional and transformatory democratic movements, eludes the NGOs, but it must not be foregone by the people. NGOs are funded for implementing specific projects in particular geographical and social spheres. Such plethora of project work can at best set up models and these models and their modes of implementation are a penny a dozen. But when the state abdicates its role in universalising and/or standardising such models of empowerment, these models lose relevance and value to wider segments of their targeted and non-targeted beneficiaries. Intervention of oppositional democratic movements remains crucial to exerting pressure on the state to do the needful in this regard.

In the past, many NGOs had themselves joined campaigns and movements on many issues such as sex-selective abortion, hazardous contraceptives, implementation of domestic violence-related laws, etc. In recent times, however, there are few project-based professional NGOs who would be ready to hit the road on the impact of various retrogressive government policies on women. For instance, the last two central budgets have made severe cuts in welfare schemes meant for disadvantaged and backward women. This is going to affect adversely the ICDS and Mid-day Meal Schemes and make implementation of the laws relating to domestic violence and sexual harassment hugely problematic. It would also curtail and restrict whatever benefits women may have been getting so far (as a result of movements and agitations) from the National Rural Employment Guarantee Scheme (NREGS) and push them further into the grossly exploitative, insecure and hazardous world of informal employment and make them more prone to enforced migration and trafficking (AIDWA Publication 2015, pp. 6–9).

There are of course movements and campaigns against these developments in different parts of the country, but very few NGOs are joining them. There have been recent amendments to the Child Labour Act which are likely to consign thousands of children, particularly girl-children, to so-called domestic enterprises and 'entertainment industries', which will hamper their school-education and rob them of their childhood. A section of NGOs, who work with children, have indeed got together with other organisations initially to prevent the amendment and when that failed, to engage in overt protests against these pieces of anti-child legislation. But other major NGOs have dragged their feet over the issue and even joined the bandwagon. The unified thrust of opposition and outrage, which is highly expected in a democratic country, is missing. It is not for nothing that the Central Government, in its draft policy on domestic workers, proposes to elide the role of trade unions with that of placement agencies, reducing the capacity of organised labour movements by changing the former into NGO-like mediatory bodies. This is a blatant an instance of the implicit subversion of democratic institutions which might have had some real effect on the existing structures of power and would have advanced the cause of empowerment of the disempowered.

The concept of civil society is a democratic one. It's most obvious political connotation becomes evident particularly when the concept is subjected to the rhetoric of restriction. This signifies the devaluation of the different institutions that embody civil society, leading further to the devaluation of democracy. Empowerment of women stands impossible in such a situation. Gender inequality and gender injustice constitute an integrally connected set of perennial social problems, which arise from the socially embedded politics of patriarchy with its entangled considerations of class, caste, religion, etc. Empowerment of the disempowered sections of society, including that of women, cannot happen outside this extremely uneven playing field wherein inhospitable and/or hostile social and political forces conspire constantly against women. It can never be possible to invest women with power from above. It is only through a broadening of the democratic space and revitalisation of the different institutions of civil society that we shall be able to proceed firmly in the direction of empowering women in the truest sense of the term.

References

Armstrong, Elizabeth. 2013. *Gender and Neo-liberalism: The All India Democratic Women's Association and Globalization Politics*. New Delhi: Tulika, 58–69.

BJP's Big Bang Reforms: Booting Women out of the Budget. 2015. All India Democratic Women's Association Publication, 6–9.

Country Report submitted to the Fourth World Conference of Women, Beijing, 1995, Delhi: Government of India, Department of Woman and Child Development, Ministry of Human Resource Development, 1.

Mazumdar, Vina. 2010. *Memories of a Rolling Stone*. New Delhi: Zubaan, 68–70.

Sarkar, Tanika. 1998. Heroic Women, Mother Goddesses: Family and Organisation in Hindutva Politics. In *Secular Challenge to Communal politics: A Reader*, ed. P.R. Ram, 184. Mumbai: Vikas Adhyan Kendra.

CHAPTER 4

NGO Activism and Women's Empowerment in India

Biswajit Ghosh

THE CONTEXT

The context of analysing the role of non-governmental organisations (NGOs[1]) in development in general and for women's empowerment in particular became critical in India amid the retreat of the state and domination of market forces since the advent of economic liberalisation in the early 1990s. The role of the 'third sector' to mitigate discontents of the marginalised was, however, visualised globally during the late 1970s when the Structural Adjustment Programme (SAP) was put forward by the Bretton Woods institutions. The new model of 'neo-liberalism', being an adjective to global capitalism, was argued to be a 'discourse' including 'new technologies of rule' beyond the economic. It had its impact on politics of gender and its associated movements. As the developing countries like India started reshaping their 'development regimes' according to neo-liberal principles from 'welfare' and 'planning'

B. Ghosh (✉)
The University of Burdwan, Purba Bardhaman, India
e-mail: bghoshbu@gmail.com

© The Author(s), under exclusive license to Springer Nature Singapore Pte Ltd. 2024
A. K. Sarkar and S. Das Gupta (eds.), *Understanding Women's Empowerment in South Asia*,
https://doi.org/10.1007/978-981-16-7538-6_4

to 'empowerment' and 'market competition' during the 1980s, NGOisation became an ubiquitous reality. Changes in the visions of justice from welfare and state protection to the affirmation of the new notion of individuated, entrepreneurial middle-class woman added new dimensions to the concepts like 'empowerment' and 'agency'.

By making market the organising principle of society, neo-liberalism has put emphasis on individual merit of women (and other marginalised sections) rather than on equality for everyone (Brown 2015). New buzzwords in development practice then initiated a shift in language from 'exploitation' to 'efficiency', which emphasises the role of individual or autonomous women for doing or changing things. All these led to a celebration of the strength and capabilities of the poor woman (Chaudhuri 2012a). In other words, gender rights then got transferred as individual liability or 'self help' rather than the responsibility of the government. It is, therefore, not a matter of coincidence that UN had celebrated 1975 as the *International Women's Year* and the years from 1976 to 1985 were earmarked collectively as the *United Nations Decade for Women*.

The Indian state, as a part of the 'World Plan of Action', then set up the National Committee to look at the 'status of women' in the country. The Committee published its report entitled *Towards Equality* in 1974. The report exposed the abysmal conditions of women in respect of declining sex ratio, increasing rate of female mortality and morbidity, economic marginalisation and the evils of discriminatory personal laws. It made several recommendations vindicating the role of the government in achieving 'gender equality'. In due course, the Indian state also amended the constitution (73rd amendment bill accepted in 1993) to allow one-third right of representation of women in the Panchayati Raj Institutions (PRIs). The whole process was taken to its heights when the feminists all over the country, belonging primarily to the upper/middle caste/class, could carry the cause of the women across the streets. Steady rise in violence against women, during the 1970s and 1980s, led women activists attached to NGOs and political parties to assert their voices against crimes like dowry, domestic violence, rape, property rights, uniform civil code and the like. All these initiated a new beginning and greater visibility of Indian feminists in the recent decades of globalisation (Chaudhuri 2012b).

As against female activists attached to different organisations, for whom handling of women's problems remained subservient to the wider programmes of their parental bodies, the autonomous women's movements, largely spearheaded by the educated middle class, took up several issues connected to the cause of 'shared sisterhood': 'facilitating' the 'other' woman and often speaking on her behalf. These autonomous NGOs left their earlier institutional form and became completely separate from the state regulatory frameworks and scrutiny. The state was then seen as inherently oppressive and not to be trusted. But, they had to pay the price of remaining informal and small due to limited access to resources (Kilby 2011). Interestingly, 1990s also witnessed the rise of NGO activism on contradictory issues like the notion of 'victimized Hindu woman[2]', the identity of dalit and tribal women, rights of Queer group members as well as issues of women adversely affected by forces of globalisation (Chaudhuri 2016).

On the whole, the decade of the 1990s witnessed increasing recognition of the centrality of the gender question in the development discourse, even though there were allegations of women's movement being 'coopted' by NGOs. As Maitrayee Chaudhuri (2012a, pp. 131–132) argues, there was a paradigm shift of the gender question in the 1990s when capital and market began to acquire ascendancy in different forms of public discourse. This shift in public discourse reconfigured the notions of both class and gender in the national imaginary and, therefore, necessarily in the priorities of developmental endeavours. Along with these developments, the 1990s also saw an increasing visibility of previously marginalised sections like dalits with their own distinct response to the paradigm shift in developmental visions. Choudhuri feels that the women's movement then became able to make gender a major issue in the public sphere. Major actors such as states, civil society, market, international institutions did have to take cognisance of the varied considerations of gender inequality. New laws were passed to combat violence against women, even though very little could be achieved in implementing them (Ghosh 2013). Thus, there has often been not just a de-link with visions of justice articulated by women's movement earlier but also significant reconfigurations of the very ideas of freedom, justice, equity, autonomy, choice, activism, empowerment that women's movements had raised earlier. Rather than seeking radical transformation in gender relations, mobilisation for women's empowerment then became a professional, expert-based and policy-oriented activity (Roy 2015, p. 101).

Interestingly, such reconfiguration reposed faith on NGOs and other Civil Society Organizations (CSOs). These organisational entities were then argued to be very useful not only to empower women but also to mitigate social discontents because of the widespread processes of dispossession due to the very operation of market liberalism and upward distribution of wealth. Proliferation of NGOs worldwide since the 1980s thereby signifies the emergence of a new discourse on rights as against the exclusionary tendencies of the market led 'growth'. Obviously, during the last few decades, there have been several researches on the working of the NGOs and their role in the development sector in general and women's empowerment in particular. Feminist scholars have claimed that mainstream economic paradigm is androcentric (Beneria and Feldman 1992). Scholars have also emphasised several complexities and contradictions in the functioning of the NGO sector. Structurally, dependency of a particular type of NGO on those very international institutions that questioned the state-centric welfarist model of development has come under serious attack (Roy 2004). If neo-liberalism posits faith on the market as the best institution for social development, including empowerment of women, what role could NGOs really play for the spread of feminist values and ideals?

It is obvious that the way arguments favouring NGO model were put into action by the mainstream agencies of development could generate many contradictions. Thus, on the one hand, they are seen as 'extension counter of the state' to fulfil several of its own obligations, particularly handling of issues of the marginalised sections like women. But NGOs have also historically challenged the state-led developmental paradigms and policies while arguing for the agenda of good governance, democracy and empowerment. This double-edged nature of NGO work puts it in a perpetual state of suspicion (Visvanathan 2014). NGOs depending on the external donors for executing certain policies and programmes of development also very often become targets of social and political criticism. It is worth mentioning here that in recent times, the Indian state has cancelled FCRA registration of selected NGOs and put several curbs on their activities by accusing them of being anti-development, anti-India and anti-Hindu. There is also a growing vulnerability of NGOs—particularly the larger ones that are dependent on foreign funding—to state scrutiny and the state's capacity to cut off NGO resources (Kilby 2011, p. 19). It is in this context that this chapter will try to critically reflect on the importance of the NGO sector, particularly with reference to the question of women's empowerment in a country like India.

Rise of NGOs as Part of CSOs

Increasing concerns for social justice, inclusive growth and empowerment of the poor and marginalised, particularly in the wake of 'market globalism' in the world today, have paved the way for spectacular rise of NGOs as a part of CSOs. It is worth noting here that cutting across intellectual boundaries, arguments in favour of NGOs are linked to the failure of the modern state to guarantee autonomy of individuals, protection of individual rights, equal citizenship and access to decision-making apparatus and participatory framework (Ghosh 2012). If a strong, vibrant and lively civil society is the foundation of a modern and open democratic polity, NGOs remain the very life force of the former. Civil society and NGOs seem to go together and one cannot exist without the other (Baviskar 2001, p. 7). NGOs are considered to be a means of strengthening civil society and fostering good governance (Bebbington and Riddell 1995). They are essential for the dissemination of new ideas and concepts with regard to social and economic development and empower women through participation, agency and gainful initiative. It is worth mentioning here that since the 1990s, the World Bank has not only encouraged member governments to work with NGOs on development projects, but has also increased its direct funding of such projects (Ghosh 2009).

Simultaneously, with the onset of an alternative paradigm of development that attaches more importance to issues like gender, health and education, our focus has shifted to alternative agenda like human development, gender development, community development, sustainable development, capacity building and the like. As NGOs work for all these, it is quite commonplace to argue for the entry of this 'third sector'[3] for the 'enlargement of people's choices', 'people-friendly' grassroots movement as well as 'empowerment' of the marginalised. The new development strategies perceive poor people, including women as active agents of their own development. Hence, instead of a top-down and hegemonic character of development under both the capitalist and state socialist models, it calls for a bottom-up participatory approach where development 'experts' become 'facilitators' working with marginalised women in particular rather than directing them (Chambers 1997; Munck 1999; Freedman 2000).

It should, however, be acknowledged that even though the distinguishing features of NGOs as against the state lie in their being autonomous, non-profit, relatively independent and self-propelled organisations, they differ from each other in terms of size, membership, funding, approaches, strategies and outcomes. Hence, a generalised statement about functioning of NGOs is bound to be problematic, and consequently, scholars have attempted to classify NGOs in several different ways (Baviskar 2001, p. 5; Oommen 2004, p. 15).

Role of NGOs in Women's Empowerment

In the historic Beijing Declaration in 1975, it was argued that women's empowerment is fundamental for achievement of equality, development and peace. The term 'empowerment' is, however, a very broad notion. It literally means capacity to influence decisions or participate in the decision-making process (Pramanick 2012). It refers to a range of activities from individual self-assertion to collective resistance, which challenge basic power relations. The process is also aimed at redistribution of 'power' that challenges patriarchy and male domination. While the notion of power can simply be defined as 'control' over external resources, there is also a strong and intrinsic sense in which it means something that women have to do for themselves internally. So empowerment gets manifested in several spheres and aspects of one's life like education, awareness and self-confidence.

In a broad sense, therefore, one may argue that unless the structural forces that lead to disempowerment—social, cultural, economic or political—are challenged and changed, real empowerment will not happen. Women's empowerment, therefore, is a continuous process aiming at changing the nature and direction of systemic forces which marginalise women in a given context (Sharma 1998, p. 7). It entails a qualitative transformation in social relations leading to women's access to resources, development of capability and ability to take decisions for assuming control over one's life.

Given the broadness of the notion of 'empowerment', questions are often raised about the extent to which NGO activism (or even membership of powerful elected bodies like parliament) would ensure that women are empowered. In the context of political empowerment of women in local bodies, Nirmala Buch (2010, p. 13) has argued that the power system has a tendency to incline in favour of the groups which can control the economic expectations of the people of villages. Empowerment, then, is a multi-sectoral issue having its ramifications in all areas of society. The process would remain incomplete unless women are both individually and collectively allowed by men to take decisions, directing and shaping her own life and are able to participate on an equal footing with men in all spheres of life—economic, social and political (Kumari 1992, p. 143).

Discussions on the role of NGOs in ensuring women's empowerment are often centred on the potential of NGOs (as compared to the state) to facilitate grassroots 'participatory' and 'sustainable' development at local levels. The merits of NGOs being autonomous, non-profit, relatively independent, spontaneous and self-propelled entities are brought in to support such a view. It is, therefore, argued that NGOs have the added advantage to facilitate women's empowerment in the following ways: (a) reach and unite them effectively, (b) involve women volunteers to listen to them and counsel them, (c) make proper assessments of their needs, (d) react to any calamity immediately, (e) monitor and guide progress of any development or welfare scheme closely, (f) arouse a sense of leadership and personality among them, (g) provide them with skills, training and other necessary abilities to act effectively, (h) contribute to sustenance of any plan of action, (i) remain responsive and committed to their cause, and (j) perform their tasks with greater efficiency and dedication.

Apart from such advantages of the NGO sector, voluntary actions are also considered to be helpful in increasing diversity of opportunities for women in society. By providing variety and autonomy in associational choice, they promote the formation of interest groups that can challenge monopolistic tendencies and poor performances of state enterprises (Bebbington and Riddell 1995, p. 56). From such a point of view, NGOs do not just attempt to replace the state; they rather try to democratise and politicise the civil society more than any other institution. Hence, the key justification for the expansion, growth and importance of NGOs seems to be 'their ability to be what the state is not and cannot be' (Zaidi 2004, p. 191).

Given the atmosphere of NGO activism that prevailed in the country by the mid-1990s, the agenda of women's empowerment became a part of the lexicon of varied civil society endeavours, and many NGOs felt they had to subscribe to it, often with little idea of what it meant (Kilby 2011, p. 18). A key feature of most NGO work in India at that time was focusing on income generation potentials of poor women through self-help groups (SHG[4]) and microfinance. SHG members can reap economic benefits through mutual help, solidarity and joint responsibility. The utility of SHGs as a successful strategy for not only women's empowerment but also participatory development was then commented upon quite pointedly (Paul 2015). Women hailing from poor families were argued to be committed to save money within a group and use those savings to procure additional credit for gainful investment. Such a scheme was seen to be helpful not only for generation of additional incomes but also to tackle poverty in that process. Even the use of such income for improved health and education was argued to be of some worth.

At the same time, microfinance through self-help groups is considered one of the effective strategies for poverty alleviation and economic empowerment. Microcredit is based on the premise that the poor have skills which remain unutilised or underutilised. For Muhammad Yunus (2003) of the famous Grameen Bank, charity is not the answer to poverty. It only helps poverty to continue. It creates dependency and takes away the individual's initiative to break through the wall of poverty. So, for him, unleashing of an individual's energy and creativity through microcredit is the answer to poverty. It is worth noting here that many multi- and bi-lateral donors including USAID, World Bank also spoke in favour of microfinance as the 'best practice' for 'empowering' women and other marginalised groups. This is because in developing countries like India, a large number of rural poor continue to remain outside the fold of formal banking system and thereby remain outside the credit-linked poverty alleviation programmes. Another reason for favouring women is that they are found to be better placed in repaying their loans as compared to men and tend more often to benefit the whole family. As 70% of the world's poor are women, the World Bank has also suggested removal of both gender inequality and poverty through microfinance and SHGs.

Various studies have also suggested that the existing policies and procedures of our banking sector very often do not meet the needs of the hardcore and asset-less poor. Contrarily, the mechanisms of microcredit are found to be helpful particularly for quick recovery. The loans given are also useful to initiate or run a small business of women vendors or those living below the poverty line. In turn, these efforts may raise their income levels and improve their living standards, while relieving them from the clutches of exploitative money lenders operating in informal sector economies and charging exorbitant interest rates. So the alternative model of credit delivery is argued to be simple, efficient, non-exploitative, financially sustainable and self-managed.

SHGs emerged as important players in the microfinance sector in 1992 when *National Bank for Agriculture and Rural Development* (NABARD) had introduced a pilot programme. It then linked SHGs and banks to enable poor households to take credit to meet their financial needs. In 1997, at the *World Micro Credit Summit*, the programme received a boost when a global target was set for supporting 100 million of the world's poorest families, especially women, with micro-credit by 2005. Later in 1999, the Govt. of India's Ministry of Rural Development introduced *Swarna Jayanti Gram Swarozgar Yojana* (SGSY) to promote self-employment of primarily rural women through SHGs. Similar programmes for urban women were also launched later in 1997.

The SHG system is seen as very effective in offering women the possibility of generating income and thereby contributing to the wellbeing of their families. According to NABARD (2017), there were 8.5 million SHGs in the country in 2016–2017 and nearly 90% of them were women's groups. As Paul (2015) reports, significant changes in the living standards of SHG members have taken place in terms of increase in income levels, assets, savings, borrowing capacity and income-generating activities. Such income generation is very often found to be positive for changing the status of women within family and allowing them to voice their opinions and take decisions. Being a bottom-up approach, it also has the potential of eradicating poverty through self-reliance and empowerment. Interestingly, SHGs are also graded according to certain criteria related to their activities and initiatives in four different stages, and the better ones are rewarded with revolving funds as well as loans for entrepreneurship development. There are many successful stories of the way SHGs have changed women's lives. As a corollary, many NGOs have started promoting the SHG mechanism and linking it to various other development interventions.

Notwithstanding such positive feedback about the role of SHGs and microfinance for women's empowerment, a certain body of critical literature on the issue has highlighted some serious limitations of the project. It is to be noted at the outset that microfinance has especially targeted poor women in a context of growing 'feminisation of poverty'. Large-scale informalisation and casualisation of jobs has taken place in liberalised India wherein women predominantly outnumber men and, hence, it cannot also be treated as 'empowering' because such low-income jobs do not make women free from vulnerabilities. Rather, the lives of vulnerable women have now become more vulnerable (Horn 2009; Oxfam 2010).

Given such contextuality, we shall have to review the role of NGO activism in forming and guiding SHGs and facilitating microfinance more critically. Dash and Saran (2012, p. 180) have argued that the knowledge about the real 'social impacts' of microfinance institutions (MFIs) is partial and contested and assessments of microfinance programmes are not always supported by credible results. This is because MFIs do not reach out to the poorest, as it is so often claimed. Frances Sinha's (2007, p. 76) research and several other studies on Indian SHGs clearly show that in terms of the number of poor women involved in the SHG movement, around half of SHG members are still below the national poverty line.

Theoretically, SHG membership is supposed to enable women to (a) go out of houses, (b) help family members financially, (c) gain family respect, (d) attend village meetings, (e) deal with officials, (f) engage in business, (g) get involved in social advocacy, and (h) influence/challenge community values and institutions. But in reality, only a handful of women are able to achieve success on all such counts. Due to poor socio-economic backgrounds, these women are not able to generate sufficient income. This is because women invest mostly in insecure activities having low profitability. The issue of leadership and relations among members of SHGs remains vital for the success of SHGs. But scholars have seen that in many instances, leaders remain self-centred and do not share critical information with members. Herein comes in the question of social, economic, religious and political affiliations of a member. Identities based on caste, class, religion and party do affect relations even within SHGs.

Hence, it would be foolish to think that formation of an SHG may guarantee its success. For reasons beyond the control of members, an SHG may become defunct due to internal conflict. Group homogeneity, cohesion and commitments are significant requirements for any SHG to perform and sustain. In fact, very few of our SHGs have crossed the second stage to qualify for additional funding and facilities. This is also because of the fact that being a government-pushed model, SHGs are mostly formed through political and administrative initiatives and once the target is fulfilled, bureaucrats or panchayat members do not find time to enquire about them. Given the non-spontaneous character of the SHG movement, the attitudes of the panchayat leaders and bureaucrats as well as political willingness of the ruling party leaders matter very crucially for making SHGs effective.

Ironically, formation of a huge number of SHGs in West Bengal since the 1990s did not either lessen incidences of violence against women or foster strong campaigns against such violence. Surveys done on SHG members also listed problems like non-cooperation by bank officials, lack of training and skill, lack of marketing avenues, lack proper planning and management, borrowing for non-productive purposes (often dictated by husbands) and lack of interest of defunct members for their failures to improve their group performance (Das 2012; Sambhaji 2016). Ahamad and Hemlata (2015) have found that despite certain positive developments, all SHG groups are not equally involved in intervening into matters like health and education of women and also taking little interest in the functioning of Gram Sabhas. So SHG membership does not necessarily translate into questioning gender biases within families and in social settings at large.

In a comparative study of 15 NGOs with experiences of running SHGs, Kilby (2011) has found that while NGOs can act as facilitators for activities relating to women's empowerment, these results were not uniform across different social groups. He noted two important factors affecting the NGOs' capacity to affect empowerment outcomes. First, the number of years a group remains in existence is important as it enables women to build confidence and trust to take power and responsibility within SHGs, make choices and take actions. But funders put pressures on NGOs to limit their engagements with particular groups to a specific time-period in order to direct and expand their reach to new communities. To Kilby, this dilemma can lead to NGOs focusing their support on those groups in society which can produce quick and early results, such as those who may be better off, thus excluding the more marginal and less resourceful ones. Obviously, such 'superficial interventions' turn out to be unsustainable. Second, NGOs, in their work for the poor and marginalised communities, remain quite forthright to follow mechanisms of accountability for SHG members.

The consequence of this 'dependent' relationship is that the poor are less likely to demand stronger accountability mechanisms as long as the services get delivered in fair and reasonable manners. Unlike membership-oriented organisations such as cooperatives or unions, where members can demand accountability, NGOs, which are non-membership bodies, may avoid doing so. This 'service-delivery approach', according to Kilby, leads to a simplistic interpretation of the term 'empowerment'. He, therefore, argues that a voluntary reversal of the power relationship between NGOs and the people to whom they are providing services is required if high levels of empowerment are to be attained. But such a reversal of power is difficult, if not impossible, particularly for larger NGOs.

Provision of microcredit is defended in development rhetoric, though it only enables money to get quick and superficial results having little long-term impacts. Feminist scholars have shown that the issue of empowerment is extremely complex and cannot be explained in any reductionist way. Obviously, access to credit does not automatically translate into empowerment. Focusing on *access*, therefore, provides only a partial view of the success because it ignores the structural and cultural barriers women face in transforming access to resources into control over them (Kabeer 2005). It is certainly not a 'Magic Bullet' for women's empowerment. Amartya Sen (1999) has powerfully argued that 'capability' is a better conceptual tool in contrast to income for understanding the multi-layered issue of well-being. Research on the functioning of SHGs in India or elsewhere has shown that credit alone doesn't enable women to challenge patriarchy and change the complex structures of subordination, inequalities and discrimination within households or in markets or in wider societal spaces. Growing suspicion about NGO-run empowerment programmes is now being emphasised even by the donors who acknowledge that effective poverty alleviation requires, at the bare minimum, the participation of beneficiaries in development activities rather than their remaining passive recipients (Kilby 2011, p. 20). Failure of the NGO sector, in general, to empower women does not, however, mean that there is no success story. In fact, there are plenty of it. Let me present some brief case studies to uphold this contention.

Some Success Stories

The success story of voluntary activism of many NGOs may be cited to argue that they are best suited for showcasing models of alternative development. The self-help approach to development was pioneered in India in the 1970s by NGOs like *Self-Employed Women's Association* (SEWA) of Ahmedabad, *Mysore Resettlement and Development Agency* (MYRADA) of Karnataka and *Annapurna Mahila Mandal* of Mumbai. The SEWA's endeavour is most widely known among these cases, and it has gained international recognition for being an illuminating model of women's empowerment through self-help.

Let me first discuss the case of SEWA. It is pertinent to note that beginning its journey as a trade union in 1972, SEWA has used microfinance strategically as an entry point for wider social and political mobilisation of women around gender issues and gradually kept expanding its activities to serve as a true representative of self-employed women in the unorganised sector. By 2015, nearly 14 lakh poor women have been organised to achieve the two basic goals of full employment and self-reliance. SEWA now provides diverse opportunities to the families of its members, including food, income and social securities. Ila Bhatt, the renowned founder of the SEWA, is considered a 'pioneer' of the microfinance movement in the South Asian sub-continent. Three years later Muhammad Yunus founded Grameen Bank, another milestone in the history of mobilisation of poor and disadvantaged people for a goal of self-help and cooperative activities. Interestingly, unlike the *Grameen Bank*, SEWA has been regulated by the Reserve Bank of India, staying strictly within the law and seeking no special dispensations.

In 2015, SEWA had a working capital of nearly 218.71 crores and its audit classification has been consistently 'A' grade (SEWA 2015). SEWA has successfully linked microfinance movement with much needed support services like insurance, health care, childcare, legal aid and training to reduce women's vulnerabilities. It has also raised voices against domestic violence, male alcohol abuse and dowry. As Oommen (2004, p. 120) argues, civil society organisations like the SEWA are not always and necessarily anti-state; sometimes they are neutral and occasionally they are even pro-state. Therefore, to posit that civil society is necessarily and always anti-state and thereby 'anti-development' is at variance with facts.

SEWA's approach to women's empowerment has, however, come under some criticisms. Thus, according to Appell (1996, p. 225), SEWA is "more ideological than practical". Appell noted several gaps in its ideology and accomplishments: (a) SEWA cannot create jobs, (b) it does not assist members in formal sectors, (c) it is not participatory, and (d) more importantly, middle-class workers are in most of the high-level positions in the organisation. Yutaka Sato (forthcoming) argues that the capacity-building programme of the SEWA in the slums of Ahmedabad calls for a refinement of feminists' notion of politics in development on two contrasting grounds. One is the livelihood approach of SEWA in the SNP, which has not only mitigated women's work burden but also increased the self-worth of women in the slums, who had previously been deprived of life-chances such as marriage due to discrimination against them. The other is its expanded, yet short-term, programmes carried out in collaboration with the state, which have created space for 'individualised' empowerment among the female leaders, in contrast to the 'collective' empowerment that members of the SEWA movement have reportedly achieved. More importantly, community participation as part of a project-specific NGO programme contributes to intensifying stratification in terms of opportunities among residents and does not readily remove such social barriers.

The *Kagad Kach Patra Kashtakari Panchayat* (KKPKP) provides another radical example of NGO activism for upliftment of a marginalised community. It is a trade union-cum-NGO of waste-pickers in Pune, Maharashtra. The aid-recipients—women and child waste-pickers—led this movement from the very beginning since 1993 (Kilby 2011, p. 67). As a result of networking and close collaboration between the Centre for Continuing Education of the Women's University (SNDT) and the waste-pickers, the issues arising out of some lived realities of the waste-pickers got highlighted. When the SNDT staff first met the waste-pickers, they realised that their main issue was less about their income levels, but more about the terms and conditions of their work. Instead of opting for the NGO model of stressing on livelihood issues, SNDT team and the waste-pickers opted for a long-term strategy of forming an organised group for mass action on their rights as 'waste pickers'. As waste-pickers were seen as scavengers and harassed by police and officials and were also treated badly by scrap dealers, the legitimacy of their work was being questioned. KKPKP, therefore, adopted a rights-based approach and started claiming legitimacy of and respect for their work and identity. They then stressed on the alternate identity of 'workers' as scrap collection is socially relevant, economically productive and environmentally beneficial. An INGO provided institutional support grant to work with waste-pickers with a relatively open-ended scope for the types of activity that would be undertaken. From being a marginalised and oppressed group, the waste-pickers could, over a period of ten years, claim their central role in the revamped waste collection system of the Pune city (ibid., p. 68).

The proto-union model helped KKPKP secure recognition of the identity of waste-pickers (Ghosh and Choudhuri 2016). Like SEWA, KKPKP has tried to provide for socio-economic benefits to its members. It also mobilised its members for direct political action and lobbying. At yet another level, the union has explored viable channels of marketing efficiently by engaging in the waste-recycling business. The KKPKP has instituted credit cooperatives, group insurance, a cooperative store and self-help groups for its members. It has organised educational and literacy programmes. Along with protests against unjust governmental actions, it has, at the same time, gone into issue-based collaboration with different government agencies and departments. Because of its growing influence, at present, the union is represented in a number of decision-making bodies in the Pune city (Routh 2016).

The establishment of a Cooperative Scrap Store in 1998 was a milestone for these waste-pickers to challenge the monopoly of the local scrap dealers (Kilby 2011, p. 72). The women selling their scrap items were then given a share in the profits of the Cooperative at the end of the year, half of which went into a provident fund and the other half was spent on giving a cash dividend. The accumulated reserves from the store of Rs.175,000 enabled KKPK to expand, and within a period of ten years, another three stores were opened across the city. Similarly, the establishment of a Savings and Credit Co-operative helped these women to avoid money lenders and take loans at a lower rate. From 2002, the union no longer required institutional support from external donors as by then it became self-funded from fees and incomes from interests. Later on, when the *Solid Waste Collection and Handling (SWaCH) Cooperative* was established in 2007 by the Pune Municipal Corporation as the umbrella organisation for the waste-pickers involved in doorstep collection, KKPK members were given the first priority. As a result, they had a greater income with easier and greater access to waste, enhanced security in employment, improved safety and gained formal recognition as an established entity among the city's waste management functionaries (ibid., p. 78).

There are plenty of other successful NGOs in the country who have made their presence felt in the society through constructive social work for women's welfare and rightful entitlements. They have been able to create a space of freedom, participation, activism, dissent and creativity for women. The Lawyer's Collective of Delhi, for instance, was instrumental in drafting the famous domestic violence law (The Protection of Women from Domestic Violence Act (PWDVA), 2005), and it has seriously and consistently worked for gender justice and gender equality. Being professionally competent to deal with the chronic shortcomings and pitfalls of the legal system of the country, this NGO has put substantial pressure on the Indian governmental authorities over a variety of issues relating to the country's justice delivery systems in general and violence against women in particular. The contributions of many other small and big NGOs in India are conspicuous by their salience. Thus, to name only a few, organisations like Working Women's Forum, Shakti Vahini, Sanchetna, Jagruti, Centre for Social Research, Majlis, North-East Network, International Centre for Research on Women, Bharatiya Grameen Mahila Sangh, Vimochana—Forum for Women's Rights, Azad Foundation, SNEHA Mumbai, Chainyard, Sanlaap, Durbar Mahila Samanwaya Committee, Bhartiya Patita Udhar Samiti, Prerana, Bhoruka Public Welfare Trust, Karnataka Integrated Development Society, Grama Vikas, Prakruthi and the like, have quite successfully intervened in enlarging the scopes of varied rights-oriented activities for disadvantaged and marginalised women and children who are victims and survivors of trafficking and other forms of social and sexual abuse and assault as well as of hunger, illiteracy and other vagaries of economic and cultural exploitation.

Failures of NGOs and Challenges Ahead

Having recognised the contributions of many notable NGOs working for women's welfare and empowerment in India, we should equally acknowledge that there are vast areas of darkness, shortcomings and failures of the NGO sector. Had this not been the case, India would have achieved tremendous success in gender development index during the last three decades. But mushrooming of NGOs did not lead to any change in the socio-cultural and relational spheres of our 'patriarchal' way of life. One way to recognise the limits of NGO activism is to argue that the hype about this sector during the 1980s and 1990s itself was exaggerated. Like the state, NGOs have their limitations. Hence, barring a few exceptions, 'they have failed at making a substantial impact upon their perceived and targeted beneficiaries' (Zaidi 2004, p. 191). Even the successful ones have their shares of drawback and failure. Gupta (2014) has shown that when grassroots NGOs expand their capacities and resources to consolidate their positions in the development regime, they face the challenge of increasing bureaucratisation of organisational structures and functioning, and come to create new relations of patronage that serve the purpose of self-preservation of these NGOs. Some of the criticisms labelled against SEWA are related to its growth and professionalisation. Niumai (2006) has also shown that whenever an NGO tries to expand and focus on the rights of its employees, it faces 'routinisation' and consequent decline of voluntarism.

The NGOisation of the feminist movement since the 1990s is particularly critiqued on the ground that autonomous women's movements of the 1970s and 1980s, which were a crucial force in social transformation despite certain limitations, have now lost all vigour and strength (Tellis 2012). Srila Roy (2015) has voiced her concern for this issue as NGOs have come to dominate the Indian women's movement in such a manner that a precise demarcation of the boundaries of Indian feminism as a social movement from that of NGOs is not always possible. Doubts about the role of transnationalised and professionalised NGOs in women's empowerment are expressed because they are argued to be 'less representative of a specific kind of feminist politics' (ibid., p. 98). Mushrooming of NGOs working on women's issues does not signify any ideological and moral improvement; they are rather identified as 'harmful' for feminism (Hodzic, quoted in Roy 2015).

These NGOs are least spontaneous and autonomous as they rely on paid employees, on the one hand, and external donors, on the other, to manage project-based assignments. In this sense, the new variety of 'project NGOs' are opposed to feminist perspectives and progressive ideals. Visvanathan (2014), too, has argued that NGOs are not angelic groups and many of them have become institutions, which have turned seriatim protest ventures into a career. Many of these groups have advocated transparency and responsibility in dealing with gender issues but failed to apply it to themselves. Niumai (2006, p. 235) has found that two out of five NGOs working on women's issues in Tamenglong district of Manipur were 'more accountable to the government and foreign funding agencies than to the local community and beneficiaries'. One, therefore, needs to be careful in making either positive or negative generalisations by looking into some individual cases (Kaimowitz 1993, p. 1139).

The perceived effectiveness of NGOs is also linked to their approaches towards short-term and long-term gains. Thus, Viswanath (1991), who conducted a study of two NGOs, namely *Gram Vikas* and *India Development Service* (IDS), to determine their effectiveness in serving the needs of women, found that Gram Vikas' strategy of short-term gains was more realistic and visible to the beneficiaries as compared to the IDS' long-term strategies. But, at the same time, ignorance of long-term needs like education and awareness hinders sustainability and empowerment, and encourages dependency. NGOs seeking positive results are, therefore, caught in a jam.

One major argument against many NGOs is: they are the creation of funding agencies and hence 'their entire existence, not merely dependency, is on donor money, which comes almost always from above' (Zaidi 2004, p. 192). And these donors are not necessarily pro-women. It is safe to argue that the extraordinary mushrooming and gendering of NGOs over the last few decades is linked to 'donor's likes'; hence, such 'NGO-isation' hardly enhances the ideology of civil society activism (ibid., p. 193). When donors dictate the choices of NGOs, an agenda of 'non-priority' for the people may find 'priority' for NGO activism. Often big NGOs are favoured by donors because of their good connections and 'power' and not on the basis of efficiency and accountability (Jerath 2010). It is in such a context that Nilanjana Biswas (2006) has argued that women's movement is a largely funded affair today and hence the voluntarism of the voluntary sector is an oxymoron. In the venture to become autonomous so as to keep safe distance from party politics or state control, NGOs have become dependent on foreign funding (as internal finding is very often limited) and thereby have been 'sold out' to the 'imperialist' forces of the West (Karat 1984) forces. Did this not constrain the culture of open and critical thinking, which is an essential aspect of NGO activism?

The patron-client relationship emerging out of such a model of development raises numerous questions about the accountability and legitimacy of the work done by NGOs who remain accountable mainly to their funders and not to their women beneficiaries whom they are expected to serve in full confidence. Misappropriation and utilisation of funds earmarked for activities on women's empowerment for other purposes are an argument often made against some NGOs. There are many instances of women and children getting abused in 'shelter homes' run by NGOs. A 'puppet' NGO, in spite of its best records, is bound to betray the very spirit of women's empowerment and replace accountability by accountancy (Edwards and Hulme 1996, p. 968). This also reduces NGOs to the position of mere 'sub-contractors' who have to rely on external agencies, including governments, for launching and managing projects on women and shift from one problem to the next, depending on the availability of funds and donor's choice. Obviously, the kind of commitment required for empowering women cannot be delivered within a given power structure. To the best, 'activism' becomes another routine work for these paid employees. The issue of external funding also gives the state a convenient leverage over NGOs, and there are instances of governments supporting or threatening NGOs (Baviskar 2001, p. 12).

Research has proved that the issue of leadership also becomes a crucial factor in NGO activism. The kind of leadership, commitment, vision and quality of work afforded by the founder member(s) of an NGO is often not replicated by others. When this happens, NGOs fail to maintain the zeal after the demise of its charismatic leader(s). Also, the very specific and local factors (caste, class, gender) that led to the success of NGO activity in any region may not be replicable in a different region due to changes in socio-cultural and political atmospheres from one region to another.

Let me cite here an interesting case reported by Nagar and Raju (2003, p. 4). They found that far from challenging the exploitation of low-caste women by upper castes, a particular NGO in Punjab was actually reinforcing such hierarchies by supplying condoms to landlords indulging in unsafe sex with low-caste agricultural labourers. This NGO candidly admitted that they do not have the capacity to deal with such complex issues as class and caste. And, in any case, social change was not on their agenda. So, not all NGOs qualify for missions and ideals of spirited social engineering, which are theoretically ascribed to the 'third sector' entities and agencies. Challenging the age-old caste-class structure is, however, a daunting task. As Nagar and Raju show, some NGOs are using available spaces to bring about such changes without talking explicitly about women's subordination or exploitation. But the experience of Mahila Samakhya (MS) of Uttar Pradesh proves that such empowerment also generates mixed results (ibid., p. 7). Thus, this particular NGO trained women from the most exploited sections of the Harijan castes and Kol tribe as hand-pump mechanics in the drought-prone regions of Banda in UP. As a result, on the one hand, marginalised women who were the last ones to have access to village tube-wells are now regarded by uppercaste landlords as *mistry-ji* (Madam Mechanic), and these men now invite women to sit on cots and serve them tea. While such a change reveals a marked shift in terms of social equations, in other realms, women's exploitation continued or rather worsened. Thus, these women are paid less than half of what government agencies pay to male mechanics for the same work. The nature of their work also took them away from their homes, children and fields into a totally different kind of monetised and bureaucratised sector in which they felt marginalised in new ways.

Often the 'success' of an NGO to empower women may not produce desirable results. NGO inputs from Gujarat led Nagar and Raju (2003) to argue that self-esteem and confidence of women through activities like opening bank accounts, meeting officials, going to markets or similar activities, which the male members of their families used to do (leading to double burdens), did not make them free from sexual and physical exploitation at home. This proves that women achieving a certain degree of empowerment may not get really empowered in the end. So the "empowerment processes do not occur in a linear progression and can sometimes have contradictory effects" (ibid., p. 8). Factors like history, geography and political culture also become critical in fulfilling such needs.

The authority structure of NGOs also gives rise to questions about transparency and democratic participation. It should be acknowledged that many NGOs are highly idiosyncratic, paternalistic and authoritarian in nature, and it is almost difficult, if not impossible, to penetrate into these deep-seated structures of individual and social maladies. Tensions and conflicts between elite (professional) and grassroots workers are also seen to be very common in big NGOs. Radical shifts of the organisational structures of many NGOs in recent times speak clearly of the rise of professionally competent (English-educated and computer literate) workers in place of dynamic grassroots social activists. In other words, "the existence and need for spirited workers have given way to those who can sell the NGO to funders, rather than those who can really connect with the people in the 'project areas' in terms of their languages, struggles, and issues and who can help achieve concrete social goals" (Nagar and Raju 2003, p. 10).

Conclusions

It appears that the task to empower women through NGOisation has serious limitations. It is certainly not the panacea for all ills. This holds good despite the fact that many of our NGOs have contributed significantly for promoting gender justice and gender equality. For some[5] grassroots activists, working for the good and benefit of others is a passion. Yet, the onus is now on the NGO sector as a whole, which is really turning quite frustrating for those seriously engaged in developmental work. A clear hint is found to have been made at this sorry and challenging state of affairs in a document prepared by Save the Children (2016):

There is one NGO for every 400 people in India. However, not every NGO out there is engaged in serious social welfare work. Many are fraudulent and many are there without much serious intent. Amidst this, NGOs doing real work face several challenges. They face situations where they have to repeatedly vouch for their credibility, struggle to reach out to donors and have trouble in collaborating with government agencies.

It is true that our qualitative assessments of NGO activism have also changed from time to time. Today we have come to realise that issues like women's empowerment cannot be dealt with only by NGOs and 'project NGOs' are far removed from achieving this goal. Mushrooming of NGOs can neither reduce gender disparities nor can promote civil society activism. More importantly, the process of women's empowerment is very complex and nuanced. Any external intervention in the form of SHG formation or microfinance, though often needed, cannot in any way do away with gender inequality prevalent in our society for centuries. They rather create serious dependency and 'under-development'. Multi-layered concerns and considerations, arising out of caste, class, religion, culture, market, etc., also hinder such processes of empowerment. A mere shift in the language of development and coinage of suitable terms or techniques meant to govern development agenda may give rise to a false paradigm of developmentalism. There are also myriad 'bread and butter' and other existential issues facing the poor and disadvantaged women that go on to make adverse commentaries of ways in which 'development' is sought to be planned and brought about. There is, therefore, no shortcut to women's empowerment. The more our women protagonists, civil society activists and policymakers understand these pitfalls and dilemmas of development, the better it would be for society as a whole.

Notes

1. A non-governmental organisation (NGO) is normally defined as a non-profit, voluntary citizens' group that is organised on a local, national or international level. A World Bank key document, *Working with NGOs* (1995), goes on to maintain that, "In wider usage, the term NGO can be applied to any non-profit organisation, which is independent from government. NGOs are typically value-based organisations that depend, in whole or in part, on charitable donations and voluntary service. Although the NGO

sector has become increasingly professionalised over the last two decades, principles of altruism and voluntarism remain key defining characteristics".
2. The emergence of fundamentalist movements such as the Hindutva led to large-scale divisions in the NGO movement in recent times.
3. Several other terms, like Independent Sector, Non-Profit Organisations, Voluntary Citizen's Group, Voluntary Development Organisations (VDOs), Community-Based Organisations, Grassroots Organisations, etc., are suggested to refer to NGOs.
4. A 'Self Help Group' is a collective of individuals belonging to a certain number of households, who decide to work together for common interests to achieve a common goal. SHGs are mostly voluntary associations of women residing in the same area, formed democratically and without any political purpose or motive. According to NABARD, SHG is a group of 20 or less people from a homogeneous class who are willing to come together for addressing their common problems. Banks lend these members credits in certain multiples of their own savings and without any demand for collateral securities.
5. Take, for instance, the case of Sindhutai Sapkal, affectionately known as the "Mother of Orphans". She is known particularly for her work in raising orphaned children in India, has nurtured over 1,050 orphaned children and runs a Sanmati Bal Niketan, at Manjari (Budruk), Pune, Maharashtra.

REFERENCES

Ahamad, Tauffiqu, and Ananta Narayana Hemlata. 2015. Role of NGOs in Women Empowerment: With Special Reference to Uttar Pradesh. *International Journal of Applied Research* 1 (10): 115–118.

Appell, V. 1996. The Self-Employed Women's Association: Ideologies in Action. PhD thesis, Department of Anthropology and Sociology, University of British Columbia, Vancouver (published by UMI Press).

Baviskar, B.S. 2001. NGOs and Civil Society in India. *Sociological Bulletin* 50 (1): 3–15.

Bebbington, A., and R. Riddell. 1995. The Direct Funding of Southern NGOs by Donors: New Agendas and Old problems. *Journal of International Development* 7 (6): 879–893.

Beneria, L., and Shelley F (Eds.). 1992. *Unequal Burden: Economic Crisis, Persistent Poverty, and Women's Work*. Boulder: Westview Press.

Biswas, Nilanjana. 2006. On Funding and the NGO Sector. *Economic and Political Weekly* 41 (42): 4406–4411.

Brown, W. 2015. *Undoing the Demos: Neoliberalism's Stealth Revolution*. New York: Zone Books.

Buch, Nirmala. 2010. *From Oppression to Assertion*. New Delhi: Routledge.

Chambers, Robert. 1997. *Whose Reality Counts? Putting the First Last*. London: Intermediate Technology Publications.

Chaudhuri, Maitrayee. 2012a. Gender and Globalisation: Shifts in Developmental Paradigms. In *Interrogating Development: Discourses on Development in India Today*, ed. Biswajit Ghosh, 131–151. Jaipur: Rawat Publication.

Chaudhuri, Maitrayee. 2012b. Feminism in India: The Tale and Its Telling. *Revue Tiers Monde* 1: 19–36.

Chaudhuri, Ritu Sen. 2016. Women's Movement in India. e-pg-pathshala Module, Social Movement Paper, Sociology, UGC.

Das, Lipishree. 2012. Microfinance in India—Self Help Groups—Bank Linkage Model. MPRA Paper No. 38755, May. http://mpra.ub.uni-muenchen.de/38755/. Accessed on 14 May 2018.

Dash, Anup, and Souvagya Laxmi Saran. 2012. Women, Poverty and Empowerment: Rethinking Microfinance After the Global Crisis. In *Interrogating Development: Discourses on Development in India Today*, ed. Biswajit Ghosh, 173–196. Jaipur: Rawat Publication.

Edwards, M., and D. Hulme. 1996. Too Close for Comfort? The Impact of Official Aid on Non-Governmental Organisations. *World Development* 24 (6): 961–973.

Freedman, J. 2000. *Transforming Development*. Toronto: University of Toronto Press.

Ghosh, Biswajit. 2009. NGOs, Civil Society and Social Reconstruction in Contemporary India. *Journal of Developing Societies* 25 (2): 229–252.

Ghosh, Biswajit. 2012. Development Through Voluntary Actions: The Paradigm of NGO-isation. In *Discourses on Development*, ed. Biswajit Ghosh, 104–128. Jaipur: Rawat Publication.

Ghosh, Biswajit. 2013. How Does the Legal Framework Protect Victims of Dowry and Domestic Violence in India? A Critical Review. *Aggression and Violent Behaviour—A Review Journal* 18 (4): 409–416.

Ghosh, Biswajit, and Tanima Choudhuri. 2016. Social Movement Unionism: The Case of India. e-PG-Pathshala Module, Social Movement Paper, Sociology, Inflibnet, UGC.

Government of India. 2016. Receipt of Foreign Contributions by Voluntary Associations. FCRA Annual Report 2015–2016, Ministry of Home Affairs, New Delhi.

Gupta, Saurabh. 2014. From Demanding to Delivering Development: Challenges of NGO-Led Development in Rural Rajasthan, India. *Journal of South Asian Development* 9 (2): 121–145.
Horn, Z.E. 2009. No Cushion to Fall Back On: The Global economic Crisis and Informal Workers. Inclusive Cities Project, Cambridge. MA: Women in Informal Employment: Globalizing and Organizing (WIEGO): 20.
Jerath, Arati R. 2010. Grassroots Gold Mine. *The Times of India*, The Crest Edition, September 20, Kolkata.
Kabeer, N. 2005. Is Microfinance a 'Magic Bullet' for Women's Empowerment? Analysis of Findings from South Asia. *Economic and Political Weekly* XL (44 and 45): 4709–4718.
Kaimowitz, D. 1993. The Role of Non-Governmental Organisations in Agricultural Research and Technology Transfer in Latin America. *World Development* 21 (7): 1139–1150.
Karat, Prakash. 1984. Action Groups/Voluntary Agencies: A Factor in Imperialist Strategy. *Marxist* 2 (2): 19–54.
Kilby, P. 2011. *NGOs in India: The Challenges of Women's Empowerment and Accountability*. Oxon; New York: Routledge.
Kumari, Ranjana. 1992. *Women in Decision Making*. New Delhi: Vikas Publishing.
Munck, R. 1999. Deconstructing Development Discourse: of Impasses, Alternatives and Politics. In *Critical Development Theory: Contributions to a New Paradigm*, ed. R. Munck and D. O'Hearn. London: Zed Books.
NABARD. 2017. Status of Microfinance in India, 2016–17. https://www.nabard.org/auth/writereaddata/tender/1307174808status%20of%20microfinance%20in%20india%202016-17.pdf. Accessed on 14 May 2018.
Nagar, Richa, and Saraswati Raju. 2003. Women, NGOs and the Contradictions of Empowerment and Disempowerment: A Conversation. *Antipode* 35 (January): 1–13.
Niumai, Ajailiu. 2006. Non-government Organisations in Development: A Sociological Study of Selected NGOs in Manipur. PhD theses, CSSS, Jawaharlal Nehru University, New Delhi.
Oommen, T.K. 2004. *Nation, Civil Society and Social Movements—Essays in Political Sociology*. New Delhi: Sage.
Oxfam. 2010. *The Global economic Crisis and Developing Countries: Impact and Response*. Oxford: Oxfam International.
Paul, Sujit Kumar. 2015. *Rural Development: Concept and recent Approaches*. New Delhi: Concept Publishing Company.
Pramanick, S.K. 2012. Political Empowerment of Women in India: Discourse and Reality. In *Interrogating Development: Discourses on Development in India Today*, ed. Biswajit Ghosh, 152–172. Jaipur: Rawat Publication.

Routh, Supriya. 2016. Informal Workers' Aggregation and Law. *Theoretical Inquiries in Law* 16 (2): 283–320.

Roy, A. 2004. Public Power in the Age of Empire. *Socialist Worker*. http://socialistworker.org/2004. Accessed on 12 May 2018.

Roy, Srila. 2015. The Indian Women's Movement: Within and Beyond NGOization. *Journal of South Asian Development* 10 (1): 96–117.

Sambhaji, Jadhav Baburao. 2016. NGOs and Micro-Credit Institution: A Study of Dalit Women Empowerment in Nanded District. Ph.D. thesis, Department of Sociology, SRTM University, Nanded, Maharashtra.

Sato, Yutaka. Forthcoming. Power in Participatory Development: Gender, NGOs and the Unequal Social Relations in the Slums of Ahmedabad. In *Development and its Social Repercussions*, ed. M.N. Panini. New Delhi: Orient Longman.

Save the Children. 2016. Challenges Faced by NGOs in India. https://www.savethechildren.in/articles/challenges-faced-by-ngos-in-india. Accessed on 12 May 2018.

Sen, A. 1999. *Development as Freedom*. New York: Alfred A. Knopf.

SEWA. 2015. Annual Report. www.sewa.org/.../SEWA-ANNUAL-REPORT-2015-ENGLISH%20DT-12-8-016.pdf.

Sharma, Kumud. 1998. Transformative Politics: Dimensions of Women's Participation in Panchayati Raj. *Indian Journal of Gender Studies* 5 (1): 23–47.

Sinha, F. 2007. SHGs in India: Numbers Yes, Poverty Outreach and Empowerment, Partially. In *What's Wrong with Microfinance?*, ed. Thomas Dichter and Malcolm Harper, 73–82. Rugby: Practical Action Publishing.

Tellis, A. 2012. Wanted: A New Feminist Movement in India. *Sify New*. http://www.sify.com/news/wanted-a-new-feminist-movement-in-india-news-col umns-mm5lMlgcabfsi.html. Accessed on 14 May 2018.

Visvanathan, Shiv. 2014. NGOs of the Mind. *The Hindu*, June 30.

Viswanath, V. 1991. *NGOs and Women's Development in Rural South India: A Comparative Analysis*. Boulder: Westview Press.

World Bank. 1995. *Working with NGOs: A Practical Guide to Operational Collaboration between the World Bank and Non-Governmental Organizations*. Operations Policy Department. Washington, DC: The World Bank.

Yunus, Muhammad. 2003. Expanding Microcredit Outreach to Reach the Millennium Development Goals. International Seminar on Attacking Poverty with Microcredit, Dhaka, Bangladesh, January.

Zaidi, S. Akbar. 2004. NGO Failure and the Need to Bring Back the State. In *Indigeneity and Universality in Social Sciences: A South Asian Perspective*, ed. P.N. Mukherji and C. Sengupta, 187–202. New Delhi: Sage.

CHAPTER 5

Women's Participation in Rural Local Governance of Bangladesh: Progress and Challenges

Soma Roy Chowdhury and Mohammad Rejaul Karim Siddiquee

INTRODUCTION

Bangladesh has made steady progress in the areas of economic development and women's empowerment in recent years. The country has witnessed a sharp rise in the number of women emerging in leadership roles in public and political life. The year 1997 is significant from the perspective of grassroots women's leadership as it paved the way for legislative reforms in the local government laws of Bangladesh. The Local Government (Union Parishad) (Second Amendment) Act, 1997 afforded

S. R. Chowdhury (✉)
Independent Consultant & Associate, The Governance & Justice Group, London, England
e-mail: soma853@yahoo.com

M. R. K. Siddiquee
International Disability Alliance (IDA), Geneva, NY, USA

© The Author(s), under exclusive license to Springer Nature Singapore Pte Ltd. 2024
A. K. Sarkar and S. Das Gupta (eds.), *Understanding Women's Empowerment in South Asia*,
https://doi.org/10.1007/978-981-16-7538-6_5

the opportunity and legitimacy to aspiring women candidates in rural Bangladesh to formally contest elections for the reserved seats in the Union Parishad (electoral representation in the lowest tier of the local government).

Politically, the country is divided into eight divisions which are divided again into sixty-four districts. Districts are divided into four hundred and ninety-one Upazilas and four thousand five hundred and fifty-four Unions. Each Union is further divided into nine wards and wards are divided into villages. The Union Parishad is headed by a chair, called Chairman, and consists of nine general members plus three women members, elected from the reserved seats. The Local Government Ordinance of 1976 initially provided for the reservation of two seats for women in each Union Parishad. Pursuant to an amendment in 1983, the number of reserved seats has been increased to three. The Union Parishad (Second Amendment) Act, 1997 repealed the provision for nomination and introduced direct elections to the reserved seats. Since then, an unprecedented number of women candidates have participated in the local Union Parishad elections. However, despite holding public office within local political structures, their meaningful and effective participation in local governance continues to remain largely circumscribed in practice compared to their male counterparts. The purpose of this article is to explore and identify some of the progress, challenges and way forward around women's participation in rural local governance of Bangladesh.

CONSTITUTIONAL AND LEGAL PROVISIONS FOR WOMEN'S PARTICIPATION IN LOCAL GOVERNMENT UNITS IN THE RURAL SETTING

Bangladesh is a unitary, independent and sovereign Republic. The Principles of nationalism, socialism, democracy and secularism, together with the ideologies derived from those, as set out in Part-II of the Constitution, constitute the Fundamental Principles of State Policy. According to clause (2) of Article 8 of the Constitution, these principles shall be fundamental to the governance of Bangladesh; shall be applied by the State in the making of laws; and shall be a guide to the interpretation of the Constitution and of other laws of Bangladesh. It is further laid down that although these principles form the basis of the work of the State and of its citizens, they cannot be judicially enforced.

Article 11 of the Constitution clearly lays down that the Republic shall be a democracy in which the fundamental human rights and respect for the dignity and worth of the human person shall be guaranteed, and in which effective participation by the people through their elected representatives in administration at all levels shall be ensured. In furtherance of the Fundamental Principles of State Policy, the Constitution provides that the local government in every administrative unit of the Republic shall be entrusted to bodies composed of persons elected in accordance with law. According to the Constitution, the administrative units are to perform such functions within their jurisdiction areas as shall be prescribed by the Act of Parliament. The Constitution enlists some functions of the local government units as below:

- Administration and the work of public officers;
- The maintenance of public order;
- The preparation and implementation of plans relating to public services and economic development.

Article 60 of the Constitution enshrines that with a view to giving full effect to the provisions of Article 59, the Parliament shall, by law, confer powers on the local government bodies referred to in that Article, including power to impose taxes for local purposes, to prepare their budgets and to maintain funds. However, the expression "administrative unit" in Article 59 has been defined in Article 152 (1) to mean a district or other areas designated by law for the purpose of Article 59. Hence no designation is necessary in case of a district as Article 152 (1) itself designates districts as administrative units, but designation by law is necessary in case of areas other than districts to qualify as "administrative unit" within the meaning of Article 59. The Parliament may or may not set up a local government body in an administrative unit, but if a local government body is set up two conditions must be fulfilled—(1) it must be constituted in an administrative unit, and (2) it must be composed of elected persons.

In Bangladesh, the local governance system remained abolished for a period of sixteen years since 1975 and was revived in 1991. The Constitution (Fourth Amendment) Act, 1975 amended Article 11 and omitted the words "and in which effective participation by the people through their elected representatives in administration at all levels shall be ensured" from it and repealed the entire chapter III (Articles 59 and 60) of Part IV of the Constitution. The Constitution (Twelfth Amendment) Act, 1991 re-inserted the omitted words in Article 11 and restored Articles 59 and 60.

Given the Constitution expressly prohibits discrimination on the grounds of religion, race, caste, sex or place of birth; people regardless of their socio-economic status are equally entitled to enjoy their rights to participate in administration at all levels of the Republic. Clause (2) of Article 28 of the Constitution affirms that women shall have equal rights with men in all spheres of the State and of public life. Therefore, the Constitution makes it obligatory for the State to ensure equal participation of both men and women in local governance too by removing barriers of systematic inequality and subordination of women.

LOCAL GOVERNMENT LAWS

Currently, rural local governance in Bangladesh are governed by the following laws:

1. The Local Government (Union Parishad) Act, 2009;
2. The Upazila Parishad Act, 1998 (amended in 2009);
3. The Local Government (Municipality) Act, 2009;
4. The District Council Act, 2000; and
5. The Local Government (City Corporation) Act, 2009.

UNION PARISHADS

The Union Parishads formed under Section 10 of the Local Government (Union Parishad) Act, 2009 (hereinafter referred as LGUPA) are the smallest administrative units of Bangladesh. They constitute the lowest tier of the local government. As mentioned above, the Union Parishad is comprised of one Chairman, nine members elected from general seats and three female members elected from reserved seats. In theory, there is no legal barrier for any woman to be elected as a Chairman or a member from general seats. The law stipulates that the Chairman and all members shall be elected through direct voting, and they shall be entitled to an honorarium determined by the government. With a view to encouraging women's participation and decision-making in political life and local governance, reservations or quota systems were introduced. The reservations were intended as a temporary special measure (CEDAW Article 4.1) to overcome historical disadvantage experienced by women in general.

Notably, the LGUPA has incorporated special provisions with a view to encouraging potential women candidates to hone their skills and capabilities around contesting elections from general seats and discharging their duties effectively in the long run. The LGUPA has incorporated the following affirmative provisions for potential women candidates:

1. Appointment as Ex-officio Advisor of Ward Shobha (Sec.5);
2. Mandatory membership in Chairman Panel (Sec.33);
3. Making Rules regarding duties and functions (Sec.38, 47);
4. Maternity leave as per government policy (Sec.40);
5. One-third of Standing Committee to be presided by women members elected from reserved seats (Sec.45);
6. One-third of Development Project Implementation Committee to be presided by women members elected from reserved seats (Sec.47);
7. Making Rules regarding powers and special functions for women elected from reserved seats (Sec.96);
8. Making *Probidhan* or by-laws regarding regulation of issues and functions of Standing Committees (Sec.97).

These special provisions have been included to enable potential women elected from reserved seats to effectively participate in mainstream rural local governance. They also intend to strengthen women's position and voice within the Union Parishads. Such measures if implemented on the ground would go a long way in building their skills and confidence over time so that they could dispel age-old negative perceptions regarding their ability to effectively participate and contribute in mainstream local politics.

Women's Participation in Various Fora of Local Government Units in Rural Bangladesh: The Gulf Between Theory and Practice—Women's Participation as Ex-officio Advisor in Ward Shobhs

Ward Shobhas or mass gatherings at the local level are a unique feature of the Union Parishad. According to the LGUPA, every Union is divided into nine wards and one member of Union Parishad shall be elected for each ward. Every three wards shall form a consolidated ward for electing one reserved seat member. According to the law, one "ward shobha" shall be convened by the voters of the concerned ward. 5% of the total population in a ward is required to constitute quorum for these meetings. The reserved seat member shall be the ex-officio advisor of the ward shobha while the general seat member shall be responsible to preside over the meetings. Section 6 lays down the functions of the Ward Shobha. Exploring information around development planning; determination of priority schemes for each ward; screening and assessment of the people based on their eligibility criteria under social safety net programs; awareness building on conservation of environment, prevention of social crimes including corruption, environment pollution, dowry, child marriage, acid-throwing and narcotics related crimes are some of the most significant functions of the Ward Shobha.

The role and responsibility of the position of "Advisor of Ward Shobha" has not been clearly articulated in the LGUPA. As a result, women members elected from reserved seats are precluded from playing their role properly in the Ward Shobha and, in practice, they are often largely ignored by their male counterparts. There is no budgetary allocation to organize a Ward Shobha. Owing to budgetary constraints, a Ward Shobha is seldom organized which eventually impedes elected women to actively engage with people at the local level.

Women's Participation as Panel Chairman

According to the LGUPA, every Union Parishad shall elect three members on the Chairman panel within thirty days of the first meeting held and out of these three, one shall be a member from the reserved seats. Panel members are to be elected from the twelve members by themselves. In the absence of the Chairman, the first panel member assumes the responsibilities of the Chairman. Likewise, the second and the third member gets opportunities to preside over Parishad meetings. It is common in most Union Parishads that women elected from reserved seats assume the third position while their male counterparts take over the first and second positions as panel members. Consequently, they hardly get any opportunity to head the Union Parishad. This impliedly silence their voice in decision-making despite having membership in the Chairman Panel.

Rules Regarding Rights, Duties and Responsibilities

Due to the absence of respective "Rules" until recently the female members from reserved seats have been unable to discharge their duties and responsibilities properly. They have to submit to the will of the Chairman who enjoys absolute and unfettered powers and privileges. Section 38 describes the rights and responsibilities of the Chairman and Members of the Union Parishad. Section 47 and Schedule-2 lists the activities of the Union Parishad. Section 47(3) empowers the government to assign duties and responsibilities to members elected from reserved seats through formulating Rules. Section 96(a) of the Act delegates the power to the government to formulate Rules regarding the powers and responsibilities of the Chairman and members. Section 96(b) empowers the government to formulate rules regarding powers and special functions of those elected from the reserved seats. After six years of enactment of the LGUPA, the government has formulated Rules namely "Union Parishad (Power and Special Functions of Reserved Seat Members) Rules, 2016. These rules merely iterate the provisions from the Parent Act. However, they have failed to address the concerns around gender discrimination and power imbalance within the local governance structure.

Women's Participation in Standing Committees

The LGUPA provides for the formation of thirteen Standing Committees to oversee finance, accounts, audit, tax, education, health, family planning, sanitation, law and order, etc. (Section 45). Such Standing Committees are comprised of five to seven members. Although the law stipulates that one-third of total Standing Committees are to be headed by women, it has been found that women are seldom heading them. As per law, Standing Committees shall meet at least once in every two months. The recommendations made by the Standing Committees are to be adopted by the Union Parishads in its next meeting. If they do not adopt them, they must inform the Standing Committees in writing with proper reasoning for non-adoption. However, in practice the Standing Committees are mostly dysfunctional, and this has apparently, no effect on the Union Parishad activities. Hence reservation for the position of Chair in one-third Standing Committees has no impact. Most Union Parishads do not have *Probidhan* or by-laws regarding functions and regulation of Standing Committees.

A study by WFP-Bangladesh in 2000 noted that about 16% of female members chair the Standing Committees of the Union Parishads. The situation has been improved by government and NGO initiatives to promote and encourage participation of women members in the Union Parishads. It was found in 2007 that 80% female members serve as Chair in at least one committee and all female members are attached to more than two committees.

According to a research report published by Bangladesh Legal Aid and Services Trust (BLAST) in 2016, only 136 Standing Committees out of 585 (in 45 surveyed UPs) are chaired by women members who have been elected from reserved seats whereas the women members are entitled to head 195 Standing Committees as per law. It has been found that 50% of the total number of Standing Committees have not been duly constituted. Most Union Parishads have failed to form all Standing Committees as per law.

Allocation of business responsibilities is often gender discriminatory. Female members elected from the reserved seats are precluded from equally participating in the distribution of the social safety net facilities which are usually dealt with by their male counterparts. Likewise, contrary to the existing legal provisions which entrust female members to distribute the maternity allowances under the local government, it has been found that these tasks are assigned to the male members.

Women's Participation in Development Projects

The law lays down that one-third of Development Project Implementation Committees are to be headed by women elected from the reserved seats. According to the BLAST survey report, it has been found that only two hundred and fifty-one development projects are being headed by women elected from the reserved seats even though they were entitled to head three hundred and sixty-two projects within the surveyed area. Another practical caveat is that most women elected from the reserved seats lack necessary knowledge and skills required for discharging their responsibilities effectively. Their capacity gaps are illustrated by the fact that most survey respondents are unable to name the projects which they are heading.

Women's Participation in Local Dispute Resolution Fora

Entrenched social norms and gender discriminatory governance practices at the local level preclude a large majority of female local government representatives to participate in decision-making at the traditional dispute resolution forums. Recent research on the justice-seeking behavior of Bangladeshis in general and the socially and economically disadvantaged groups suggests that majority of people prefer Union Parishads for settlement of disputes at the local level. However, women members elected from reserved seats continue to face discrimination within the traditional dispute resolution forums including the Village Courts and the Arbitration Councils in their efforts to assume the role of local mediators or arbitrators. In the absence of continued opportunity for their skills training and capacity building, sometimes the male relatives (including the husbands of the female members elected from the reserved seats) play an active role in the dispensation of justice at the local dispute resolution forums on their behalf.

Women's Participation in Upazila Parishads

Upazila Parishads constitute the second lowest tier of the local government in Bangladesh. The Parishad is comprised of a chairman, two vice-chairmen, chairmen of all Union Parishads within the territory of the concerned Upazila, mayor (s) of Pourasava (s) or municipalities (if any) and members/councilors elected from the reserved seats of the Union Parishads and Pourasavas. The law stipulates that number of members from the reserved seats will be one-third of the total number of Union Parishads and Pourasavas of the concerned Upazila. Out of two vice chairman positions, one is reserved for women. Both the Chairman and Vice-Chairman are required to be elected through direct vote.

The Ministry of Local Government through a circular issued on 31 May 2015 notified that 3% of the total annual budget of any Upazila Parishad shall be allocated for the members of the Nari Unnoyan Forum (a forum comprised of women including the female Vice-Chairman and elected female members from the reserved seats of the Union Parishads). It further stated that 25% development projects shall be led by female members. However, the ground reality is very different. According to a news report published in a leading Bengali daily on 27 February 2016, one Shahida Begum who was elected as Vice-Chairman of Zianagar Upazila of Pirojpur district in 2009 and 2014 for two consecutive terms was deprived of her entitlement. The Zianagar Upazila Parishad received 42 metric tons of rice from the government for implementation of development projects during the 2015–2016 fiscal year. Although Shahida Begum submitted ten project proposals, she was not given any allocation for those. The report noted that the Upazila Chairman arbitrarily rejected the projects submitted by Shahida in violation of the aforesaid circular. Following the news report, BLAST offered to provide legal support to Shahida Begum for initiating legal action against the alleged discrimination but she declined.

Challenges Impeding Women's Participation in Local Governance at the Rural Level Safe Workplace

The absence of a safe and secure workplace acts as a major impediment in women's participation in the local government. The LGUPA is silent about the safety and security measures that should be in place to encourage women to actively participate in the affairs of running the rural local government units. Despite an Apex Court ruling and guidelines to combat sexual harassment at workplace, the local government is yet to take appropriate measures toward implementation of this milestone judgment. According to a news report, a female member elected from a reserved seat was allegedly raped by her male colleague (a general seat member) on 6 April 2017 at her workplace (in the Union Parishad office in Bajubagha Union under Bagha Upazila in Rajshahi). She had to be admitted for medical treatment in the One Stop Crisis Center under the Rajshahi Medical College Hospital. Though police arrested both the accused member and the accomplice (the panel chairman), however, recurrence of such incidents discourages women from working with their male colleagues in the Union Parishads. An indigenous woman member of Fasiakhali Union Council of Lama Upazila at Bandarban in the Chittagong Hill Tracts was beaten up by her male colleague on 8 May 2017 while she was visiting an area under an ultra-poor employment project. The victim complained that she was assaulted because she was getting actively involved in local projects.

Entrenched Social Norms and Gender Discriminatory Practices

Entrenched social norms and gender discriminatory practices seriously impede women's participation in politics and public affairs. According to a BIGD report, the factors that have been commonly identified as barriers to women's participation in public life include political violence, gender stereotypes and outright discrimination, personal obstacles such as lack of confidence, culturally prescribed domestic roles, lack of education, lack of financial and economic capital and balancing family and public life. In most Union Parishads, the female members are neglected and ignored by the Chairmen and other male members. As such, women feel discouraged to attend their office and sometimes they are even accompanied by their husbands. Panday observed that inconvenient schedules, location, distance and the lack of escort are major impediments for women elected as representatives to attend meetings. Another study carried out by Panday in 2013 found that 62.5% of survey respondents identified physical mobility as a stumbling block and 50% UP Chairs opined that lack of family support were barriers for women's participation. Panday pointed out that most women who were surveyed noted ambiguity in existing laws regarding the role of women as one of the biggest constraints for their effective participation in politics and public life.

It has been observed by survey respondents that female members are often compelled to sign on meeting resolutions even if they have been absent in those meetings. Women elected to reserved seats who participated in the survey opine that they are often regarded as "second class" representatives with limited power and credibility. In most cases, the Chairman does not share government notifications, meeting decisions and other necessary information with the female members of the Union Parishad.

Power Imbalance

The Chairman of a Union Parishad is elected directly by the voters of the concerned union (nine wards constitute a union) while the reserve seat members are elected by voters of a consolidated ward (three wards constitute a consolidated ward). Since the Chairman represents all nine wards and she/he is elected directly by the voters, she/he is vested with unbridled powers by the law. Consequently, the Chairman assumes the role of an autocrat in most cases and tends to exercise his powers rather arbitrarily. Though the general seat members are elected from one ward, they tend to dominate the reserved seat members due to general perceptions that the reserved seat members only have an ornamental role to play in local governance. According to the BIGD report, the Chairman is the chief executive of a Union Parishad. He decides on all matters. He assigns work, approves sanctions of development works and presides over all meetings, committees. Without his support and favor nothing is possible and both male and female members have to maintain good working relations with the Chairman. This is despite that the law has neither accorded superior status to the general seat members nor discriminated between the general and reserved seat members.

Women's Limited Ability to Exercise Their Autonomy Around Voting Rights

Even though Bangladesh has made steady progress in ensuring women's presence in the local government, still many women in rural Bangladesh continue to face challenges in exercising their right to vote. In Bangladesh (the then East Pakistan), women were conferred voting rights since 1958. However, in practice, many women in remote areas of Bangladesh are not allowed to exercise their voting rights independently due to social and family restrictions. They are often discouraged to go to the polling centers to cast their votes. Against this backdrop, Bangladesh National Women Lawyer's Association (BNWLA) had to invoke a Writ Petition in the form of public interest litigation in 2001 to ensure voting rights of women in twelve villages under *Surat* union of Jhenidah district.

Weaknesses in Implementation of Existing Legal Provisions

Although special provisions were incorporated in the LGUPA for the gradual empowerment and meaningful participation of women in rural local government units, nonetheless the following gaps pose a challenge toward its effective implementation:

1. Loopholes, ambiguities within existing laws and regulations;
2. Lack of oversight by the concerned Ministry;
3. Social resistance including patriarchal values and mindset which tend to undermine women and their participation in public life;
4. Lack of skills and knowledge accounting for incompetence and dearth of capacity among the female members elected from reserved seats to effectively participate in local governance.

Challenging Gender Discrimination in Public Office: Shamina Sultana Case

In response to a writ petition challenging a discriminatory circular issued by the Ministry of Local Government, the Supreme Court iterated that all citizens are equal in the eyes of the law and are entitled to equal protection before the law and that the circular contradicted the Fundamental Principles of State Policy which seeks to ensure the participation of women in all spheres of state affairs. The impugned circular sought to exclude female ward commissioners from discharging key functions including serving on the Law and Order Committees, issuing certificates relating to birth and death; succession and nationality and overseeing local infrastructure projects. The Court also directed that once elected, the Commissioners, whether in the general seats or in the reserved seats, male or female, are equal in all respects and they shall be treated alike by all concerned. Likewise, they must enjoy same and equal power, responsibility, dignity and jurisdiction of work.

While delivering the milestone judgment former Chief Justice ABM Khairul Haque noted "(A) woman always has to adjust her position, sometimes with her husband, sometimes she has to compromise between her children and her job. Unlike a working man, a working woman of necessity has always to keep an eye on her family. This is how a woman is thrown and pushed in a discriminatory situation."

It has been noted with concern in different NGO meetings that even after a decade since the passage of the monumental judgment, women members/councilors elected from reserved seats continue to face gender discrimination in discharging their functions as elected representatives. There is limited scope, resources and opportunity for training and capacity building of women members.

THE WAY FORWARD: SETTING PRIORITIES TO ELIMINATE CHALLENGES

Quotas or reservations will merely ensure women's representation in local government units. However, representation is not a sufficient condition for effective participation. Partnerships between government and non-governmental organizations must be developed to eliminate gender discrimination, biases and barriers to effective participation of women in local politics. Strong institutional mechanisms are required to further explore and strengthen women's participation in local governance at the rural level. The following is a raft of recommendations which may be considered and adopted by the policymakers to strengthen the role of women in local government:

1. Legislative Reforms

- The existing laws should be amended with a view to curtailing the unfettered powers conferred upon the Chairpersons within the local government structure. Enabling provisions for punitive action and holding the Chair accountable for arbitrary exercise of powers should be incorporated within the LGUPA.
- Prepare and/or revise all Rules under the LGUPA in conformity with the spirit of the affirmative provisions.
- The newly drafted rules should be revised to eliminate the practical challenges faced by elected women members (emanating from gender discrimination and power imbalance within the existing local government structures) in consultation with grassroots women leaders, women rights activists and NGOs with a commendable track record of working with elected local government representatives.

2. Increase Budgetary Allocations

- An appropriate investment plan should be prepared by the concerned Ministry for allocation of adequate resources toward implementation of the various functions envisaged under the Ward Shobha and Standing Committees.
- Benefits and resource allocation for each reserved seat member should be revised so that the proposed allowance is proportionate to the jurisdiction and population of the constituency to be led by the reserved seat members which is practically three times more than a general seat member.

3. Capacity Building of Women in Local Government

- An overwhelming number of rural women are being elected to the reserved seats within local government units. However, many of them are not aware, educated and skilled to perform their duties as elected representatives. Owing to lack of information, knowledge and skills, their male counterparts often tend to exploit and undermine their participation in local government. The government, NGOs and development partners should coordinate and develop strategies and action plan for consistent engagement and building the capacities of elected women representatives so that they are able to play an active role in decision-making at all forums of the local government units.

4. Introduction of a Code of Conduct

- A code of conduct should be prepared and implemented for both general and reserved seat members in all local government units to ensure elimination of gender discrimination and gender stereo-typing in discharge of their regular duties as elected representatives within the local government.
- There should be an oversight body comprising of government and NGO representatives that will jointly monitor and report progress and compliance to the Ministry of Local Government.

5. Formation of Sexual Harassment Prevention Committees

- Sexual Harassment Prevention Committees at the local level should be urgently formed in compliance with the Supreme Court guidelines under Writ Petition No. 5916 of 2008 headed by qualified women. Likewise, a Complaint Committee should be set up within every Union Parishad that would expeditiously take appropriate measures to redress grievances relating to sexual harassment.

6. Strengthening the Knowledge Base to Inform Policy and Strategy Development

- It is imperative to build a robust evidence base that would inform policy and development of strategies to eliminate the practical impediments faced by women in local government. The government and development partners should coordinate their efforts to provide support and assistance to NGOs and academics for the systematic collection, dissemination and publication of data on caveats which impede effective participation of women in local government.

7. Closing the gap between international human rights covenants and national laws, policies and practices

- It is the ultimate responsibility of the State to ensure that all national laws, policies and practices conform to international standards and principles of non-discrimination and equality. It is incumbent upon the State to take necessary measures for correcting the environment which deter women from meaningfully participating in decision-making in all forums of the local government in Bangladesh through systematic and sustained action backed by strong institutional reforms.

Notes

1. Bangladesh National Portal, The People's Republic of Bangladesh, accessed on December 10, 2017, http://www.bangladesh.gov.bd.
2. Ibid.

3. Article 1, The Constitution of the Peoples' Republic of Bangladesh (Printed with last amendment, April 2016), Legislative and Parliamentary Affairs Division, Ministry of Law, Justice and Parliamentary Affairs, Government of the People's Republic of Bangladesh, p. 2.
4. Article 8, The Constitution of Peoples' Republic of Bangladesh (Printed with last amendment, April 2016), p. 4.
5. Article 59 (1), The Constitution of the Peoples' Republic of Bangladesh (Printed with last amendment, April 2016), p. 19.
6. Article 59 (2), The Constitution of the Peoples' Republic of Bangladesh (Printed with last amendment, April 2016), p. 19.
7. Kudrat-E-Elahi Panir V. Bangladesh, 44 DLR (AD), p. 319.
8. Ibid., p. 336.
9. Section 2, The Constitution (Fourth Amendment) Act, 1975 (Act II of 1975).
10. Section 4 (b), The Constitution (Fourth Amendment) Act, 1975 (Act II of 1975).
11. Sections 2 and 3, The Constitution (Twelfth Amendment) Act, 1991 (Act XXVIII of 1991).
12. Article 28 (1), The Constitution of the Peoples' Republic of Bangladesh (Printed with last amendment, April 2016), p. 8
13. Section 8, The Local Government (Union Parishad) Act 2009 (Act No. 61 of 2009), Laws of Bangladesh, Ministry of Law Justice and Parliamentary Affairs, accessed on December 17, 2017, http://bdlaws.minlaw.gov.bd/bangla_all_sections.php?id=1027.
14. Sub-Section (1) of Section 10, the Local Government (Union Parishad) Act, 2009.
15. Section 3(1), Local Government (Union Parishad) Act, 2009.
16. Section 3(2) and 13 (9), Local Government (Union Parishad) Act, 2009.
17. Section 4, Local Government (Union Parishad) Act, 2009.
18. Ibid.
19. [Unpublished] Report of Expert Consultation Meeting on "Need for Rules regarding Special Functions of Reserve Seat Members of Union Parishad for Ensuring Effective Participation of Women in Local Governance System", (Dhaka: Bangladesh Legal Aid and Services Trust-BLAST, June 25, 2015).
20. Rejaul Karim Siddiquee, Reservation of Seats in Local Government Units for Women's Empowerment: Evaluation of four and

half decades, Eposode-2 (Dhaka: The Daily Sangbad, Date: March 19, 2017, p. 14).
21. Section 33(1), Local Government (Union Parishad) Act, 2009.
22. Siddiquee, Reservation of Seats for Women's Empowerment, Eposode-2, (Dhaka: The Daily Sangbad, Date: March 19, 2017, p. 14).
23. SRO No. 296-Act/2016, Bangladesh Gazette, Local Government Division, Ministry of Local Government, Rural Development and Co-operatives, Published on October 2, 2016.
24. Sub-Section (4) of section 45, Local Government (Union Parishad) Act, 2009.
25. Sara Hossain and T. Islam, Women's Participation in Local Governance and Local Justice (Dhaka: Bangladesh Legal Aid and Services Trust-BLAST, 2016), pp. 5–6.
26. Siddiquee, Reservation of Seats for Women's Empowerment, Episode-2 (Dhaka: The Daily Sangbad, Date: March 19, 2017, p. 14).
27. Tanjeela Mumita, Achieving Equal Rights (Dhaka, The Daily Star, dated: March 8, 2010), accessed on 18 May, 2017, http://www.thedailystar.net/news-detail-129088.
28. Ibid.
29. Sara Hossain and T. Islam, Women's Participation in Local Governance and Local Justice (Dhaka: Bangladesh Legal Aid and Services Trust-BLAST, 2016), pp. 5–6.
30. Ibid.
31. Safiul Azam, Review of Local Government Laws (Dhaka: Munni Publication, 2015) p. 33.
32. [Unpublished] Report of Sharing Meeting with Members of Union Council, Paroikora Union, Anwara, Chittagong (Meeting held on May 11, 2015, organized by BLAST).
33. Report of Expert Consultation Meeting on "Need for Rules regarding Special Functions of Reserve Seat Members of Union Councils for Ensuring Effective Participation of Women in Local Governance System"; (Dhaka: Bangladesh Legal Aid and Services Trust-BLAST, June 25, 2015).
34. Caritas Development Institute, *Role of Traditional Institutions in Conflict Resolution in Rural Bangladesh, unpublished report* (2012); CLS, *Measuring Community Perceptions on Access to Justice in CLS Intervention Areas* (Perception Study 2013), (research

outsourced by Community Legal Services, a project funded by UK Aid and implemented by Maxwell Stamp PLC, British Council and the Center for Effective Dispute Resolution).
35. The Village Court (VC) is a quasi-judicial body working at the grassroots level having jurisdiction to adjudicate petty offences and civil disputes. The VC is formed under the Village Court Act, 2006 and comprised of a Chairman and four members (each party in dispute is to nominate two members, out of whom one must be a UP member). The Chairman of the concerned Union Parishad generally acts as the Chairman of Village Court. During his/her absence any member of the UP except him/her who has been nominated by both parties in dispute shall act as Chairman of the VC. If the dispute involves interest of minor or women, the concerned party shall nominate one female member.
36. The Arbitration Council (AC) is formed under the Muslim Family Laws Ordinance, 1961 and deals with adjudication of family disputes relating to divorce, dower, maintenance and polygamy. The AC is comprised of a Chairman and two members (one is nominated by the husband and the other is nominated by the wife). No divorce can be executed without serving notice to the AC. AC's prior permission is a must for contracting multiple marriages.
37. Section 6, Upazila Parishad Act, 1998 (amended in 2009), Act No. 24 of 1998, Laws of Bangladesh, Ministry of Law, Justice and Parliamentary Affairs, accessed on December 17, 2017, http://bdl aws.minlaw.gov.bd/bangla_all_sections.php?id=827.
38. Woman Vice-Chairpersons have been denied allocations (Dhaka: The Daily Prothom Alo, date: 27 February 2016), accessed on December 10, 2017, http://www.prothom-alo.com/bangladesh/article/781804.
39. Bangladesh National Women Lawyers Association (BNWLA) v. Bangladesh, 14 BLC, Writ Petition No 5916 of 2008.
40. UP Member Raped in her Office (Dhaka: the Daily Prothom Alo, dated 7 April 2017)
41. Woman UP Member assaulted at Lama (Dhaka: Online news portal Somoyer Khobor, dated: 8 May 2017) accessed on May 8, 2017, http://www.somoyerkonthosor.com/2017/05/08/128004.htm.
42. Women's Participation in the Union Parishads, Local Governance Programme Sharique-III, BIGD Special Publication Series No. 04 (2016).

43. Panday, P.K. (2008) 'Representation without Participation: Quotas for Women in Bangladesh', International Political Science Review 29.4: 489–512.
44. Panday, P.K. (2013) "Impact Study on Women Empowerment through Effective, Transparent and Inclusive Local Governance" [Report prepared for Sharique, Local Governance Programme].
45. Women's Participation in the Union Parishads, Local Governance Programme Sharique-III, BIGD Special Publication Series No.04 (2016).
46. Report of Expert Consultation Meeting on "Need for Rules regarding Special Functions of Reserve Seat Members of Union Councils for Ensuring Effective Participation of Women in Local Governance System"; (Dhaka: Bangladesh Legal Aid and Services Trust-BLAST, June 25, 2015).
47. Women's Participation in the Union Parishads, Local Governance Programme Sharique-III, BIGD Special Publication Series No. 04 (2016).
48. BNWLA V. Bangladesh (Writ Petition No. 964 of 2001).
49. Women's Participation in the Union Parishads, Local Governance Programme Sharique-III, BIGD Special Publication Series No. 04 (2016).
50. Bangladesh National Women Lawyers Association v. Bangladesh, 14 BLC (2009) p. 694.

REFERENCES

Azam, Safiul. 2015. *Review of Local Government Laws*. Dhaka: Munni Publication.
Bangladesh National Portal. 2017. The People's Republic of Bangladesh. http://www.bangladesh.gov.bd. Accessed on 10 December 2017.
Bangladesh National Women Lawyers Association (BNWLA) v. Bangladesh, 14 BLC (Writ Petition No. 5916 of 2008).
BNWLA V. Bangladesh (Writ Petition No. 964 of 2001).
The Constitution of the Peoples' Republic of Bangladesh. 1972 (Printed with last amendment, April 2016). Legislative and Parliamentary Affairs Division, Ministry of Law, Justice and Parliamentary Affairs, Government of People's Republic of Bangladesh.
The Constitution (Fourth Amendment) Act. 1975 (Act II of 1975).

The Constitution (Twelfth Amendment) Act. 1991 (Act XXVIII of 1991).
Hossain, Sara, and T. Islam. 2016. *Women's Participation in Local Governance and Local Justice*. Dhaka: Bangladesh Legal Aid and Services Trust-BLAST.
Kudrat-E-Elahi Panir V. Bangladesh, 44 DLR (AD), p. 319.
The Local Government (Union Parishad) Act 2009 (Act No. 61 of 2009), Laws of Bangladesh, Ministry of Law Justice and Parliamentary Affairs. http://bdlaws.minlaw.gov.bd/bangla_all_sections.php?id=1027. Accessed on 17 December 2017.
"Measuring Community Perceptions on Access to Justice in CLS Intervention Areas" (Perception Study 2013), *(research outsourced by Community Legal Services, a Project Funded by UK Aid and Implemented by Maxwell Stamp PLC, British Council and the Center for Effective Dispute Resolution)*.
The Muslim Family Laws Ordinance. 1961 (Ordinance No. VIII of 1961). Laws of Bangladesh, Ministry of Law Justice and Parliamentary Affairs. http://bdlaws.minlaw.gov.bd/print_sections_all.php?id=305. Accessed on 17 December 2017.
"Need for Rules Regarding Special Functions of Reserve Seat Members of Union Parishad for Ensuring Effective Participation of Women in Local Governance System". Unpublished Report of an Expert Consultation Meeting. Dhaka: Bangladesh Legal Aid and Services Trust-BLAST, June 25, 2015.
Panday, P.K. 2008. Representation without Participation: Quotas for Women in Bangladesh. *International Political Science Review* 29 (4): 489–512.
Panday, P.K. 2013. *Impact Study on Women Empowerment through Effective, Transparent and Inclusive Local Governance* [Report prepared for Sharique, Local Governance Programme].
"Role of Traditional Institutions in Conflict Resolution in Rural Bangladesh". 2012. Unpublished Report. Caritas Development Institute.
Siddiquee, Rejaul Karim. 2017. *Reservation of Seats in Local Government Units for Women's Empowerment: Evaluation of Four and half decades*, Eposode-2. Dhaka: The Daily Sangbad, Date: March 19, 2017, p. 14.
Sharing Meeting with Members of Union Council, Paroikora Union, Anwara, Chittagong, Unpublished report (Meeting held on May 11, 2015, organized by BLAST).
Shamima Sultana Seema Vs. Bangladesh, 57 DLR (HCD) 2005, p. 201 (Writ Petition No. 3304 of 2004).
SRO No. 296-Act/2016, Bangladesh Gazette, Local Government Division, Ministry of Local Government, Rural Development and Co-operatives, Published on October 2, 2016.
Tanjeela Mumita. 2010. Achieving Equal Rights. *The Daily Star*, March 8, Dhaka. http://www.thedailystar.net/news-detail-129088. Accessed on 18 May 2017.

"UP Member Raped in Her Office". 2017. *The Daily Prothom Alo*, April 7, Dhaka.

The Upazila Parishad Act. 1998 (amended in 2009). Act No. 24 of 1998, Laws of Bangladesh, Ministry of Law, Justice and Parliamentary Affairs. http://bdlaws.minlaw.gov.bd/bangla_all_sections.php?id=827. Accessed on 17 December 2017.

The Village Court Act. 2006 (Act No. 19 of 2006). Laws of Bangladesh, Ministry of Law, Justice and Parliamentary Affairs. http://bdlaws.minlaw.gov.bd/bangla_all_sections.php?id=938. Accessed on 17 December 2017.

Woman Vice-Chairperson Have Not Been Given Allocations. 2016. *The Daily Prothom Alo*, February 27, Dhaka. http://www.prothom-alo.com/bangladesh/article/781804.

Woman UP Member Assaulted at Lama. 2017. Online News Portal. *Somoyer Khobor*, May 8, Dhaka. http://www.somoyerkonthosor.com/2017/05/08/128004.htm.

Women's Participation in the Union Parishads. 2016. Local Governance Programme Sharique-III, BIGD Special Publication Series No. 04.

CHAPTER 6

Reproductive Health of Women and Human Development in Nepal Practical Challenges and Policy Implications

Ishara Mahat and Kamal Gautam

INTRODUCTION

The concept of "reproductive health" acquires different meanings to different people and especially to the vulnerable groups of the developing world, it gets integrally connected with an entire range of socio-cultural taboos. In its most commonly accepted form at the global level, 'reproductive health' focuses on the following indicators: (1) every sexual act should be free of coercion and infection; (2) every pregnancy should be intended; and (3) every birth should be healthy (NRC 1997). However, such concept, though based on women's rights and objectivity of ideal gender relations, doesn't always take into account the socio-economic

---

I. Mahat (✉)
University of Ottawa, Ottawa, ON, Canada
e-mail: imahat@uottawa.ca

K. Gautam
Tribhuvan University, Kirtipur, Nepal

© The Author(s), under exclusive license to Springer Nature Singapore Pte Ltd. 2024
A. K. Sarkar and S. Das Gupta (eds.), *Understanding Women's Empowerment in South Asia*,
https://doi.org/10.1007/978-981-16-7538-6_6

contexts and social relations prevailing in most countries of the developing world where problems of reproductive health would be integrally connected with considerations of social stigma and shame, all of which remain heavily embedded in the culture of lived realities. Sex-selective abortions in India and China, for instance, have incurred large social costs in terms of losses of freedom of conjugal choices and deteriorating maternal health conditions (Sen 1999). Under such circumstances, affected people hardly worry about the choices in reproduction and furthermore, about autonomy as long as children remain a source of their integration into a family unit (Mumtaz and Salway 2009).

Given such stigma and sensitivity, the maintenance of reproductive health turns out to be severely problematic. Apart from the biological risks, social forces and arrangements often let women down and constrain their choices on reproductive health (Sen 1994). These include, for instance, multiple constraints on accessing available care from their spouses or partners, families and communities as well as being able to afford transportation even before the healthcare system is reached. Hence, reproductive health awareness becomes very crucial in the cultural context of the Nepalese society, which can lead to positive outcomes for individuals, families and communities at large.

According to an estimate made by the WHO (2011a), 30% of adolescent girls in low and middle-income countries get married by the age of 18, and it enhances the risk of adverse health conditions of early pregnancy. Similarly, unmet needs for modern contraception are high in the least developed countries, where the risk of maternal mortality is the highest. In addition, women with unintended pregnancies are more likely to receive delayed pre-natal care, which also has an adverse impact on maternal and infant health (Darroch and Singh 2012). Young women remain particularly vulnerable in situations where access to effective methods of contraception gets restricted only to married women, and where the incidence of non-consensual sexual intercourse is high (WHO 2011b). In addition, 13% of pregnancy-related deaths are attributed to unsafe abortion, which is also prevalent in the developing world (WHO 2011b).

Nepal is one of the countries with the highest maternal and infant mortality in South Asia. Given the poverty-driven socio-economic realities intertwined with the cultural, geographical and political specifics of the country, the reproductive health awareness among the youths and adolescents is far from satisfactory. The adolescents remain especially disadvantaged in the rural settings with limited access to information, health and educational opportunities and also discernibly handicapped in terms of several retrogressive social and cultural norms and practices. Early marriage and early pregnancy are the norms of a traditional society that leave couples less prepared for making better reproductive choices based on adequate literacy about family planning, including maternal and infant care (Khatiwada et al. 2013). The legal age of marriage for women and men with and without the consent of parents is 18 years and 21 respectively. The sexual debut for the vast majority of girls occurs during adolescence, and within the context of marriage. Early marriage can have numerous complications, including unplanned pregnancy and exposure to sexually transmitted infections (STIs) that do have adverse impacts upon women's health (WHO 2011b). Nevertheless, giving birth within the first few years of marriage brings a sense of joy to the whole family, especially, when the baby is a boy.

The unmet needs of contraception are high in Nepal as only 14% of married adolescent girls aged 15–19 and 24% of married women aged 20–24 are using the modern methods of contraception (MOH & New Era 2012). Unsafe abortions followed by post-abortion complications and post-bleeding are one of the major causes of maternal mortality in Nepal (Thapa et al. 1994). Although abortion is legalized in Nepal since 2002, 20% of maternal mortality is caused by unsafe abortions as women seek clandestine abortions because of the ingrained societal fears and shame attached to the very act of abortion (MOH & New Era 2007).

As discussed above, reproductive health is one of the detrimental factors for human development in terms of ensuring good health conditions of women of reproductive age, and the infants born. Nepal is one of the countries with low human development index, which can be attributed to poor maternal and infant health among the other health indicators.

Reproductive health has a direct association with issues of maternal and infant health. Poor health conditions of women and children not only restrict their participation in economic and social activities but it also equally impacts the well-being of the whole family and overall human development. There exists a large gap between the reproductive health policy and everyday practices, which demands serious attention from various global and national authorities. This paper looks into the practical and policy challenges pertaining to women's reproductive health, and its analysis draws upon a study of specific issues facing a particular ethnic community, which was done in 2015.

Reproductive Health and Human Development: A Conceptual Framework

Reproductive health has been a global phenomenon especially in terms of protecting the reproduction rights. For instance, couples should be free to decide on the number of births, timing and spacing with sufficient information and means to do so. The reproduction rights necessitate all the decisions on reproduction to be free of discrimination, coercion and violence (UN 1994). They include, for instance, safe pregnancy, as well as the rights to support for reproduction (care for maternal health by providing antenatal and post-natal care and infant health) and also the abortion rights (UN 1994). While these concepts on reproductive health and rights are ideally accepted by the global authorities, operationalization of such rights becomes critical, given the diverse socio-economic and cultural contexts of the developing countries around the world. Reproductive health has a direct connection with the well-being of a family, which is embedded in the aspects of human development.

The human development approach devised by the UNDP in 1990 is based on the capabilities approach, coined by Amartya Sen (1999), in which individuals must have a freedom or capabilities to pursue the life they value. This notion emphasizes on the freedom or capabilities that are entangled with other factors, which in aggregate makes human development possible. For instance, they include resources for enabling the individuals to have the opportunities for health and education, and at the same time, they must be able to pursue those opportunities without any restrictions from the other members of the household, given the intra-household power disparities (Kabeer 2005). In this sense, gender inequality at the household level is an example of the incapability for women to participate in the economic and social fronts such as participation in health services for better health options, including the information on the reproductive health.

This illustrates how the intra-household power relations restrict the capabilities of women to utilize the so-called reproductive rights, which not only hinder their individual health but also their capacity to nourish the future baby and the family as well as their responsibilities for social reproduction (Nussbaum 2003). The major challenge is that global policy on reproductive health and rights is less oriented toward the ground realities prevailing in most developing countries. It is almost impossible to address the reproductive health issues in isolation from the rights-based perspectives without paying attention to the overall human development or to the well-being perspectives. There is a significant association between the reproductive health and human development as reproduction roles are overburdened on women both biologically and socially. For instance, while a woman cannot deny giving a birth nor can she undermine her responsibilities of motherhood, but her rights to be a healthy mother with access to information and health services are often jeopardized. Such a situation further harms her social reproduction capacity as well as biological reproduction affecting negatively on the well-being of the family.

Right Based Approach

As discussed earlier, the reproductive health issues have had a great impact on the rights-based perspective since the adoption of the International Conference on Population Development (ICPD) Program of Action in Cairo in 1994. This perspective has been recognized as integral to sustainable development as well as fundamental human rights. It has created a dominant discourse in the post-2015 development agenda at the UN General Assembly with the adoption of sustainable development goals, which got reflected on the millennium development goals (Haslegrave 2013). Despite the controversy around the reproductive health rights, which failed to set a clear demarcation on the rights related to reproductive health, (e.g., sexual health, family planning, abortion rights as women's rights, etc.), it remained a central agenda in the international conventions. On the other hand, the reproductive rights agenda has gradually been depoliticized since 2000. The larger INGOs have been demotivated to push forward these rights, considering the unfavorable political climate. Especially, the religious fundamentalists and the conservative governments have made a serious effort to weaken the rights-based resolutions, especially the one on abortion rights (Nowicka 2011).

Nevertheless, the ICPD has devised a number of progressive resolutions such as the 2012 resolution on adolescents and youth that provided a firm basis for negotiations for their reproductive rights. Such resolutions were found to be more successful at the regional level such as the Maputo protocol (African Charter of human rights covering the rights of women in Africa) that addressed the issue of unsafe abortions, calling for safe abortion services (Miller and Roseman 2011). However, the implementation of such plans lagged behind due to a number of constraints at the local level such as the absence of skilled staffs, lack of medicines and other necessary equipments, etc. Civil society, especially, the NGOs have taken lead roles in promoting sexual and reproductive health and rights even before the ICPD, 1994. These roles led to the formation of, for instance, the International Women's Health Coalition (IWHC), the International Planned Parenthood Federation (IPPF), the Development Alternatives with Women for a New Era (DAWN) and the Asia–Pacific Resource Centre for Women (ARROW); some of these bodies playing important roles in advocacy at national and international levels and others in carrying crucial research activities (Haslegrave 2013).

The two UN bodies primarily engaged in making the rights-based treaties were the CEDAW(Convention on All Forms of Discrimination against Women) and the Convention on Economic and Social and Cultural rights (CESCR). While the CEDAW interpreted reproductive rights as human rights that refer to the women's ability to choose the number and spacing of children (Article 6) (Miller and Roseman 2011), the CESCR treated the reproductive health issues as rights to health and addressed the importance of reproductive health as problems of health in general. In line with the ICPD, and the Beijing Convention, 1995, the CESCR emphasizes on the reproductive health rights as "right to control one's health and body including sexual and reproductive freedom" (CESCR 2009). The CESCR is primarily concerned with economic, social and cultural rights of all men and women without discrimination based on the sexual orientations, which include health as the right of everyone and so is the reproductive health.

While rights-based models have got a special emphasis on post-2015 development agenda, and the reproductive health rights have become a part of the sustainable development and millennium development goals, their practical implications are yet to be examined from the grassroots perspectives (Berer 2013). The global authorities are very much convinced of the efficacy of the rights-based models in protecting the universal rights of women, which generate further discourses among the practitioners, policymakers and academics of the South as to whether the rights of women can really be universal as envisioned by the western elites (Sen 2014), and concerns have been expressed over how far the reproductive rights of women have been conceptualized on the basis of empirical knowledge and the ground realities facing the grassroots-level women of the South.

Human Development and the Capabilities Approach

Poverty alleviation has been the main priority of the Millennium Development Goals (MDGs) in developing countries, including Nepal. However, it is ironic that the poverty reduction framework has often failed to incorporate the human dimensions of poverty despite the efforts that are in place to address human development (UNDP 2006). Nobel laureate Amartya Sen (1999) argues that poverty is more than having low income and is closely connected with deprivation of basic capabilities, which diminish the overall well-being of people, especially women. The capabilities approach thus recognizes the significant connections between income-poverty and capabilities, and considers the former as instrumental in achieving the latter. For instance, education and health are important means of reducing income-poverty while being the end results of these activities (Greene and Merrick 2005). Sen claims that the issues of social justice have created both income and gender inequalities, which directly affect people's livelihood systems elsewhere (Nussbaum 2003; Robeyin 2003). Gender relations, for instance, highlight the dimensions of capabilities. Women in rural settings in Nepal are often unable to access the pre- and post-natal care not only because of the unavailability of health services but also due to the restricted mobility to access health services in the distant locations.

In some cases, women were not able to pay the transport cost to travel to distant health clinics and hospitals, while in other cases, women were not allowed to seek the healthcare services, and to travel long distances away from home. In this situation, the rights-based policies are less meaningful for protecting the maternal and infant health rights and thereby ensuring human development. There is a complex interconnectedness among various kinds of freedoms. For instance, women's freedom to work outside the home is critical for their capability to access health care, reproductive health information, education, social and political activities. Sen (1994) contends that gender inequalities can be better reflected by comparing the functioning and capabilities that matter intrinsically with the means to achieve them such as resources. For instance, men and women do not enjoy equal benefits from development services such as health and education, which leads to the deprivation of their basic capabilities. Educated mothers, for instance, have the ability to know and utilize health information, and decision-making capabilities for utilizing better health services to reduce child mortality (Ruger 2004). Supporting Sen's view on capabilities, Robeyins (2003) makes the contention that capabilities constitute potential functioning, which is basically doing and being out of the freedom they generate.

All the capabilities together bring overall freedom that people have reasons to value. Thus, capabilities are freedom and functioning and achievement are same as opportunities and outcome, the former being instrumental for and the latter being constitutive of freedom (Agrawal et al. 2003; Pettit 2001). In this view, it can be argued that women cannot be very efficient for individual as well as social reproduction and contribute to family well-being unless they are free to engage in social and economic activities outside the household environment (Sen 1999).

Alternative Strategic Model on Reproductive Health

An alternative concept of reproductive health emerges from a detailed investigation of socio-cultural realities of the developing world, which differs from the concept of reproductive health based on the notions of women's rights on a global scale. Unlike the global concept of reproductive health as women's rights, this alternative concept (knowledge based) addresses the social bases of reproductive health problems that concern the majority of women in the developing world. This is more relevant in terms of widening the need-based health services as well as enlarging the qualities of reproductive health that helps to increase the human capabilities required for ensuring the well-being of a family. Although the global concept of reproductive health is dominant largely due to its authoritative status, it is believed that the alternative concept has a wider application for addressing the reproductive health problems.

As stated earlier, reproductive health to a large extent depends more on social and cultural factors than economic conditions. While physical access to reproductive health services may not be adequate to cover the wider population, even those available services are not always widely used for different reasons. The utilization of health services is often minimal in the rural areas due to lack of information and awareness as well as to the inability to afford the cost of transportation, user fees and restricted mobility of women outside the home. If women can access and utilize the available reproductive health services, it can reduce fertility and at the same time improve the maternal and infant health that in turn can increase their capabilities for production and reproduction, which ultimately ensures the well-being of a family and human development in general. A real challenge lies in building enabling health services that will have a wider reach at least among the vulnerable groups of society. Health policies and interventions that don't address the social realities of the developing world are unlikely to be successful in handling the problems of maternal health and maternal mortality of these populations.

Moves Beyond Autonomy
The global concept of reproductive health greatly emphasizes women's autonomy in making reproduction choices, which is not available to the women in most developing countries. The alternative concept focuses on socio-cultural integration based on certain specific ground realities. In the South Asian context, the freedom to give birth is least important for women as what matters is their integration into a family regardless of the sex of a child (Kabeer 2005; Sen 1999). Women value more their integration into a family unit with the support from the family members and are least concerned about making the reproductive decisions on their own (Mumtaz and Salway 2009). And such autonomy is thus considered less likely to produce family peace and harmony. Women would rather be involved in joint decisions with their spouses provided they are equally respected in a family. Such practices help to maintain the familial and societal integration, which ultimately leads to the overall well-being of a family.

Research-Based Knowledge
The alternative concept of reproductive health aims at bringing up issues that emerge through specific socio-cultural realities on the ground, which receive least academic attention at present in the mainstream policy formulation activities. As stated earlier, reproductive health problems in the developing world relate largely to social factors such as deteriorating maternal health due to abortion of the female fetus or connecting fertility with preference for the male child, inadequate care and nutrition, mobility constraints in matters of accessing health services in the absence of support from spouses and family members and so on (Filippi 1998; Sen 1999).

In addition, problems such as miscarriage, prolapsed uterus and obstetric fistula leave women with disability to reproduce and thus lead to their disintegration from a family unit, while their causes often relate to inadequate care and nutrition, domestic violence and limited reach of health services (Graham and Campbell 1992; Estelle and Guskin 2003).

Until and unless such realities are addressed, the problems of maternal and infant mortality are likely to continue in the developing countries. Hence, the alternative concept focuses on the critical research needs to identify and analyze the social bases of reproduction in order to design policies and programs that are reachable to the wider groups of population in general and more acutely to the vulnerable groups in particular.

Education and Awareness
The global concept of reproductive health based on the rights-based approach is supply-oriented and services here are structured to reorganize health facilities that do not guarantee equal access for the vulnerable groups. For instance, the right to abortion is highly advocated for preventing unintended pregnancy. However, they still have poor maternal health with frequent abortion practices. It is even worse in the developing countries with poor health facilities in most of the remote regions. In the developing world, youth pregnancy often is not a choice but it occurs through coercion arising out of stigma and shame (Mathur et al. 2004). In addition, such abortion is far from being safe even if health facilities are available for two reasons; (a) lack of trained health workers and enough equipments, (b) confidentiality of such abortion due to stigma and shame (Bearinger et al. 2007). Thus, priorities should be rather on promoting education and awareness to prevent violence practices that lead to unintended pregnancy, sexually transmitted infections and worsening women's health. So the alternative concept of reproductive health emphasizes prevention rather than treatment.

REPRODUCTIVE HEALTH POLICY CHALLENGES IN NEPAL

The National Health Policy (1991) was implemented in Nepal with an emphasis on preventive, promotive and curative measures to provide basic health services, including those of reproductive and maternal health. Since then, the medium-term strategic plans, the National Reproductive Health Strategy (1995), the Adolescent Health and Development Strategy (2000) and the Nepal Health Sector Program II (NHSPII) (2010–2014) highlighted the broad strategies for reproductive health in Nepal. For instance, the National Adolescent Sexual and Reproductive Health Program has made an effort to link itself with several other programs that provide specific services, including safe motherhood, family planning, HIV/AIDs and STI programs. Similarly, a new HIV/AIDs

National Strategy (2011–2015) has been developed and approved by the government. Additional policies for research, information, education and communication (IEC), safe motherhood and adolescent reproductive health are in place. The national health sector policy also devised the operational guidelines for reproductive health care at all levels (from village to district and national) (NHSPII 2010) with increased attention on training and management.

All these efforts have been conducive to improving the quality and efficiency of health services, including the ones for reproductive health. The different layers of health system at the community level are organized effectively in cooperation with local and district organizations (Gautam 2015). Better arrangements are made at the community level to expand reproductive health services through primary healthcare centers and a nationwide network of female community health volunteers (FCHs). At the national level, the health indicators reflect an important progress in meeting reproductive health needs of the diverse populations of Nepal, although they still remain the lowest in Asia (UNFPA 2010). In addition, the functional aspect of health services to provide better care, and to cover wider segments of the population is still quite problematic. Due to the difficult topographic conditions, and lack of infrastructures such as communication and transportation, health services reach for the majority of the population rather inadequately. On the other hand, the available health services are not well equipped in terms of having sufficient skilled medical personnel, health equipments and medical supplies that lead to low quality of services resulting in little motivation for many patients to avail themselves of the health services (Gautam 2015).

The general health policy at the national level is not based on the knowledge or evidence coming from the pressing ground realities to cater to the needs of the diverse populations around the country. Although the national health policy has focused on the reproductive health needs of the adolescent and the youth, and has identified them as vulnerable groups requiring specific services, there aren't many programs and projects to that effect (Khatiwada et al. 2013). Different government departments have collaborated with bilateral, multilateral and non-governmental agencies to reach the young population with appropriate sexual and reproductive health information and services. However, such services remain largely insufficient in reaching mainly the rural masses (MOHP 2012). At the same time, to ensure better implementation of reproductive health services, effective monitoring and evaluation, it's critical to have continuous support generated through the varied experiences and insights gained from the community, members of the projects' staff and the volunteers.

REPRODUCTIVE HEALTH PRACTICES: ISSUES AND CHALLENGES IN NEPAL

Reproductive health specifically deals with women's health, and it addresses the critical issues of maternal and infant mortality in Nepal. While maternal mortality ratio (MMR) has declined in Nepal, it still stands at the second highest in South Asia (WHO 2014). A female child is discriminated since her birth and it continues till she reaches adulthood, and even beyond her reproductive age. Mortality rate under 5 years' age is higher (112.4:104.8) for the females as compared to the males (NDHS 2008). It is often women who take the burden of unwanted pregnancy as they continue to give births for the preference for male children. On the one hand, rural health centers are not well equipped with adequate reproductive health services, and there is information gap for utilizing the health services and information for better maternal and infant health. To a large extent, the utilization of health services varies between advantaged and disadvantaged people based on their different socio-economic conditions. For instance, the ethnic minorities like *Magar* and *Dalit* have a poor access to health services as well as very inadequate health awareness. In addition, the people of the plains are more privileged to access the health centers as compared to those living in the hilly and mountain areas due to inhospitable topographic conditions.

The use of contraceptives by married women is higher among the high-income groups (53.9%) as compared to that for the low-income groups (30.3%) (NDHS 2008). 16.5% of women have adopted voluntary sterilization as compared to only 7% of men. Similarly, the use of family planning services varies by geography and education as well. For instance, 33.5% of women with no education use modern contraceptives as compared to 46.4% of women with education. In addition, the poor utilization of contraceptives can be attributed to the misconceptions about contraceptives due to the socio-cultural factors like the ethnic beliefs and attitudes of people (NDHS 2008).

Although abortion has been made legal since 2002 in Nepal, 20% of maternal mortality is caused due to unsafe abortions taking place in the absence of trained health personnel and lack of equipments. This situation is much worse in rural health clinics. Abortion-related complications constitute almost 40% of total gynecological admissions in maternity hospitals and 10% of them have induced abortion (Sharma 2004). On an average, 3% of pregnancies end with abortion and about 10% with miscarriage. More than half of abortions and miscarriages associated with complications are among the women of the low socio-economic groups who have the least chance of getting urgent medical services (MOH & New Era 2007). In addition, young-age pregnancy exacerbates the health risk of mothers as evident from the South Asian situation. In Nepal, 6.6% of births take place under the age of 18 years causing the risk of the life of mothers and fetus 2.24 times higher than faced by women above the age of 18 years.

The antenatal care that provides for risk detection, prevention and treatment of anemia and for immunization against tetanus has been limited in most urban centers. Only 44% of pregnant women attend antenatal checkups with trained personnel and among them only 29% attend the recommended four check-up visits (NDHS 2006). Only 48.4% urban and 11.8% of rural women get the prescribed 4 antenatal visits. Around 17% urban and 53% rural Nepalese women do not receive any antenatal care due to unavailability of services as well as lack of awareness of the importance of such care. Similarly, proper delivery and care during childbirth are highly critical for maternal and infant health. While institutional delivery within the healthcare system has been growing over the years with increasing facilities, many are still adopting the traditional method of delivery in rural settings, resulting in high risks of maternal death. The dominant reasons for maternal death in the rural communities were identified as hemorrhage, obstructed labor, pre/eclampsia, sepsis, abortion, ectopic pregnancy, all of which were preventable (MOH 1998).

Only 21% of new mothers receive the post-natal care and only 17% of mothers receive the post-natal care within two days of delivery (Yamasaki et al. 2001). Utilization of post-natal care is crucial not only in terms of monitoring the maternal and infant health but also for prevention of repeated pregnancies and the increasing use of contraceptives. However, there is minimum use of post-natal services due to the factors relating to poverty, ethnicity and socio-cultural practices such as maternal seclusion after delivery apart from low access to modern health services (Mesko et al. 2003).

FINDINGS FROM CASE STUDIES

This paper draws upon the data coming from the case studies conducted in 2015 for a Ph.D fieldwork among three ethnic groups in one of the remote districts of Nepal. The groups are *Magar, Dalits and Tharus* who represent, demographically, the ethnic minorities having their unique socio-cultural attributes. The ethnic orientation for the study was based on the assumption that these minorities would fall into the lower socio-economic stratum, and have different perceptions and values of the reproductive health problems.

Magar

Magar belongs to the Tibeto-Burman family known as *Adibasi* who represent the largest ethnic groups (20%) spread around the country. These groups of people believe in the value system of Prima and Porima meaning to lend an arm to others in need. Cross-cousin marriage is popular among *Magars*, retaining the strong dual kin affiliations (Molnar 1984). Women enjoy higher economic independence with their rights over the properties they get from their parents (*pewa*). They have a strong belief in the supernatural world and illness is often treated by traditional healers known as *Dhami Jhankri*. Childbirth is normally given at home with the help of experienced women from the neighborhood (*Ama*), who can identify child positioning in the womb (Molnar 1984). Their traditional belief often prevents the women from going to health centers or hospitals for the delivery as well as for the pre- and post-natal care.

Dalits

Dalits are the occupational groups known as *achoots* (from whom water is not accepted and whose touch requires the sprinkling of holy water to become pure) who fall at the bottom of the social hierarchy in Nepal. They represent 12% of the total population, however, are deprived of equal opportunities throughout from time immemorial. *Dalits* are not the original inhabitants of Nepal but were brought from India, who were descendants of the untouchables from outside the *varna* system (social caste) and they operate at the lowest rung of the division of labor, cleaning toilets, scavenging, etc. (Ahuti 2004). *Dalits* in Nepal are highly discriminated against the upper castes and most other Jan jati people under the feudal social system of the Hindu society (Pathak 2006; Tamrakar 2006). They are deprived of religious, social and political rights. For instance, the *Dalit* people are not allowed to enter into the temples despite their integration into the Nepalese society. Similarly, in view of a very low literacy rate, their occupation is restricted within the traditional periphery. Only a few individuals from the Dalit community are represented in the national parliament (Ahuti 2004). The *Dalits*, however, believe in the Hindu value system and perform similar birth and death rituals.

Tharus

Tharus of Nepal comprise one of the ethnic tribes scattered over the Southern foothills of the Himalayas and in the neighboring areas of India (Meyer and Deuel 1999). *Tharus* are a small isolated community that lives by following an egalitarian way of livelihood. They remain in extended households and perform household and business activities under the one roof. A village council is formed representing each household and a leader is elected for a one-year tenure, who makes important decisions (e.g., land disputes, marital disputes, etc.) on behalf of the community (McDonaugh 1997). *Tharus* worship the household god (*kurma deuta*) in the village shrines (*bhuiya*) for protecting themselves against all illnesses and misfortunes. They feel less safe outside their village boundaries as they think they wouldn't be protected by their deities. They rely on the traditional healers (*Bharra, Guruwa*) for curing any sickness that is assumed to cause by evil spirits. In this ethnic group, there is high gender equality as compared to what exists in the higher caste groups. For instance, girls are not kept in seclusion during menstruation (not allowing them to prepare food and worship), and the mother and the new born are not considered as impure to be secluded from the family members for the first few days (Gurung and Kittelsen 1999). Although there are some beliefs and practices that relate to the ritual of blood pollution among some groups of the *Tharus*, they are not exactly the same as those of the orthodox Hindus.

The delivery of a child is assisted by a traditional birth attendant, and a woman known as *Sornniya* is assigned for the care of the mother and the infant on a daily basis. *Sornniya* takes the ritual bath once she completes her care work. Households with women of child-bearing age worship the deities twice a year and also offerings are made to the natal household when a woman is giving birth of the first child with a belief that the infant can get sick due to the actions of a malevolent spirit (rath lausari)

(Gurung and Kittelsen 1999). There is a practice of consulting *Ghar-guruwa* (holy person/priest/healer), when women are in pain during pregnancy (delivery and post-partum). *Tharu* women, unlike their high-caste Hindu counterparts, are not bound by the ideology of female ritual impunity and perform the kurma rituals in both paternal and maternal families (Thapa et al. 1994).

Awareness of Contraception

Among all the *Magar, Tharu* and *Dalit* communities, the majority still follows traditional birth practices and doesn't use contraceptives, although a change is taking place now to that effect. The reasons behind the low use of contraceptives can be attributed to the deep-rooted cultural belief in the deities (especially among the *Magars* and the *Tharus*), lack of proper information about the birth control devices, fear of not knowing how to use these devices, lack of time for visiting the health centers due to workload, and lack of understanding between couples. For instance, among the *Dalit* community, women were interested in using birth control devices for birth spacing but their husbands did not support them. Young and educated couples were using contraceptives and among those user groups, the female-oriented devices such as Depo-Provera, pills and Norplant were in common use for reasons of reliability and durability. Pills and Depo-Provera were easily accessible with the help of female health volunteers. Male contraceptives were used in rare cases. Although many people were aware of the birth spacing practices, especially for protecting women's and child health, the progress made in this direction was negligible due to the factors mentioned above. The use of contraceptives was almost nil until the first birth, even though some couples preferred to delay the first pregnancy.

Abortion Practices and Pregnancy

Early marriage and early pregnancy are the general norms of the Nepalese society, which have a detrimental effect on maternal health. The average age of marriage for girls falls between 16 and 18 years. In each of the three communities, the first pregnancy occurs within the first and second years of marriage, unless the family suggests postponing it due to the risk of young pregnancy, which is the case in the *Tharu* community. In this community, the parents guide their children not to have a child before

16 even if they are married at that age. However, young pregnancy is very common among all ethnic groups in Nepal, which have multiple adverse impacts on the mothers' health as well as that of the newborns. For instance, the newborns from young mothers are predisposed to illness and death, and teenage mothers are more likely to experience complications during pregnancy as they are less prepared physically, psychologically and emotionally to deal with the pregnancy-related challenges, leading to maternal illness and death. Their early entry into the fold of reproduction and child-bearing denies them the opportunity to pursue academic or professional goals (Ahmad 2012). It is very common that women can lose the fetus either in the womb or immediately after birth and so are likely to lose their own lives and those of the babies (Silwal 2011).

Among the *Magar and Tharu* communities, abortion is still considered a shameful act, although there is some evidence of unwanted pregnancy and against the unwanted female gender. However, both safe and unsafe abortions are not reported enough as these are kept secret, even if prevalent in the communities. While many informants were against the abortion practices considered unethical and with potentials for encouraging illegal and permissive sexual activities, a few informants were in favor of the free-of-cost legal abortion for saving the mothers in difficult pregnancy. However, many preferred to use contraceptives rather than abortion that might cause further health complications to mothers. Especially, the *Tharu* community follows certain egalitarian livelihood activities and there were no gender-based discriminatory practices. So there was no willingness for pre-determination of sex of the fetus and abortion of the female fetus. There was no evidences of any abortions except the miscarriages in some cases, although some opined that the provision of safe abortions might be helpful to save mothers involved in cases of complicated pregnancy.

Abortion practices were rare among the *Dalit* community as they also see it as a sinful practice. In some cases, they were not aware of the abortion provisions even if such needs arise as they rarely visit the hospitals. Women continued to give births even through unplanned pregnancy. So there is no evidence of both safe and unsafe abortions in the community. Most members of the community see abortion as a sinful activity that might encourage unethical sexual activities and in turn, have an adverse impact on women's health.

Antenatal and Post-natal Care

Antenatal and post-natal care have significant impacts on the health of mothers and infants. Antenatal care has been very much accessible to the community with the help of Community Health Volunteers (CHVs), who consult and assist the pregnant women for antenatal visits. Most of the informants from the *Magar* community talked about the increasing trend of antenatal care as many women were made aware of the importance of such checkups by the Community health volunteers. However, almost half of the pregnant women in the community are still out of such services especially due to their increasing workload. Some women work in the construction site as wage labor while others work in their fields, and they still have to perform their household work. Similarly, middle-aged women hesitate to visit the health posts as they are not supported by the family members unwilling to shoulder their workload. They are also shy of visiting the health posts. However, there is an increasing trend for antenatal checkups due to both the safe motherhood allowance and the awareness created by the CHVs who visit every family to have consultations with the pregnant women. Despite an increasing trend of giving birth in health institutions, half of the births takes place at homes with the help of traditional birth attendants because some families still prefer home-based deliveries due to lack of transportation, financial resources and traditional beliefs. Once a delivery takes place, the mother and the baby are kept in a separate room for 11 days until the naming ceremony. Family members, especially the female members, do the cooking, and oiling the mother and the baby, while the fathers-in-law and the husbands manage the marketing of necessary supplies such as meat, fruits, fish and medicines. Depending on the socio-economic background, some families can afford longer maternity care (2–3 months), while some mothers have to start working within a couple of weeks.

Among the *Dalit* community, antenatal checkups are very rare as they are from the low socio-economic class. Although few young women visit the health posts for antenatal care under the influence from the higher caste people, the majority does not use the health facilities unless serious complications arise. Because of their low status in society, *Dalit* women do not share the news of their pregnancy with the health personnel. The delivery of the baby often takes place at home with the assistance of the mothers-in-law or traditional birth attendants or experienced women from the neighborhood. Many women in this community are not aware of safe the motherhood allowance, and so they do not come to the health institutions for delivery. The scenario of the post-natal care is almost the same for the *Magar* community.

Among the *Tharu* community, a special care is provided after 7 months of pregnancy by letting them do light work inside the home. But they work actively both inside and outside the home up to 6–7 months. Most of the pregnant women rarely visit the health posts for antenatal care, delivery and post-delivery matters unless any serious problems arise. However, there is a changing trend of post-natal visits for the purpose of immunization.

Challenges for Utilization of Health Services

In all the three communities, there is low utilization of health services for issues of reproductive health even if facilities exist in the community. First of all, they have more faith in the traditional healers at the community level, whom they consult first in any sickness and who all can be easily accessible at low cost. In the health posts, only basic medicines are supplied free of cost, and sometimes these are in short of supply. In addition, many people do not have faith in the efficacy of these medicines as they are used to taking traditional medicines prepared at home. Only when a sickness cannot be treated in traditional ways, they visit health clinics.

Reproductive health issues are far more sensitive and women are often too shy to express their problems regarding sexuality, pregnancy and family planning especially among the *Tharu*, *Magar* and *Dalit* communities as they are illiterate, and from the low socio-economic class. On the one hand, their low socio-economic conditions get inextricably tied up with certain cultural norms to prevent them from utilizing health services, while, on the other, these women find it rather hard to spend their time and money to afford health care at institutions. Because of the poor transportation system, they have to travel almost a day to reach the health posts that excludes the waiting time, which is even more costly for many women from low-income families. It is especially critical for the *Dalit* women who have to wait in long queues in the health posts. In addition, as reported by some of the informants, the health posts are not well equipped in their areas. Lack of diagnostic facilities, medicines and impolite attitude of the health staffs as well as irregular staffing discourage many in utilizing these services. Also, the discriminatory behavior in the health posts is very much directed against the *Dalit* castes, which deter them from utilizing these services.

IMPLICATIONS FOR HUMAN DEVELOPMENT

Reproductive health, especially in relation to early marriage practices, unplanned pregnancy and abortion has a huge negative impact on maternal and child health, affecting negatively the overall human development in Nepal. As stated earlier, the younger age of marriage indicates a higher fertility as well as higher mortality for both mothers and infants, which contributes to low human development index (WHO 2011a). Reproductive health is more burdened for women than men not only because of the biological factor (that women have to give birth) but also because of the gender expectations of motherhood from family members, including husbands and higher social reproduction responsibilities (e.g., nurturing and caring for children and, in-laws, cooking and cleaning, etc.) (Akhtar and Winkvist 1997). In addition, women's health deteriorates with multiple pregnancies due to the preference of sons in South Asian societies that restrict their capabilities to participate in both production and reproduction roles, impacting negatively on human development (Sen 1999). Due to the absence of effective health services and lack of awareness among the populations, reproductive health issues (e.g., use of contraception and fertility, unwanted pregnancy and abortion) have the severe impact on human development. As observed from in our case study, many women were not informed of the safe abortion facilities while unsafe abortions were rarely reported.

The majority of the informants in all three ethnic communities consider abortion as unethical and sinful due to the likelihood of arising out of immoral sex. Women from the higher socio-economic class are inclined to have the sex-selective abortion that impacts negatively on population distribution and human development. While clinical abortions are rare, there are likely to be unsafe abortions not noticed publicly, especially among unmarried teenagers that often lead to further complications, putting their life at risk (George 2003). Antenatal cares were never a priority among all the ethnic groups, and pregnancy was just taken for granted, so regular checkups and special dietary practices were almost non-existent. The *Magar* community was utilizing more antenatal and post-natal care as compared to the other two communities.

However, women were given less workload after 7 months of pregnancy among the *Tharu* community as part of a traditional belief in protecting the mother and the child. Regular antenatal care service promotes safe motherhood and delivery with improved maternal and neo-natal outcomes (UNICEF 2009). It often presents first contact opportunities for pregnant women as an entry point for integrated care promoting healthy home practices, influencing care-seeking behaviors and linking women with pregnancy complications to referral systems, thus impacting positively on maternal and fetal health (Bulatoo 2000). Similarly, among the *Tharu* and *Dalit* communities, most of the deliveries took place at home as compared to those in the *Magar* community. Safe delivery is critical for both mother's and infant's health, affecting them in later lives, and yet many were out of reach of such practices. Post-natal care existed at two different levels, which are very significant for improving maternal and infant health. At the first level, the ethnic cultural practices of caring for the mothers and the newborns that prevailed in each community were based on their socio-economic resources. On the other hand, post-natal care based at the health institutions was again very negligible especially for monitoring the maternal and infant health and preventing any kind of infection at an early stage of maternity. Among all the ethnic groups, the traditional practice involves keeping the mother and the baby separate from the family members in a secluded area that often discourages women to go for post-natal checkups (Smith and Neupane 2011). Such a situation indicated a high risk of morbidity and mortality, affecting negatively the overall health of women and children and thereby their capabilities.

The reasons behind not using antenatal and post-natal care services were mainly their traditional beliefs in local medicines, lack of support from husbands and mothers-in-law for visiting health posts and ineffective and discriminatory services in the health posts. For instance, the *Tharu* community believes that their village boundary is protected by their deities, and did not feel safe to move beyond that boundary to utilize the health services. However, the fact of such low access to the modern health facilities is supported by the evidence coming from many of the developing countries, which goes on to indicate that women from poorer households have worse reproductive health outcomes and make less use of health services that further restrict their capabilities for production and reproduction (DHS 1998). On the other hand, among the rich households, the intra-household disparity and gender inequality still result in high fertility, morbidity and mortality, generating negative impact on human development (Anand and Morduch 1998).

POLICY IMPLICATIONS

Alternative Development Strategy

As indicated earlier, the reproductive health of women largely depends on the accessibility, affordability and availability of health services, which, to a large extent, is the responsibility of the state, and it should make necessary investments and/or provide subsidies in both the education and health sectors. There is a link between economic development and progress in education and health, which are the true indicators of human development. In this context, the state needs to devise alternative strategies to have equitable development of the different sectors and among the diverse segments of the population living in the rural and urban regions of the country.

Research on Understanding the Social Bases of Reproductive Health

It is very urgent that the reproductive health issues are appropriately identified at the grassroots level to accommodate the maternal health needs of the majority of populations in the developing countries. Beyond the limitation of health services and facilities, much needs to be done in addressing maternal health problems that have been a major barrier against improving the reproductive capacities of women. So in-depth research and analysis are required so as to initiate strategic interventions in the varied spheres of the social bases of reproductive health.

Promotion of Gender Awareness and Education

Promoting awareness and education at the levels of family and community would be absolutely crucial. It is more about educating people for sociocultural integration by reducing gender inequalities and dealing effectively with power relations. Once the society, family and community understand the integral importance of mother's and child health (regardless of sex) in terms of the present and future connotations of these vital indicators of human developments, there will be less restrictions on mobility for attending health clinics, less preference for child marriage, less priority for male children and less adoption of the techniques of risky abortion and so on. Hence, awareness and education should be a top priority of the preventive approach to combating violent practices as well as abuses in sexual health.

Appropriate Interventions in Health Services

It is imperative that a due emphasis—medical supplies to ensure access to proper health services. In the remote regions of a developing country like Nepal, health facilities are often located in urban centers, and even if they are located in the rural areas, they are without enough supplies and insufficient health workers. At any cost, reproductive health workers should be very mobile and be able to attend delivery cases very promptly. For this purpose, there should be incentives for the health workers to make them remain in the remote regions or to train the local community members to attend to such health problems. The other alternative would be to run mobile clinics for basic medication such as providing vitamin A and Folic Acid for pregnant women, immunization services, and for antenatal and post-natal services.

Monitoring and Evaluation

In order to check the efficiency and effectiveness of reproductive health services, there should be a regular system of monitoring at the local and regional levels. This can be done in partnership with different stakeholders such as local community organizations, schools, non-governmental organizations and government institutions. Such monitoring and evaluation practices help policy formulators and executing agencies identify the challenges facing relevant practices (e.g., irregular staffing, inadequate supplies, lack of equipments, etc.) and also document the best practices, make corrections for continuous improvement in modes of practice.

Conclusions

Reproductive health need is one of the basic human needs similar to those for food and shelter that are so very fundamental to survival. It especially restricts women's capabilities to function for the well-being of their ownselves and of their families. The challenges lie not only in developing physical infrastructures, but also in confronting socio-cultural factors such as son-preference, low mobility, family support, attitude of health workers and community support. In rural settings, women are often unaware of their health problems and are prevented from making reproductive decisions to enjoy the freedom of leading a satisfying sex life. These problems do aggravate and worsen for the marginalized and disadvantaged ethnic groups.

Despite concerted efforts of the global authorities to address the reproductive health problems from the rights-based perspectives, maternal and infant mortality is still quite high in South Asia. On the one hand, there is high investment in modern health services and equipments to increase the quality of reproductive health through inventions of diagnostic techniques and family planning methods and on the other, large sections of society remain severely constrained in accessing the basic reproductive health entitlements such as antenatal and post-natal services. This has created severe bottlenecks in the reproductive health measures that are focused on sustainable and millennium development goals.

Nevertheless, it is critical to address the reproductive health issues from the broader perspectives of the complex social and cultural realities that have multiple implications on reproductive health. The socio-cultural dimensions remain particularly instrumental in enlarging the reproductive health problems, which restrict the productive capabilities of women, leading to negative impacts on the well-being of families and communities at large. A balanced orchestration of policies and practices at the local, regional, national and international levels is required to make sure that reproductive health needs and priorities are identified properly at the community level and effective services are designed and delivered to meet, both quantitatively and qualitatively, the reproductive health requirements of the poor and the marginalized. Community-based organizations and local NGOs can contribute positively to build an effective mechanism for community mobilization aimed at a creating massive awareness of utilizing antenatal and post-natal services to be delivered as part of integrated local health packages.

REFERENCES

Agrawal, Bina, Jane Humphries, and Ingrid Robeyins. 2003. Exploring the Challenges and Work of Amartya Sen: Ideas and Work. *Feminist Economics* 9: 3–12.
Ahmad, Ahsan M. 2012. *Primary Antenatal Care Services, Maternal Health and Birth Outcomes in Rural Pakistan*. A PhD dissertation submitted to the Faculty of Medicine, Dentistry and Health Science, The University of Australia, Melbourne.
Ahuti. 2004. *Hindu Samajma Dalit Jatiya Muktiko Prasna, in Nepalko Sandarvama Samajshastriya Chintan*. Ed. Mary Desh and Pratyoush Onta, 475–521. Lalitpur: Social Science Baha.
Akhtar, H. Zareen, and Anna Winkvist. 1997. Images of Health and Health Care Options among Low Income Women in Punjab, Pakistan. *Social Science and Medicine* 45 (10): 1483–1491.
Anand, Swamy, and Jonathan Morduch. 1998. Poverty and Population Pressure. In *Population and Poverty in Developing Countries*, ed. Massimo Livi-Bacci and Gustavo de Santis, 9–24. Clarendon: Oxford University Press.
Bearinger, H., E. Reneet. Linda, Jane Ferguson Sieving, and Vinit Sharma. 2007. Global Perspectives on the Sexual and Reproductive Health of Adolescents: Patterns, Prevention, and Potential. *Lancet* 369 (9568): 1220–1231.
Berer, Marge. 2013. A New Development Paradigm post 2015, a Comprehensive Goal for Health that includes Sexual and Reproductive Health and Rights, and Another for Gender Equality. *Reproductive Health Matters* 21 (42): 4–12.
Bulatoo, Rodolfo. 2000. *Rating Maternal and Neonatal Health Programs in Developing Countries*. MEASURE Evaluation Project. Chapel Hill, NC: University of North Carolina, Carolina Population centre.
CESCR. 2009. *Concluding Observations of the Committee on Economic, Social, and Cultural Rights*. Poland.
Darroch, E. Jacqueline, and Susheela Singh. 2012. *Adding It Up: Costs and Benefits of Contraceptive Service, Estimates for 2012*. New York: Guttmacher Institute.
DHS. 1998. *Maternal Mortality and Morbidity Study in Nepal*. Department of Health Services, Family Health Division, Kathmandu Nepal.
Filippi, Veroniqque. 1998. Near Misses: Maternal Morbidity and Mortality. *Lancet* 351 (10): 145–146.
Gautam, Kamal. 2015. *Existing Practice and Perception of People on Maternal Health*. Ph.D Thesis submitted to faculty of Education, Tribhuvan University, Nepal.
George, Asha. 2003. Accountability in Health Services: Transforming Relationships and Contexts. *Working Paper Series* 3 (1).
Graham, J. Wendy, and R. Oona Campbell. 1992. Maternal Health and the Measurement Trap. *Social Science and Medicine* 5 (8): 967–977.

Greene, E. Margaret, and Thomas Merrick. 2005. *Poverty Reduction: Does Reproductive Health Matter?* The World Bank.

Gurung, M. Ganesh, and C. Tove Kittelsen. 1999. *Symbol of Tradition, Sign of Change, Marriage Customs among the Rana Tharus of Nepal, Kathmandu.* Kathmandu: Educational Enterprises.

Haslegrave, Marianne. 2013. Ensuring the Inclusion of Sexual and Reproductive Health and Rights under a Sustainable Development Goal on Health in the Post-2015 Human Rights Framework for Development. *Reproductive Health Matters* 21 (42): 61–73.

Kabeer, Naila. 2005. Gender Equality and Women's Empowerment: A Critical Analysis of the Third Millenium Development Goal. *Gender and Development* 13 (1): 13–24.

Khatiwada, Naresh, R. Pushkar Silwal, Rajendra Bhadra, and M. Tirtha Tamang. 2013. *Sexual and Reproductive Health of Adolescents and Youth in Nepal: Trends and Determinant.* Kathmandu: Ministry of Health and Population.

Mathur, Sanyukta, Manish Mehta, and Anju Malhotra. 2004. *Youth Reproductive Health in Nepal: Is Particiation the Answer?* International Centre for Research on Women (ICRW).

McDonaugh, Chris. 1997. Breaking the Rules: Changes in Food Acceptability among the *Tharu* of Nepal. In *Food Preferences and Taste: Continuity and Change*, ed. H. Macbeth. New York Oxford: Berghahm Books.

Mesko, Natasha, David Osrin, Suresh Tamang, P. Bhim Shrestha, Dharma Manandhar, Madan Manandhar, Hilary Standing, and de M. Costello. 2003. Care for Prenatal Illness in Rural Nepal: A Descriptive Study with Cross-Sectional and Qualitative Components. *BMC International Health and Human Rights* 3 (3): 1–12.

Meyer, W. Kurt, and Pamela Deuel. 1999. Who Are the Tharu? National Identity and Identity as Manifested in Housing Forms and Practices. *Bibiliotecha Himalayaica*, Vol. 16, Series, iii. Kathmandu: Education Enterprises.

Miller, M. Alice, and J. Mindy Roseman. 2011. Sexual and Reproductive Rights at the United Nations: Frustration or Fulfillment. *Reproductive Health Matters* 19 (38): 102–118.

MOH. 1998. *Maternal Mortality and Morbidity Study, Nepal.* Kathmandu, Nepal: Family Health Division, Department of Health Services, Ministry of Health.

MOH & New Era. 2007. *Nepal Demographic and Health Survey 2006.* Calverton, Maryland: Ministry of Health and Population, New Era, and ICF International.

MOH & New Era. 2012. *Nepal Demographic and Health Survey 2011.* Calverton, Maryland: Ministry of Health and Population, New Era, and ICF International.

MOHP. 2012. Nepal Adolescents and Youth Survey 2010/11. Kathmandu, Nepal: Ministry of Health and Population.
Molnar, Alex. 1984. Female Ambiguity and Liminality in Khan Magar Belief. *Himalayan Research Bulletin*, Iv 2: 31–45.
Mumtaz, Z., and S. Salway. 2009. Understanding Gendered Influences on Women's Reproductive Health in Pakistan: Moving beyond the Autonomy Paradigm. *Social Science & Medicine* 68 (7): 1349–1356.
National Research Council. 1997. *Reproductive Health in Developing Countries*. Washington, D.C.: National Academy Press.
NDHS. 2008. *Nepal: 2008 Demographic and Health Survey Key Findings*. Maryland, USA: Measure DHS, ICF International.
NHSP-IPII. 2010. Nepal Health Sector program Implementation Plan II (2010–2015). Kathmandu, Nepal: Ministry of Health & Population.
Nowicka, Wanda. 2011. Sexual and Reproductive Rights and the Human Rights Agenda: Controversial and Contested. *Reproductive Health Matters* 19 (38): 119–128.
Nussbaum, C. Martha. 2003. Capabilities as Fundamental Entitlements: Sen and Social Justice. *Feminists Economics* 30 (2–30): 33–59.
Pathak, S. Ram. 2006. Adolescence Reproductive Health and Rights in Nepal. *Nepal Population Journal* 12 (11): 19–32.
Pettit, Philip. 2001. Symposium on Amartya Sen's Philosophy: Capability and Freedom: A Defence of Sen. *Economics and Philosophy* 17: 1–20.
Robeyins, Ingrid. 2003. Sen's Capability Approach and Gender Equality: Selecting Relevant Capabilities. *Feminist Economics* 9 (2–3): 61–92.
Ruger, P. Jennifer. 2004. Millennium Development Goals for Health: Building Human Capabilities. *Bulletin of the World Health Organization* 82 (12): 9.
Sen, K. Amartya. 1994. Population: Delusion and Reality. *New York times Review of Books* 41 (15): 62–71.
Sen, K. Amartya. 1999. *Development as Freedom*. Oxford: Oxford University Press.
Sen, Gita. 2014. Sexual and Reproductive Health and Rights in the Post 2015 Development Agenda. *Global Public Health* 9 (6): 599–606. https://doi.org/10.1080/17441692.2014.917197.
Sharma, Bishesh. 2004. Utilization of Antenatal Care Services in Nepal. *Nepal Population Journal* 11 (10): 79–97.
Silwal, Manish. 2011. *Maternal Health Practices among Indigenous People of Nepal; A Case Study of the Raute Community*, M. Phil. in Indigenous Studies, Faculty of Humanities, Social Science, and Education, University of Tromso.
Smith, L. Stephanie, and Sujaya Neupane. 2011. Factors in Health Initiative Success: Learning from Nepal's Newborn Survival Initiative. *Social Science and Medicine* 72 (4): 568–575.

Tamrakar, Tek. 2006. Reservation for the Protection of Social Economic and Political Rights of Dalits. *Dalit Women in Nepal*. Kathmandu: Feminist Dalit Organization (FEDO).
Thapa, Shyam, J.P. Thapa, and Nipun Shrestha. 1994. Abortion in Nepal: Emerging Insights. *Advances in Population: Psychological Perspectives* 2: 253–270.
UN. 1994. *Programme of Action Adopted at the International Conference on Population and Development*, Cairo, September 5–13.
UNFPA. 2010. Annual Report 2010. New York.
UNICEF. 2009. *The State of the World Children, 2009: Maternal and Newborn Health*. NewYork: UNICEF.
WHO. 2011a. *WHO Guidelines on Preventing Early Pregnancy and Poor Reproductive Outcomes among Adolescents in Developing Countries*. Geneva: Switzerland.
WHO. 2011b. *Unsafe Abortion: Global and Regional Estimates of the Incidence of Unsafe Abortion associated Mortality in 2008*. Geneva, Switzerland.
WHO. 2014. *World Health Statistics*. Geneva: World Health Organization.
Yamasaki, N., K. Ozasa, N. Yamada, K. Osuga, A. Shimouchi, N. Ishikawa, D.S. Bam, and T. Mori. 2001. Gender Difference in Delays to Diagnosis and Health care Seeking Behavior in a Rural Area. *Nepal International Journal of Tuberculosis and Lung Disease* 5 (1): 24–31.

CHAPTER 7

Role of Micro Finance in Empowering Women Entrepreneurs of Rural Sri Lanka

Rathiranee Yogendrarajah

INTRODUCTION

Micro finance plays a vital role in women's empowerment and entrepreneurship development in many developing countries like Sri Lanka (Zama, 2004, cited by Haq, Hoque and Pathan, 2008). Rural people are not able to access financial services from commercial banks because they can't give guarantees and can travel long distances to reach these institutions. Lack of education, requisite experience, proper training, high expenses on transactions of small loans and lower rates of profit are some of the reasons for the unwillingness of the commercial banks to provide financial assistance to the rural poor. Micro-lending and micro finance have afforded poor people what they need to fight out poverty through small-scale entrepreneurial activities. According to Otero (1999), micro finance is "the provision of financial services to low-income poor and very poor self-employed people".

R. Yogendrarajah (✉)
University of Jaffna, Jaffna, Sri Lanka
e-mail: rathi@jfn.ac.lk

© The Author(s), under exclusive license to Springer Nature Singapore Pte Ltd. 2024
A. K. Sarkar and S. Das Gupta (eds.), *Understanding Women's Empowerment in South Asia*,
https://doi.org/10.1007/978-981-16-7538-6_7

Women remain instrumental in the processes of societal transformation because they play a dual role in family and society. As a result of a thirty-year-long internal armed conflict, Sri Lankan women and children had lost their male relatives and had to experience huge magnitudes of displacement. A very large number of rural households in Sri Lanka are now headed exclusively by women. Most of these women are marginalized and have substantially limited access to education, health care, workplace, which can cause over-reliance on men for economic support and social status. Micro finance has catered to the capital and credit needs of their small business ventures and thereby enabled them to ensure certain standards of living amid progressive deterioration of overall economic conditions.

Micro finance has evolved as a key instrument to afford financial and non-financial facilities to the entrepreneurs. Most people think of micro finance, if at all, as being about microcredit, i.e. lending small amounts of money to the poor. Micro finance is not limited to this; rather it has a broader perspective which also includes insurance, transactional services and, importantly, savings (Barr and Michael 2005). Since micro finance organizations have a financial focus, they are expected to cause an impact in the lives of the poor (Kabeer 2005). According to Ledgerwood (2000) "Micro finance has evolved as an economic development approach intended to benefit low-income women and men. The term refers to the provision of financial services to low-income clients, including the self-employed". According to ADB (2008) "Micro finance is the provision of a broad range of financial services such as deposits, loans, payment services, money transfers, and insurance to poor and low-income households and, their micro enterprises". The Canadian International Development Agency (2002) defines micro finance as "the provision of a broad range of financial services to poor, low-income households and micro-enterprises usually lacking access to formal financial institutions". In some least developed countries in the world, Co-operative Assistance and Relief Everywhere (CARE) focuses on women, because in every society women struggle against gender norms that limit their resources and opportunities for improvement. In this respect, women's empowerment is a tremendous resource for social change and a prerequisite to fight against global poverty.

Problematics and Objectives

Empowerment of women is very much essential to achieve sustainable development. Quoting from a UNFPA report, "the State of World Population 1992", the News Letter of Bernard Van Leer Foundation expresses the opinion that there can be no sustainable development without the development of women because it is women who contribute the most to the development of children. Access to credit is an important mechanism for reducing women's poverty and ensuring their empowerment. In this regard, the delivery of micro finance is one of the approaches to empowering rural women. Poor women in rural areas have little or no access to credit that can help them to take up farm and allied activities such as keeping milk cattle, tailoring, poultry or running other independent small enterprises and handicrafts which enable them to respond to the opportunities created in various processes of development. microcredit for women has been the mantra that has worked like nothing else to pull poor women out of poverty. Under the post-war developments, the Sri Lankan Government has initiated various activities to enhance the standard of living of the women who have been affected by the war situation that killed or disabled their male partners and where they have taken the responsibilities of the family as the household head.

In addition to this, disability brings additional burdens to most of the families, especially to the female-headed households. It has been stated that some families are being run by female heads because the men are disabled or have disappeared due to the conflict situation. There are also some women whose husbands are in detainee camps and they have access to the detainees. These women are engaged in labour work and self-employment as their occupation. The *UN Security Council Resolution 1325* clearly stated that the full participation of women is essential for the rehabilitation process in the post-war situation and women's specific needs should be taken into account in the developing countries as a prerequisite to this process (Women's Action Network 2012). The Network was deeply concerned with the lack of choices for and decision-making powers of women in the formerly war-torn areas and it has demanded that the administrative functions should hand over completely to the civil authorities as a genuine proof of the government's reconciliation programme.

However, there is no sufficient research to look beyond micro finance-generated economic activities, which has looked at how it has collectively empowered people and stabilized situations. Most of the researchers investigated developments by publishing reports and articles funded or sponsored by non-governmental organizations and foreign nations. The impact of microcredit on women's empowerment has been analysed in developing countries especially in Pakistan, Bangladesh and India. Although there is a huge amount of literature covering micro finance-related developments globally, not much has been written in that regard in the Sri Lankan context. Most studies have focused on micro finance institutions (MFIs) in Sri Lanka and their impact on the rural people. There are a few studies that empirically support the role of micro finance in helping the poor for creating self-employment. There is also a certain bunch of empirical evidence which shows that the involvement of women associated with micro finance programmes has been on the increase, resulting in a greater awareness and confidence, much of which isn't properly organized.

Micro loans are provided by organizations with collective of collateral securities and women repay the same regularly but their self-employment remains a point of uncertainty. In this study, an attempt has been made to find out the impact of microcredit on women's empowerment in the war-torn areas of the Northern Province of Sri Lanka. The shortcomings identified in much of the previous research endeavour and the changing economic conditions and socio-political culture in the post-war situation have motivated the author of this article to undertake this study and it's expected that this attempt will add some new dimensions to the stock of existing knowledge. This study raises the research question: "Whether micro finance has facilitated the enhancement of entrepreneurial activity in the rural areas of Sri Lanka and thereby empowered female entrepreneurs in any appreciable measure".

Micro finance has facilitated in the creation of self-employment and growth of businesses, generating wealth. Littlefield, Morduch and Hashemi (2003) acknowledged the evidence of the impact of micro finance on health and have concluded that compared to non-users, users of micro finance have good health practices, health education and better nutrition. There are basically three important dimensions of women's empowerment at the household level, which are familial, psychological and socio-economic (Malhotra 2003). According to Malhotra et al. (2002), household-level studies have made a major progress in conceptualizing broader perspective-explicit frameworks and in signifying indicators that can be said to have captured features of agency, but considerably more work is required in this area. Noreen (2011) concluded that women's empowerment was significantly influenced by the age and education of husbands, assets inherited from fathers, marital status and the number of sons and it was statistically significant. Another conclusion was that the loan amount also contributed to women's empowerment at the household level, although its outcome was not as significant as was expected in their study. Further, this study showed that females' use of loans produced enhanced impact than that of the males. This study focused on the entrepreneurial activities of women in the post-war context of Sri Lanka.

Literature Survey and Development of the Hypotheses

Micro Finance Activities

It was identified that micro finance is an important tool to enhance women entrepreneurial activity in developing countries. It provides different services to the poor people to enhance their living conditions and hence create opportunities for empowerment. According to Ledgerwood (2000), the following activities and characteristics are important:

- Small and short-term loans
- Social collateral rather than financial collateral
- Access to larger amounts of loan if repayment performance is positive
- Search and access the real poor and their business demands
- Continuous monitoring of business
- Loan on higher interest rates due to expensive financial transactions and risk factors
- Easy way to access finance, not too much paper work, and easy and short procedures
- Offering saving services to borrowers even for the smallest amount
- Offering training services for borrowers' business development
- Literacy training for borrowers so that they can develop competence in handling daily business problems and solutions
- Health care, social services and other skill training services for borrowers for the creation of sustainable bases for their businesses.

In developing countries, people from low-income communities, like shopkeepers or household product manufacturers, have innovative ideas for their businesses but they have no financial resources to operationalize the same. Lack of financial resources lead to more poverty with poor life standards. Financial services cover savings and credit activities but MFIs work for general financial services with which they provide insurance and payment services to their clients (Ledgerwood 2000). The important aspect of MFIs is not only to provide financial intermediation but also to provide social intermediation and social services. Social intermediation and social services include trainings, management development and financial literacy activities. Furthermore, many MFIs engage experienced people who guide others by giving useful suggestions, tips and other tactics for their business. Therefore, micro finance provides financial services with social services. Normally, social services are not offered by the general banking system. It is observed that micro finance is not only simply a banking system but also a development tool, combining both financial and social intermediation (Ledgerwood 2000). The following different services have been provided by MFIs.

Financial Intermediation

This is the most primary objective of MFIs because without loans/money, social intermediations cannot work. MFIs use financial services to achieve poverty alleviation, health care and education (Ledgerwood 2000). MFIs are providing many financial services such as credit, savings, insurance, credit cards and payment services, etc. It must be noted that almost all MFIs lend credit by default. It is not necessary that every MFI should help their customers by providing all these services but MFIs in general can facilitate many or most of these processes. "The choice of which financial services to provide and the method for providing these services depend on the objectives of a MFI, demands of its target market and its institutional structure" (Ledgerwood 2000, p. 66).

Social Intermediations

This activity covers the issues of group formation, leadership training and cooperative learning, which is a secondary role for the borrowers of MFIs. Development of social capital is a basic ingredient of sustainable development, especially in the lives of the poor in the society. Ledgerwood (2000,

p. 64) defines social intermediation as "the process of building the human and social capital required by sustainable financial intermediation for the poor". Social capital acts as a link between clients of a group and those of other multiple groups, and between MFIs and their borrowers. These links are based on strong foundations of trust and cooperation (Agion and Morduch 2005). The ratio of social capital will increase with the increase in business activities among members and also with the increased financial transactions between lenders and borrowers.

Enterprise Development Services

MFIs provide support to borrowers either in groups or in their individual capacities for different enterprise development services like marketing, business and training for accounting, etc. This service can be divided into two parts, enterprise formation and enterprise transformation. In enterprise formation, MFIs provide technical support to groups or individuals for setting up business, and for its development as well as for maturing of ideas and skills. While in the transformation of enterprises, MFIs arrange training programmes for their borrowers, workshops and get together for developing new technology and skills in their business areas (Ledgerwood 2000).

Social Services

According to micro finance practitioners, poverty can be addressed by financing the poor for productive activities, which in turn creates access to the necessities of life. But financial lending is only one of the tools for poverty alleviation. The poor needs more than micro finance to address the problems of poverty and accessibility of other basic needs like food, health, family planning, education, social support network and so on. Therefore, Ledgerwood (2000) focuses on the fact of MFIs providing additional social services with financial intermediation. The best way to contact their clients is to approach them in groups, which is the easiest way of making them literate, providing health care and other facilities. These supportive services play an important role in sustainable human development and livelihood of the poor (Khan and Rahaman 1998). Social service should not get mixed up with financial services or social intermediation because financial intermediation is a primary service provided by MFIs. That means there should be no additional cut off from loans on account of social service but it should be provided by secondary means or by subsidies (Ledgerwood 2000). The following table illustrates these activities briefly:

Minimalist approach	Integrated approach
One "missing piece" credit	financial and non-financial services

Source Ledgerwood (2000)

The government of Sri Lanka has given special consideration to uplift the social and economic status of the war widows in the country. The majority of populations in Sri Lanka lives in rural areas and large number of poor people are concentrated in the rural sector. Feminization of poverty is a major problem in Sri Lanka. It is described as "the burden of poverty being borne by women in developing countries". It indicates a situation in which women constitute a disproportionate percentage of the world's poor. Due to the 30 years' conflict situation, there has also been an increase in the number of female-headed households and disabled men. There are specific impacts on the agricultural sector and communities due to lack of working men who have either been killed or have disappeared or been detained due to the conflict. A recent study on Sri Lanka, dealing with the needs of aged people, highlights the need for critical policy changes. Women live longer than men, reaching 65 years of age, longevity for men being 71% whereas for women, it's 82% (Naoko 2009). One of the findings of this report relates to the increasing economic strains borne by the families on account of bearing the burden of old and aged women dependents. Owing to the rapidly increasing elderly population of Sri Lanka, it becomes a key issue for the government to build the abilities of women by creating opportunities for contributing substantially to the processes of income generation for the families and to economic development of the country. For attaining political, socio-economic, cultural and environmental securities, women's empowerment and gender equality are important requirements (Retrieved from http://www.un.org/womenwatch/daw/beijing/pdf/BDPfA%20E.pdf) (Fig. 7.1).

Women's Empowerment

Women have to bear the brunt and burden of unpaid house work as well as unequally treated professional obligations at varied workplaces. These gender inequities are either ignored in development planning and policy formulation or are reinforced through specific development projects and

7 ROLE OF MICRO FINANCE IN EMPOWERING WOMEN ... 133

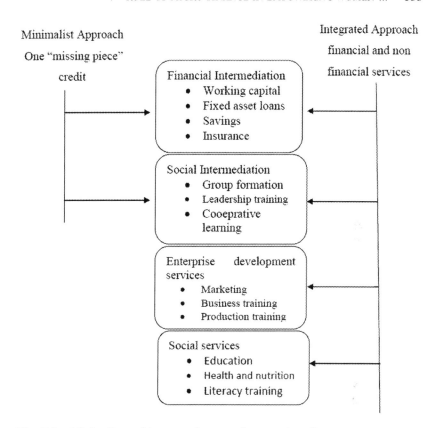

Fig. 7.1 Minimalist and integrated approaches to micro finance

policies (Sahay 1998). In large parts across the globe, women and children suffer from chronic hunger or malnutrition caused by acute poverty, deprivation and maladjustments of all sorts. A UN Secretary General's report states that women in the developing world face violence in varying degrees: forced marriage, spousal abuse, forced prostitution, infanticide and genital cutting. Nicholas Kristof, a New York Times journalist, who reports widely on human rights issues in the developing world, describes how husbands perpetrate violence on spouses for disobedience; how parents spend more on health care for infant boys than girls and how women are forced into sex trafficking. Kristof argued that "in this century the paramount moral challenge will be the struggle for gender equality around the world".

Micro Finance and Women's Empowerment

Pushpakumara (2011) concluded that micro financing is an important factor in reducing poverty since it has a positive relationship between credit usage and performance. Micro finance credit schemes lead to capital investment and savings. However, gender-wise, women are more effective than men in using microcredit facilities. Therefore, it has been recommended that more credit facilities need to be granted to female-oriented business activities in order to achieve the objective of gender justice and women's empowerment at the community level.

Khachatryan (2010) highlighted a research in progress on financing MFIs and its influence on their strategies in the context of its philosophical and methodological implications. Two-fold objectives have been covered with the help of combining both quantitative and qualitative methods. He empathized on the fact that micro financing takes place in the recently developing non-conventional financial sector which is highly heterogeneous in different countries. Certain constraints and limitations of his research methodology have also been noted. Hasan (2002) has studied the microcredit movement engineered by Bangladesh's Grameen Bank, the success of which showed a new way to the entire world in so far as women's collective participation in cooperative microcredit financing is concerned.

Based on these studies, the following hypotheses have been formulated:

H1   Micro finance has an impact on women's empowerment at the household level through engagement in entrepreneurial activity.
$H1_a$ Availability of micro loan improves entrepreneurial activity and empowers women at the household level.
$H1_b$ Increasing saving is one of the ways to empower women at the household level through engagement in entrepreneurial activity.
$H1_c$ Skill training for entrepreneurial activity leads to women/s empowerment at the household level.
$H1_d$ Educational activities strongly impact women's empowerment at the household level.

So far, 13 million micro entrepreneurs worldwide have benefited from microcredit, using their loans to increase their incomes and lift their families out of poverty. But there remain 200 million families who work hard but cannot access affordable credit (Swider Paul 2000). Edgecomb and Barton (1998) described social intermediation as the process through which investments are made for development of both human resources and institutional capital with the aim of increasing the self-sufficiency of marginalized groups and preparing them to engage in formal financial intermediation. Thus, social intermediation includes non-financial support provided to prospective borrowers to help them acquire skills and values, which they need to initiate and sustain their enterprises like training in credit norms and procedures, savings discipline, business management and assistance in getting organized into groups.

According to a study made by Bharathamma, 2005, many people improved their communication skills, leading to increased confidence level and getting respect from the society and family members by taking up income-generating activities. Further, it was mentioned that education, land holding, levels of family income and participation in social and mass media platforms have shown highly significant association with empowerment. However, age, marital status, caste, family type, family size, material possession and extent of media participation had no association with empowerment of rural women for whom the hindering factors were lack of education, overburdening with dual responsibilities, lack of proper training, family restrictions for mobility and lack of sufficient finance. She also stated that women who had never ventured outside their homes nor had spoken to outsiders could travel outside their villages because of their involvement in IGAs by SHGs. SHGs have not only helped these women to improve economically but they have also emboldened them will power and determination.

According to Gaiha, R. (2006), the indicators that have been proposed for examining the connection between social capital and micro finance, between micro finance and empowerment of the poorest people, especially women, as well as between micro finance and reduction of vulnerability through self-insurance must be tailored to specific contexts of application. Cross-validation through a mix of quantitative and qualitative data and methods is vital for a vigorous assessment. Even small samples carefully designed and analysed would yield rich and precious insights into the potential of micro finance for empowerment and economic security.

Kabeer (2005)'s "Is Micro finance a 'Magic Bullet' for Women's Empowerment?" emphasized that access to micro finance has had a positive economic impact as it has reduced poverty and increased the duration of membership as members have invested in assets rather than for purposes of consumption (Morduch and Haley 2001; Hulme and Mosley 1996). Further, she cited (Morduch and Haley 2001) to hold the contention that with regard to social impact, MFIs have discharged some important functions in the south Asian context including health nutrition and education. Her findings suggested the need for caution in talking about the impact of micro finance in general, and the need to talk about the impact that some particular organizations have had in particular contexts. MFIs vary considerably with regard to situational contexts in which they work as also with regard to their analysis of the problem of financial exclusion, the strategies they adopt to address these problems and the commitment they bring to bear in the implementation of their strategies. Regarding the pace and the extent of change they follow and bring about, she suggests that micro finance generates important and effective short-term changes on different fronts—economic, social and political and the question relating to the longer-term impact of micro finance remains unanswered.

Ayadurai (2010) concluded that the women entrepreneurs of the North East part of Sri Lanka must be recognized as important contributors to the economic growth of the country. They must be supported by international organizations working for the growth and development of entrepreneurship, especially women entrepreneurship. Their constraints must be recognized and a structured and organized strategic plan must be put in place to help them overcome these limiting factors. The Sri Lankan Government, several UN agencies, foreign and other donors, international non-governmental agencies, Sri Lankan non-governmental agencies, women's networks, international corporate organizations, international and other social entrepreneurs can greatly enhance the entrepreneurial capabilities of these women through funding and skill development.

Premaratne, 2011's "Empowerment of Women through Self Help Groups (SHGs) in Sri Lanka" emphasized that the impact of micro finance on women is substantial in building confidence, courage, skill development and empowerment but it hasn't contributed much to sustainable rural development, especially to reduction of poverty, creation of employment opportunities and creation of assets in the rural areas.

In "Accessibility and Affordability of Rural Micro finance Services in Sri Lanka", he came up with the contention that the accessibility of micro finance depends on factors such as the level of household income, distance from the serving MFI, availability of information about the technology in use, rate of interest, level of education, vocational training and the availability of collateral securities. It is further maintained that micro finance providers should think about a system of minimizing transaction costs.

Arulrajah and Philip (2011) concluded that in the perceptions of the respondents of their research exercise, INGOs and NGOs have been considered as making moderate-level contributions to what they set out to do, even though they have played a considerable role in improving the lot of the women-headed households in Sri Lanka (Manmunai South west DS Division). Further, they highlighted that considerable gaps still exist in the areas of ensuring equality and personality development.

Tilakaratna et al. (2005) have held, in "Promoting Empowerment through Micro finance in Sri Lanka", that micro finance plays an important role in the lives of poor and keen entrepreneurs. A reasonable percentage of clients, who have started up their businesses with the aid of MFIs, mentioned that the training provided to them had helped them to improve their businesses. In their study, about 45% of the clients claimed that they were satisfied with the business development services provided by their serving MFIs, although a majority commented nothing in this regard. The main reason for their satisfaction related to the training facilities they had been provided with.

Chulangani and Ariyawardana (2007) suggested that the transaction cost of borrowing declines as the size of loan increases. Their analysis showed that the Ceylinco Grameen Credit Company Limited has successfully reduced the borrowers' transaction cost due to special features of the loan procedures unlike what the Samurdhi Bank has done in the same situation. Ceylinco Grameen could be considered a successful experiment in the microcredit ventures in Sri Lanka and so by incorporating the good points of Ceylinco Grameen lending policy, Samurdhi Bank can develop their credit delivery system in an effective manner.

Maheswaranathan and Kennedy (2010) have concluded, in "Impact of microcredit on Eliminating Economic Hardships of Women", that microcredit activities led to the elimination of economic hardships of women. It was an easy way for women to obtain a loan facility in an informal method. Although microcredit was meant for the livelihood-related activities of women, it helped the beneficiaries' families to support them in fulfilling the collective needs as well. The institutionalization of microcredit ventures was made in a planned and corporative manner wherein the procurement and repayment of loans became convenient for women in economic and social disadvantage and/or distress.

Based on these studies, the following hypotheses have been formulated:

H2   There is a significant relationship between micro finance and women's empowerment at the community level.
$H2_a$ There is a significant relationship between micro loans and women's empowerment at the community level.
$H2_b$ There is a significant association between savings and women's empowerment at the community level.
$H2_c$ There is a relationship between skill training and women's empowerment at the community level through entrepreneurial activities.
$H2_d$ There is a relationship between educational activities and women's empowerment at the community level.

Research Method

Geographic and Demographic Scenarios of Sri Lanka

Sri Lanka is an island in the Indian Ocean, located to the south of the Indian subcontinent and it's separated from India by the Gulf of Mannar. It has a diverse climate, ranging from sunny beaches along the coast to cool mountains in the central south. Twenty million people of Sri Lanka are made up of various cultures, religions and languages; Sinhalese make up 74% of the population, while Tamils (18%), Muslims (7%) and Burghers (1%) (Census Report 2012). According to this census, the urban population is 2.8 million, rural population is 15.8 million and the estate population is 1.1 million. The numbers of male- and female-headed households are 3.8 million and 1.1 million, respectively. This is 23.0% of the country's total 4.9 million households (Census Report 2012).

Population of the Study

The total population of Northern Province is 997,754 and the female population of Northern Province is 517,231, which is more than 50%. Out of this, 52.6% was in the age group of 15–59 years (Census Report 2012). Most of the women entrepreneurs do not register their self-employment activities. The districts of Jaffna, Kilinochchi, Mannar, Mullaitivu and Vavuniya are situated in the Northern Province of Sri Lanka. The population of this study comprises 47,375 self-employed women-headed families in these northern parts of Sri Lanka as made available in December 2011 (Statistical Handbook 2012).

Sample Size and Sampling Techniques

The sample is drawn from the 47,375 women-headed families across the northern parts of Sri Lanka and a multi-stage sampling technique has been adopted. The purpose for adopting this sampling technique is that from among the 25 districts of the nine provinces of Sri Lanka, 5 districts of the war-torn Northern Province have been selected. This study adopts a stratified random sampling method for data collection to ensure the representation of self-employed women. The respondents were stratified randomly. This was made in order to get the information from their own experiences of empowerment through participation in microcredit activities in different circumstances.

The Northern Province includes 36 Divisional Secretariats Divisions (DS Divisions) and 861 Grama Sevaka Divisions (GS Divisions). 40 self-employed women having more than two years of experience in micro finance work were to be selected from each district. It was difficult to identify the potentially self-employed women-headed families with such experience because there were no records of registration of these activities due to lack of awareness of the need for registration and also an unwillingness for bearing the burdens of cost to that effect. However, these records were obtained from the Northern Province Industrial Department and selection was made of only the female entrepreneurs from each of the five districts. There were 1656 actively self-employed women in 2014 in the Northern Province of Sri Lanka. In this situation, after selecting some of the respondents, the snowball sampling method was also used to identify the potentially self-employed women in those divisions. And finally, the self-employable women-headed families were then randomly selected. The following Table 7.1 enumerates the sample population of the study. According to the records of the Industrial Department of the Northern Province, the numbers of women involved in self-employment in the Districts of Jaffna, Kilinochchi, Mannar, Mullaitivu and Vavuniya were 625, 275, 238, 340 and 178, respectively. However, as per the above Table 7.1, the selection of sample populations are 100, 48, 41, 53 and 28 in Jaffna, Kilinochchi, Mannar, Mullaitivu and Vavuniya districts, respectively, and a total of 270 women entrepreneurs have been selected for data collection. The samples for this study comprise of people who have been engaged in micro finance programmes for at least two years and live in the Northern Province of Sri Lanka. The women-headed families, which are involved in self-employment activities for more than 2 years and have been working with a capital Rs. 30,000 represent the sample size. Further, not only widows but also women heads of the families in which the male members were disabled or had disappeared during the war, divorced/separated women and the unemployed and the detainees are also included. So the female members of these families are the breadwinners and they have been forced to take the responsibility of looking after the families due to the incapability of the male members. After the war, the micro-level entrepreneurs gradually started their business activities. Further, this study classified the self-employable activities into categories that are in existence in the Northern Province and these are (Table 7.2).

These categories were found in the Provincial Council's Industrial Department Records, on which some of the respondents had reflected in this study.

Table 7.1 Sample population of the study

Districts	Total female self-employable women	Sample size of the population	% of sample size
Jaffna	625	100	16
Kilinochchi	275	48	17
Mannar	238	41	17
Mullaitivu	340	53	15
Vavuniya	178	28	15
Total	1656	270	15

Source Industrial Department—Northern Province—2014

Table 7.2 Categories of self-employable jobs in Northern Province

Production	Service	Business
Fisheries	Tailoring	Cigars
Palmyrah Leaf Product	Beauty Parlour	Mixture
Handicraft	Service Station	Jewellery
Food Processing	Studio	Textile
Coir based product	Watch Repair	Fancy Shop
Oil Product	Printing Work	Computer shop
Poultry farm	Tuition	Timber depot
Leather Product	Grinding Mill	Communication
Tooth powder	Video	Furniture shop
Decorative items	Vocational training	Grocery shop
Coconut shell product	Construction work	Cool bar
Broom Stick	Welding Work	Food café
Papaddam	Cake icing	Bakery
Statue product	Batik	Musical instruments
Agriculture		Textile shop
		Phone shop

Source Industrial Department—Northern Province—2012

The choice of people with experiences of participating in micro finance programmes was made because they are well informed and know much about the pros and cons of these activities, which have enabled them to reflect better on queries made in the questionnaire. They are involved in the production of packing food items (appalam, vadakam, chillies, rice powder, etc.), handicrafts, service activities (sewing, working in beauty parlours, etc.), agriculture (in home-grown gardens and tendering livestocks) and doing small businesses. In addition to this, these areas were war-affected, which required their rehabilitated in the near future. However, most of these programmes are being implemented by governmental agencies and their living conditions are pretty much critical.

The research design was also limited to covering the MFIs due to time and financial constraints. In this regard, formal MFIs were selected for the study. These formal institutions which were the SBs, RDBs and the WRDSs, were chosen because of their wide areas of coverage, involving members from Jaffna, Kilinochchi, Mullaitivu, Mannar and Vavuniya districts. For this study, a wide client base is required to provide opportunities to obtain different sets of ideas, opinions and views that can improve the undertakings in question. In addition, the assurance given by the staff and management of MFIs to provide necessary cooperation during the study was another reason for selecting these institutions.

Data Sources

Different kinds of primary and secondary data were used for the study. The primary data was collected by using the questionnaire developed by the author and with the help of direct interviews with the branch managers and field officers of micro finance institutions and other organizations (NGOs, divisional secretariat offices) and the secondary data was collected from books, journals and other reports. Besides collecting information on micro finance, entrepreneurship and empowerment, the survey collected detailed information about a variety of factors. For example, demographic information (age, sex, marital status, etc.) and socio-economic information (education, employment, food consumption, expenditure on health, etc.) were collected for all the household members. Apart from using the questionnaire, there were also interviews and discussions held with the respondents to collect authentic biographic and other types of data.

Key Variables and Measures

Micro Finance
Previous studies have used various indicators and scales to measure the micro finance activities of the respondents. For example, frequency of taking small loans, respondent's reasons for taking the loans, health care and nutrition, social welfare, have all been used as measures of the micro finance situations. However, these measures are used to ascertain poverty alleviation, standards of living and income-generating opportunities, etc. Further, some studies had dealt with the demographic factors. In this study, the questions that the respondents were asked in this regard were: Can you fulfil your expectations by participating in the micro finance programmes? Have you developed a saving habit after participating in micro finance programmes? Is skill training useful for your entrepreneurial activity? Does education generate awareness of home to work for self-actualization? Answers to these questions were vetted on a scale ranging from strongly agree to strongly disagree, marking the responses between 5 and 1. The questionnaire was developed to cover the above-mentioned variables for measuring the impact of micro finance activity.

Women's Empowerment

Empowerment is the common term which is used in all spheres like organizations, households and communities. In this study, women's empowerment is measured to ensure the development of the poor at the household and community levels. According to the proposed conceptual model, women's empowerment is a dependent variable, analysed at the household and community levels.

Similarly, women's empowerment at the community level is measured by the variables like political participation, social participation, development of social and economic collectives and appreciation from the community.

Mode of Data Analysis

The collected data was tabulated, interpreted and simplified to make them suitable for the research purpose. With regard to the quantitative analysis, the SPSS software 16 version was used for data entry and to calculate percentage values. The resulting data was then analysed and interpreted.

Regression analyses were used for an inferential analysis needed to make the study more specific. Correlation matrix is used for showing the simple correlations, r, between all possible pairs of variables included in the analysis. The diagonal elements, which are all 1, are usually omitted. Coefficient of simple and multiple correlations have been calculated in this study to measure the relationship between dependent variables (women's empowerment) and independent variables (micro finance). The technique of multiple regression is used to find out the extent of the impact of the independent variables (micro finance) upon the dependent variables (women's empowerment).

DATA ANALYSIS

Relationship Between Micro Finance and Women's Empowerment

To find out the impact of micro finance on women's empowerment, a regression analysis has been made between micro finance and women's empowerment. Table 7.3 shows the model summary in this regard.

From the above analysis, the researcher tried to find out the relationship between micro finance and women empowerment. Here, the null hypothesis is that there is no relationship between micro finance and

Table 7.3 Regression analysis between micro finance and women's empowerment

Model	R	R Square	Adjusted R Square	F	Sig.	Unstandardized coefficient
1	0.270[a]	0.073	0.070	26.247	0.000[b]	0.272

[a] Predictors: (Constant), micro finance
[b] Dependent Variable: Women Empowerment

women empowerment and the alternative hypothesis states that there is a relationship between micro finance and women empowerment. In the above Table 7.3, the results of regression analysis shows that R-square for the regression model is 0.073. R-square shows the amount of variations in one variable of micro finance that is accounted by dependent variable of women empowerment. In this case, respondents perception of increasing micro finance account for 7.3% of the total variation in the increase degree of women empowerment in the region. The ANOVA table shows that the F ratio is for the regression models. This statistic assesses the statistical significance of the overall regression models. Larger the F ratio, the more variance in the dependent variable (Women empowerment) is explained by the independent variable (Micro finance). The F ratio 26.247 indicates that the model is highly significant at the 0.000 level.

From the regression coefficient table, the "Unstandardized Coefficients" reveal the unstandardized regression coefficient for micro finance, as 0.272. The t-test tells us the regression coefficient is different enough from zero to be statistically significant at the level (0.000). According to the above analysis, the null hypothesis is rejected, which indicates that the relationship existing between these two variables of micro finance and women empowerment can be seen in the following observed cumulative probability curve (Fig. 7.2).

Multiple Regression Analysis Between the Dimensions of Micro finance and Women Empowerment

To find out the impact of micro finance dimensions on women empowerment, the regression analysis has been made among the variables. Table 7.4 shows the model summary in this regard.

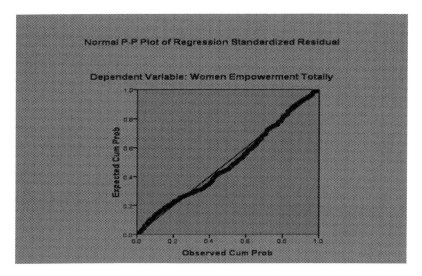

Fig. 7.2 Multiple regression between micro finance and women empowerment

Table 7.4 Regression analysis between the dimensions of micro finance and women empowerment at household level (model summary)

Model	R	R square	Adjusted R square	Std. error of the estimate
1	0.331[a]	0.109	0.099	0.65108

[a] Predictors: (Constant), Micro Loan, Micro saving, skill training and education programme

Table 7.4 model summary indicates that the value of R square for the model is 0.109. This means that 10.9% of the variation in women empowerment at household level (dependent variable) can be explained from the four independent variables. In general, R-square always increases as independent variables are added to a multiple regression model. To avoid over estimating the impact of adding an independent variable to the model, some analysts prefer to use the adjusted R square value (it recalculates the R square value based on the number of predictor variables in the model). This makes it easy to compare the explanatory power of regression models with different numbers of independent variables. The adjusted R square for the model is 0.099, which indicates only a slight overestimate with the model.

The overall regression results are shown in the ANOVA Table 7.5. The regression model is statistically significant (F ratio = 10.195, probability level 0.000). The probability level 0.000 means that the chances are almost zero and the results of regression model are due to random events instead of a true relationship.

In the above Table 7.5 women empowerment at the household level was considered as a dependent variable and the others such as Micro loan, Micro saving, Skill training and Education programme as independent variables. Here the null hypothesis states that there is no relationship between women empowerment at HH Level and Micro loan, Micro saving, Skill training and Education programme altogether. The alternative hypothesis states that Micro loan, Micro saving, Skill training and Education programme are related to the women empowerment at HH Level. Based on the above calculations, shown in Table 7.6, the impact of micro finance on women empowerment at HH Level has been explained using regression analysis.

To assess the normality of the residuals, consult the P-P Plot (Fig. 7.3) from the regression output. The residual plots show a random scatter of the points (independence) with a constant spread (constant variance). The normal probability plot of the residuals show the points that are close to a diagonal line; therefore the residuals appear to be approximately normally distributed. Thus, the assumptions for regression analysis appear to be met.

Table 7.5 Regression analysis between dimensions of micro finance and women empowerment at household level (ANOVA)

Model		Sum of squares	df	Mean square	F	Sig
1	Regression	17.286	4	4.322	10.195	0.000[a]
	Residual	140.736	332	0.424		
	Total	158.022	336			

[a]Predictors: (Constant), Micro Loan 3, Micro saving, skill training and education programme

Table 7.6 Regression analysis between the dimensions of micro finance and women empowerment at household level (coefficients)

Model		Unstandardized coefficients		Standardized coefficients	t
		B	Std. error	Beta	
1	(Constant)	3.000	0.320		9.387
	Micro Loan	−0.014	0.072	−0.013	−0.190
	Micro Saving	0.284	0.061	0.293	4.637
	Skill training	−0.185	0.092	−0.135	−2.020
	Education programme	0.147	0.062	0.159	2.360

[a]Dependent Variable: Women Empowerment at HH Level

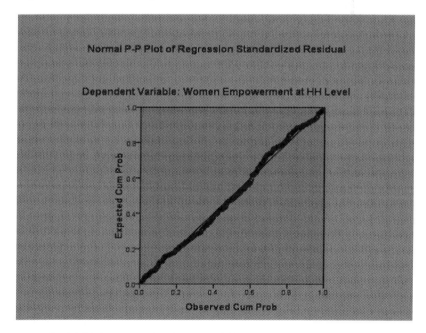

Fig. 7.3 Multiple Regression between different variables of Micro finance and Women empowerment at HH level

To meet the objective, the impact of micro finance on women empowerment has been investigated. The following model was used to investigate the relationship between dependent and independent variables.

$$Y = a + \beta_1 X_1 + \beta_2 X_2 + \beta_3 X_3 + \beta_4 X_4 + \varepsilon$$

where, Y = Dependent Variable (Women empowerment at Household Level)
Intercept term $\beta_1, \beta_2, \beta_3, \beta_4$ are regression coefficients.
X_1, X_2, X_3, X_4 represent Independent variables (Micro loan, Micro saving, Skill training and Education programme)

$$Y = a + \beta_1 X_1 + \beta_2 X_2 + \beta_3 X_3 + \beta_4 X_4 + \varepsilon$$

$$Y = 3.000 - 0.13\, X_1 + 0.293\, X_2 - 0.135\, X_3 + 0.159\, X_4 + \varepsilon$$

The significant t-value of each variable confirms the significant contribution of each independent variable rather than one (Micro saving) to the model.

The value of Beta coefficient is highest in the case of X_2 (Micro savings) explaining that 29.3% of the variation in women empowerment can be explained by this variable. Similar results are shown in other variables rather than the Micro loan. However, there is a significant relationship between Skill training and women empowerment and there is a negative coefficient. The smallest Beta in the case of X_1, i.e. 0.13 shows that the micro loan contributes least to the empowerment of women clients.

Similarly, we can discuss the empowerment at community level with dimensions of micro finance.

Table 7.7 model summary indicates that the value of R square for the model is 0.059. This means that 5.9% of the variation in women empowerment at community level (dependent variable) can be explained from the four independent variables. The adjusted R square for the model is 0.048, which indicates a slight overestimate with the model.

The overall regression results are shown in the ANOVA Table 7.8. The regression model is statistically significant (F ratio = 5.215 (which is below the F ratio of WE at HH level), $P = 0.000$).

Similarly, in Table 7.9, women's empowerment at the community level was considered as dependent variable and micro loan, micro saving, skill training and education programme as independent variables.

Table 7.7 Regression analysis between the dimensions of micro finance and women empowerment at community level (model summary)

Model	R	R square	Adjusted R square	Std. error of the estimate
1	0.243[a]	0.059	0.048	0.55928

[a] Predictors: (Constant), Micro Loan, Micro savings, Skill training and Education programme

Table 7.8 Regression analysis between the dimensions of micro finance and women empowerment at community level (ANOVA). ANOVA[a]

Model	Sum of squares	df	Mean square	F	Sig.
Regression	6.524	4	1.631	5.215	0.000[b]
Residual	103.847	332	0.313		
Total	110.372	336			

[a] Dependent Variable: Women Empowerment at Community Level
[b] Predictors: (Constant), Micro Loan, Micro saving, Skill training and Education Programme

Table 7.9 Regression analysis between the dimensions of micro finance and women empowerment at community level (coefficients)

Model		Unstandardized coefficients		Standardized coefficients	t
		B	Std. Error	Beta	
1	(Constant)	2.432	0.275		8.856
	Micro Loan	−0.100	0.062	−0.114	−1.611
	Micro savings	0.123	0.053	0.152	2.336
	Skill training	0.074	0.079	0.065	0.946
	Education programme	0.117	0.054	0.151	2.177

[a] Dependent Variable: Women's Empowerment at the Community Level

From these analysis the hypotheses developed in this study are $H2_b$ and $H2_d$, i.e. "There is a significant association between savings and women's empowerment at community level" and "There is a relationship between education activity and women empowerment at community level", respectively, are accepted however the impact relationship is low. There is a significant relationship at 0.000 level. Furthermore, $H2_a$ and

H$_{2d}$ "There is relationship between micro loans and women empowerment at community level" and "There is relationship between education activity and women empowerment at community level" which have been rejected and the null hypotheses have been accepted because it has a low impact relationship and insignificant among the variables which has a significant level at 0.108 and 0.345, respectively. The Micro loan and Skill training are not related to the empowerment at the community level.

As per the results in the coefficient table in Regression Model 2, it has been noted that the fitted model reveals the significant impact of micro finance on women empowerment at the community level. It explains that the micro finance factor of micro savings, independent variable positively influences women empowerment at community level (i.e. $\beta = 0.152$, p value < 0.05) (Fig. 7.4).

The coefficients table shows that the two independent variables that are the significant predictors of women's empowerment at the community level are micro savings and education programme. In the significant column, we have noticed that the beta coefficients for micro savings and education programme are significant. Using the beta coefficient in micro

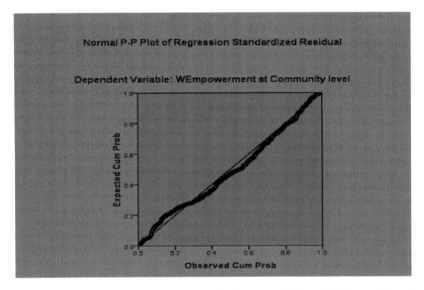

Fig. 7.4 Multiple regression between different variables of microcredit and women's empowerment at the community level

savings, for example, we can conclude that every time the amount of saving increases by 1 unit, the improvement in women's empowerment at the community level will increase averagely by 0.152 units, when the other variables are held constant. Information in the coefficients tables reveal that micro saving is the most significant predictor of women's empowerment at the community level, with a high beta coefficient 0.152 ($P = 0.000$).

However, the coefficient table reveals that educational programmes also become significant every time when the loan interest is increased by 1 unit and women's empowerment will increase averagely by 0.151. If the awareness of educational programmes increases, women's empowerment at the community level will be increased. Micro loans and Skill training are insignificant predictors of empowerment at the community level.

From these analyses, the hypotheses developed in this study that H_{1b} and H_{1d}, i.e. "Increasing saving is one of the ways to empower women at the household level" and "There is an impact of education programmes on empowerment at the household level" are accepted. However, the impact relationship is low and there is a significant relationship at 0.000 level. Furthermore, H_{2b} and H_{2d} "There is a significant association between savings and women's empowerment at the community level" and "There is a relationship between educational programmes and women's empowerment at community level through entrepreneurial activity" have been accepted and "There is a significant relationship between micro loans and empowerment at the community level" and "There is relationship between education and women's empowerment at the community level" have been rejected and the null hypotheses have been accepted because it has a low impact relationship and is insignificant among the variables which have a significant level at 0.108 and 0.345, respectively ($P > 0.05$). The micro loans and skill training are important issues in these areas which show the insignificance of empowerment at the household and community levels.

To meet the objective, the impact of micro finance on women's empowerment has been investigated. The following model was used to investigate the relationship between dependent and independent variables.

$$Y = a + \beta_1 X_1 + \beta_2 X_2 + \beta_3 X_3 + \beta_4 X_4 + \varepsilon$$

where Y = Dependent Variable (Women empowerment at Community Level)
Intercept terms $\beta_1, \beta_2, \beta_3, \beta_4$ are regression coefficients.
X_1, X_2, X_3, X_4 represent Independent variables (Micro Loan, Micro saving, Skill training and Education programme).

$$Y = a + \beta_1 X_1 + \beta_2 X_2 + \beta_3 X_3 + \beta_4 X_4 + \varepsilon$$

$$Y = 2.432 - 0.100\, X_1 + 0.123\, X_2 + 0.074\, X_3 + 0.117\, X_4 + \varepsilon$$

The significant t-value of each variable confirms the significant contribution of each independent variable rather than one (Micro saving) of the model.

The value of Beta coefficient is highest in case of X_2 (Micro saving) explaining that 12.3% of the variation in women empowerment at the community level can be explained by this variable. Similar results are shown in other variables rather than repayment of loan. The smallest Beta in case of X_1, i.e. −0.100 shows that the Micro loan contributes least to the empowerment of women clients (Table 7.10).

Key Findings

This study came out with the following findings:

1. Micro saving and education programmes influence women's empowerment both at the household and the community levels but skill training does not impact women's empowerment due to low infrastructural facilities.
2. Micro loan has no impact on women's empowerment at the household and community levels because women who are provided with loans will be considered as debtors by the society. Rahman (1999) pointed out that the empowering influence of micro finance doesn't relate to the upliftment of women's lives because credit is considered a liability for a household as it entails risk-taking.
3. Women's empowerment remains rather inadequate at the community level. Micro finance has not been successful in enhancing the political participation of women and ensuring respect for their legal rights (Mustafa and Ismailov 2008).

Table 7.10 Hypotheses testing

Serial No.	Hypotheses	Outcome dimensions Accepted/Rejected
H_{1a}	Availability of micro loan improves entrepreneurial activities and empowers women at the household level	Rejected
H_{1b}	Increasing saving is one of the ways to empower women at the household level through their entrepreneurial activities	Accepted
H_{1c}	Skill training for entrepreneurial activity leads to women's empowerment at the household level	Rejected
H_{1d}	There is a relationship between educational activity and women's empowerment at the household level	Accepted
H_{2a}	There is a significant relationship between micro loans and women's empowerment at the community level	Rejected
H_{2b}	There is a significant association between savings and women's empowerment at the community level	Accepted
H_{2c}	There is a relationship between skill training and women's empowerment at the community level through their entrepreneurial activities	Rejected
H_{2d}	There is a relationship between educational activity and women's empowerment at the community level	Accepted

It has been found that micro finance contributes only 7.3% to women's empowerment and the unstandardized coefficient illustrates 27.2%, which is consistent with the survey conducted by the author who concluded that women's empowerment, economic empowerment and social empowerment, were influenced only by microcredit 19%, 17% and 10%, respectively, in Jaffna district (Rathiranee 2011). The remaining 92.7% has been explained by other factors which have not been considered in this study. Further, Chowdhury (2008) argued that the access to microcredit programmes does not contribute to women's entrepreneurship development at the household level.

Further, it could be concluded that a small amount of loan is not enough to enhance entrepreneurial activities and improve their performance and sustainability. Although with the help of this micro loan, they are able to start businesses and repay the loans successfully, the sustainability and performance are poor due to other aspects of value addition of the products and services.

It has been found that micro finance facilities are essential in empowering women and turning them into entrepreneurs in the post-war context because most of the women-headed families are in the rural areas and for achieving all this in an effective way, micro finance services should be provided in the areas of education, health, nutrition, generating awareness of savings and insurance programmes and providing training for skill development by using modern technology. Further, micro finance institutions should provide monitoring and guiding services for specific entrepreneurial activities and awareness of the ways of improving the qualities of products by creating better facilities for marketing, packaging and advertising.

Conclusions

This study would be an important addition to the literature on micro finance and its impact on women's empowerment at the household and community levels in Sri Lanka. Besides, the recommendations will have interesting bearings on the micro finance programmes and entrepreneurial development. It is expected that the suggestions will have potentials for a sound entrepreneurial development in the Northern Province of the country and it will be helpful to the policymakers, MFIs and other institutions related to the development of these activities. Although this study focuses primarily on micro financing methodologies, the author also acknowledges that empowerment and entrepreneurial activities can be achieved through other variables as well as by encouraging further research in this area.

REFERENCES

Afrane, S., N. Islam, and S.U. Ahmed. 2008. A Multivariate Model of microcredit and Rural Women Entrepreneurship Development in Bangladesh. *International Journal of Business and Management* 169–185.

Agbonifoh, B.A., and G.O. Yomere. 1999. *Research Methodology in the Management and Social Sciences.* Benin City, Nigeria: University of Benin.

Aggarwal, S. 2014. Tackling Social and Economic Determinants of Health Through Women Empowerment. The SEWA Case Study, Draft, WHO—Searo New Delhi.

Anwar, B., M. Shoaib, and S. Javed. 2013. A Woman's Autonomy and Their Role in Decision Making at Household Level: A Case of Rural Sialkot. *World Applied Sciences Journal* 23 (1): 129–136.

Arora, S., and M. Meenu. 2011. Women Empowerment through Microfinance Intervention in the Commercial Banks—An Empirical Study in the Rural

India with Special Reference to the State of Punjab. *International Journal of Economics and Research* 2 (2): 35–45.
Arulrajah, J.A., and P.G. Philip. 2011. Equality and Personality Development of Women-Headed House Hold: The Role of INGOs and NGOs in Women Headed House Hold in Manmunai South West D.S Division of Batticaloa.
Attapattu, A. 2009. State of Microfinance in Sri Lanka. State of Microfinance in SAARC Countries.
Ayadurai, S. 2010. Report on Field Trip to Foster Collaborative Partnerships With Local Ngos, National Ngos And Ingos, to Assess and Identify Immediate and Mid-Term Needs of Returnees and Displaced Communities in North East Sri Lanka, Field Trip From 30th June 2010, To 10th July 2010 Facilitating Partner: The Green Movement of Sri Lanka.
Babajide, A., and T. Joseph. 2011. Microcredit and Business Performance in Nigeria: The Case of MFI Finance Enterprises. *International Journal of Research in Commerce & Management* 2 (11): 43–49.
Bagati, D. 2003. Microcredit and Empowerment of Women. *Journal of Social Work Research and Evaluation* 4 (1): 19–35.
Bakhtiari, S. 2006. Microfinance and Poverty Reduction: Some International Evidence. *International Business & Economic Research Journal* 5 (12). https://doi.org/10.19030/iber.v5i12.3550.
Barr, Michael S. 2005. Micro Finance and Financial Development. The John M. Olin Centre for Law & Economics Working Paper Series, University of Michigan Law School.
Bastien, M. 2007. Micro Finance Activity in Sri Lanka. IDLO MF Working Paper, University of Boston, Morin Center/International Development Law Organization (IDLO).
Brau, C.J., and M.G. Woller. 2004. Microfinance: A Comprehensive Review of the Existing Literature. *Journal of Entrepreneurial Finance and Business Ventures* 9 (1): 1–26.
Buvinic, M., and S. Yudelman. 1989. Women, Poverty and Progress in the Third World, Headline Series, No. 289, Foreign Policy Association, New York.
CARE Report. 2005. Women's Empowerment.
CARE Report. 2011. Women's Empowerment Principles, Why Business should care? UN Women, Global Combact Network, India.
Central Bank. 2004. Annual Report of Central Bank, Sri Lanka. Published by Central Bank Sri Lanka.
CEPA. 2007. Absolute and Relative Consumption Poverty in Sri Lanka: Evidence from the CFS2003–2004.
Chowdhury, M.J.A. 2000. Microcredit, Enhancement of Entitlement, and Alleviation of Poverty: An Investigation into the Grameen Bank's Role in Bangladesh, Unpublished Ph.D. Dissertation, University of Stirling, Stirling, UK.

Chowdhury, M.J.A. 2008. Does the Participation in the Microcredit Programs Contribute to the Development of Women Entrepreneurship at the Household Level? Experience from Bangladesh. Paper Presented at UNU-WIDER Workshop on Entrepreneurship and Economic Development, World Institute of Development Economics Research (WIDER), United Nations University, Helsinki, Finland.

Chowdhury, M.J.A. 2009. Microcredit, Micro-enterprises, and Self-employment of Women: Experience from the Grameen Bank in Bangladesh. Gender Pathways out of poverty Rural Employment. Paper presented at the FAO-IFAD-ILO Workshop on Gaps, trends and current research in gender dimensions of agricultural and rural employment differentiated pathways out of poverty, Rome, 31 March, 2 April 2009.

Colombage, S. 2004. *Micro Finance as an Instrument for Small Enterprise Development: Opportunities and Constraints*. Central Bank of Sri Lanka: Colombo, Central Bank Printing Press.

Colombage, S. 2010. Macro Economic Effects of International Migration: Evidence from Sri Lanka. *Journal of Humanities & Social Sciences* 6.

Daily News. 2012. Sri Lanka News. *Online Edition of Daily News, Lanka House Newspapers* 07 (10): 2012.

David, M.J.R., and K. Liyanage. 2005. Second Generation Problems at Bridging Digital Divide in Sri Lanka: Practitioner's Assessment. International Seminar on Bridging the Digital Divide: Best practices and false perceptions. Oxford, UK: Oxford Internet Institute.

Dejene, Y. 2007. Promoting Women's Economic Empowerment in Africa, AFDB Publication.

Department of Census and Statistics Report. 2013.

Deshpanda, R. 2001. *Increasing Access and Benefits for Women: Practices and Innovations among Microfinance Institutions—Survey Results*. New York: UNCDF.

Drolet, J. 2010. Women, microcredit and Empowerment in Cairo, Egypt, International Social Work, Published by SAGE.

Dubreuil, G.S., and C.T. Mirada. 2010. microcredit and Women Empowerment: An Empirical Case–Study Based in Catalonia. Presented to the 2010 ISTR International Conference, Istanbul.

Edgecomb, E., and L. Barton. 1998. *Social Intermediation and Microfinance Programs: A Literature Review*. Bethesda, MD: Development Alternatives Inc.

FAO Corporate Document Repository. 2012. Rural Women in Sri Lanka's Post Conflict Rural Economy. Regional Office for Asia and Pacific.

Fasoranti, M.M. 2010. The Influence of microcredit on Poverty Alleviation among Rural Dwellers: A Case Study of Akoko North West Local Government Area of Ondo State. *African Journal of Business Management* 4 (8): 1438–1446.

Fernando, N. 2002. Microfinance Industry in Asia: Current Status, Recent Trends and Some Thoughts on the Future.
Gayangani, Poornima, and Wasana Jayawardana. 2011. Capabilities of Rural Credit in Entrepreneurship Development among Women: A Sri Lankan Perspective. In *Annual Summit on Business and Entrepreneurial Studies (ASBES 2011) Proceeding*. Graduate School of Asia Pacific Studies, Ritsumeikan Asia Pacific University.
GTZ. 2007. Outreach of Financial Services in Sri Lanka. Promotion of the Microfinance Sector, Colombo.
GTZ. 2010a. ProMiS Partners During Phase I: TCCS Union-Jaffna. International Organizations: Caritas, FORUT, CARE, Swiss Development Cooperation, Christian Aid, World Vision, and UN Agencies.
GTZ. 2010b. Key Principles of Microfinance, Explained by Microfinance Practitioners and Promoters, GTZ & Ministry of Finance and Planning.
Habib, M., and C. Jubb. 2012. Role of Microfinance in Political Empowerment of Women: Bangaladesh Experience, Ontario International Development Agency.
Hair, J.F., R.E. Anderson, R.L. Tatham, and W.C. Black. 2003. *Multivariate Data Analysis*. New Delhi: Pearson Education.
Haq, M., M. Hoque, and S. Pathan. 2008. Regulation of Microfinance Institutions in Asia: A Comparative Analysis. *International Review of Business Research Paper* 4 (4): 421–450.
Haque, M.M., and A.M. Taher. 2007. In Search of Latent Relationship among Some Selected Variables Affecting Job Satisfaction: Bangladesh Perspective, Vol. 1(1).
Hashemi, S.M., S.R. Schuler, and A. Riley. 1996. Rural Credit Programmes and Women's Empowerment in Bangladesh. *World Development* 24 (4): 653–653.
Hilman, H., J. Gidwani, E. Morris, P.S. Subedi, and S. Chowdhary. 2007. Using Microfinance to Expand Access to Energy Services: The Emerging Experiences in Asia of Self-Employed Women's Association Bank (SEWA) Sarvodaya Economics Enterprise Development Services (SEEDS). Nirdhan Utthan Bank Limited (NUBL) and AMRET, USAID, Citi Foundation.
Hoque, M., and Y. Itohara. 2009. Women Empowerment Through Participation in Micro—Credit Programme: A Case Study from Bangladesh. *Journal of Social Sciences, Science* 5 (3): 244–250.
Howard, Z.P. 2013. Economic Empowerment and Political participation: The Political Impact of Microfinance in Senegal. Unpublished Ph.D. thesis, Colombia University.
Ishii, N. 2009. Sri Lanka: Key Persons Forum organized by the Women's Chamber of Industry and Commerce, Training and Supporting Women in Business, Speech at the Luncheon Meeting at the Key Persons Forum. Women's Chamber of Industry and Commerce, World Bank, Sri Lanka.

Jain, D., and B. Jain. 2012. Does Microfinance Empower Rural Women?—A Empirical Study in Udaipur District, Rajasthan. *Journal of Arts, Science and Commerce* 2 (1): 76.
Jamie. 2011. Literature Review: Theories of Empowerment, Village Earth News, Sustainability through Empowerment.
Jan, I., and S. Hayat. 2011. Empowerment of Rural Women through microcredit by Rural Support Programs in Pakistan. *World Review of Business Research* 1 (3): 46–60.
Johannes, A.M. 2007. Women's Empowerment as a Foundation for Social Change, Research Essay about Gender and the Development of Peace. Astrid-Margrete Johannessen.
Khachatryan, K. 2010. Financing Microfinance Institutions: Impacts on Organizational Strategy and Performance: Philosophical and Methodological Implications, Skema Business School, Soreze, France.
Khan, M.A., and M.A. Rahaman. 1998. Impact of Microfinance on Living Standards, Empowerment and Poverty Alleviation of Poor People: A Case Study on Microfinance in the Chittagong District of Bangladesh. Master thesis, diva-portal.org.
Khan, S., M.R. Sajid, and H. Rehman. 2011. Women's Empowerment through microcredit: A Case Study of District Gujrat, Pakistan. *Academic Research International Journal* 1 (2): 332.
Khandker, R.S., and M.M. Pitt. 1996. Household and Intrahousehold Impact of the Grameen Bank and Similar Targeted Credit Programmes in Bangladesh. World Bank discussion papers.
Kim, J.C., C.H. Watts, R. Hargreaves, et al. 2007. Understanding the Impact of a Microfinance Based Intervention on Women's Empowerment and the Reduction of Intimate Partner Violence in South Africa. *American Journal of Public Health* 97 (10): 1794–1802.
Ledgerwood, J. 2000. *Microfinance Handbook: An Institutional and Financial Perspective*. Washington, DC: The World Bank Publications.
Maheswaranathan, S., and F.B. Kennedy. 2010. *Impact of microcredit Programs on Eliminating Economic Hardship of Women, ICBI 2010*. Sri Lanka: University of Kelaniya.
Malathy, D.A. 2000. Changing Role of Women in Sri Lankan Society. Chapter 6, the context of the Sri Lankan Societal Conflicts.
Malhotra, A. 2003. Conceptualizing and Measuring Women's Empowerment as a Variable in International Development. Presented at Workshop on Measuring Empowerment Cross-Disciplinary Perspectives. Word Bank in Washington.
Malhotra, A., S.R. Schuler, and C. Boender. 2002. *Measuring Women's Empowerment as a Variable in International Development*. Gender and Development Group of the World Bank, World Bank's Social Development Group.

Mayoux, L. 2006. Women's Empowerment through Sustainable Microfinance: Rethinking Best Practice, Gender and Microfinance.

Michael, M., and A. Appau. 2011. *An Impact Assessment of Microfinance Institutions on Women Entrepreneurs in Small and Medium Enterprises (SMEs)*. A Case Study of Sinapi Aba Trust: OECD Publishing, OECD.

Mushtaq, A. 2008. Role of microcredit in Poverty Alleviation. Partial fulfillment of the requirement for Master of Business Administration, MBA thesis, National University of Modern Languages, Islamabad, Pakistan.

Mustafa, Z., and N. Ismailov. 2008. *Entrepreneurship and Microfinance—A Tool for Empowerment of Poor—Case of Akhuwat—Pakistan (Master Thesis)*. School of Sustainable Development of Society and Technology: Malardalen University.

Naoko, I. 2009. Sri Lanka: Key Persons Forum organized by the Women's Chamber of Industry and Commerce, Training and Supporting Women in Business. Speech at the Luncheon Meeting at the Key Persons Forum organized by the Women's Chamber of Industry and Commerce, World Bank, Sri Lanka.

Noreen, S. 2011. Role of Microfinance in Empowerment of Female Population of Bahawalpur District. In *International Conference on Economics and Finance Research IPRED*, Vol. 4. Singapore: IACAIT.

Nycander, Lotta. 2004. *"Empowerment of Women through microcredit" microcredit and Social Protection Mitigating Social Exclusion and Empowering Women*. Dhaka: ILO.

Premaratne, S.P. 2008. Entrepreneurial Networks and SME Development: A Managerial Approach. *The Peradeniya Journal of Economics* 2 (1&2): 88–97.

Premaratne, S.P. 2009. Accessibility and Affordability of Rural Microfinance Services in Sri Lanka. *Sri Lanka Economic Journal* 10 (2): 109–136.

Premaratne, S.P. 2011a. Household Labour Supply in Sri Lanka for Urban Young Couple with Pre-school Children. *South Asia Economic Journal* 12 (2): 323–338.

Premaratne, S.P. 2011b. *Female Labour Supply and Child Care: Urban Young Parents with Pre-school Children*. In Annual Research Symposium: University of Colombo.

Premaratne, S.P., S.M.P. Senenayake, and M. Warnasuriya. 2012. Empowerment of Women through Self Help Groups (SHGs): A Study of SHG Microfinance Project in Sri Lanka.

Pushpakumara, W.P.N. 2011. *Impact of Gender on Effect Utilization of the Microfinance Credit Facilities in Sri Lanka*. ICBI: University of Kelaniya, Sri Lanka.

Sara, N. 2011. Role of Microfinance in Empowerment of Female Population of Bahawalpur District. In *International Conference on Economics and Finance Research IPEDR*, 4.

Saroja Sivachandran. 2011. Sri Lanka: Battles Ahead for Women, Humanitarian news and analysis, IRIN.
Sathiabama, K. 2010. Rural Women Empowerment and Entrepreneurship Development. Student Papers Sathiabama/Women Empowerment.
Sri Lanka Action Plan. 2008–2015. SAARC Social Charter, National Coordination Committee, Prime Minister's Office, Colombo.
Sri Lanka Human Development Report. 2012. Bridging Regional Disparities for Human Development, Published by United Nations Development Programme (UNDP), Sri Lanka.
Sri Lanka Needs Micro finance to Empower Rural Micro Entrepreneurs for Sustainable Development. 2010. Microfinance Africa Leave a comment. www.sundayobserver.lk, By Lalin Fernandopulle.
Statistical Handbook. 2012. Northern Province, Sri Lanka.
Stewart, R., C. Van Rooyen, K. Dickson, M. Majoro, and T. De Wet. 2010. *What Is the Impact of Microfinance on Poor People? A Systematic Review of Evidence from Sub-Saharan Africa, Technical Report*. EPPI Centre, Social Science Research Unit, Institute of Education: University of London.
Thurairajah, N., D. Amaratunga, and R. Haigh. 2007. *Women's Empowerment in Disaster Reconstruction: Critical Perspectives on Policies and Frameworks*. School of the Build Environment: University of Salford.
Tilakaratne, G., A. Galappattige, and R. Perera. 2005. Promoting Empowerment through Microfinance in Sri Lanka, Economic and Political Empowerment of the Poor (EPEP), Country Studies of Sri Lanka.
Thilagaratne, G., U. Wickramasinghe, and T. Kumar. 2011. Microfinance in Sri Lanka: A Household Level Analysis of Outreach and Impact on Poverty. Publications Unit of the IPS.
Vulnerability of displaced Women in Post Conflict era in Sri Lanka. 2011. National Protection and Durable Solutions for Internally Displaced Persons Project. Human Rights Commission of Sri Lanka.
Women's Action Network (WAN). 2012. Sri Lanka: Tamil Women coerced into joining the military, A situation concern by the WAN, Asian Human Rights Commission, Hong Kong, China.
Woodworth, W. 2006. *microcredit in Post-Conflict*. Conflict: Natural Disaster and other difficult settings, Marriot School, Brigham Young University.
World Bank. 2009. World Bank Calls for Expanding Economic Opportunities for Women as Global Economic Crisis Continues.
World Bank Annual Report. 2003. Year in Review, The International Centre for Settlement of Investment Disputes.
World Bank Annual Report. 2005. Year in Review, The International Centre for Settlement of Investment Disputes.
World Bank Annual Report. 2012. Year in Review, The International Centre for Settlement of Investment Disputes.

World Bank Annual Report. 2013. Year in Review, The International Centre for Settlement of Investment Disputes

World Economic Forum. 2005. *Women's Empowerment: Measuring the Global Gender Gap.*

Zohir, S., and I. Matin. 2004. Wider Impacts of Microfinance Institutions: Issues and Concepts. *Journal of International Development* 16 (3): 301–330.

CHAPTER 8

Lives in Neglect, Deceit and Violence: Voices and Agencies of Trafficked Women

Satyajit Das Gupta

INTRODUCTION

Trafficking in women and minor girls takes place in cumulative conditions of deceit, violence and exploitation. It's always a continuum of processes. Men and women do it for all sorts of pecuniary gain and physical lust or pleasure. Their means could be consensual or coercive. Vulnerabilities, compulsions and choices of all types may or do coexist. Sections of law-enforcement agencies and political racketeers connive with families and governmental agencies, NGOs and rights functionaries, howsoever well-meaning they may be, often try to combat this menace with activities carried out with misplaced emphases on imperatives or goals of their actions.

Most neglected and least heard in these processes remain the voices of those who get trafficked. For instance, different major government-run anti-trafficking schemes and programmes don't quite mention, not

S. Das Gupta (✉)
Legal Aid Services, West Bengal, Kolkata, India
e-mail: satyadg085@gmail.com

© The Author(s), under exclusive license to Springer Nature Singapore Pte Ltd. 2024
A. K. Sarkar and S. Das Gupta (eds.), *Understanding Women's Empowerment in South Asia*,
https://doi.org/10.1007/978-981-16-7538-6_8

even rhetorically, the need for it.[1] Quite the same is true of various NGO and civil society polemics on rescue, rehabilitation and re-integration of victims of trafficking.[2] Stereotype notions of prevention, protection and prosecution abound in documentation of both the genres. Consequently, assertion of trafficked women's agency gets suppressed or subverted by the political correctness or moralist class prejudices ingrained in these benefactors' palliative or curative missions.

This essay is based mostly on interviews, carried out during the past two years, in one of the major catchment areas of trafficking in West Bengal, with 140 women who have been trafficked and/or re-trafficked. There were some interviews with elderly people of the area and experienced health workers. All the trafficked women were asked questions about their childhood experiences and family situations, circumstances leading to the act of trafficking, traffickers and their associates, the role of the law-enforcement agencies and local panchayats and political functionaries, their current work and future plans. Thirty-two of these women were then asked to tell their life histories, which have been written down in the form of 'biographic narrative'.

When these women shared their stories, they focused not simply on the experience of being trafficked but on a wide range of incidents and issues involving poverty, neglect, discrimination, exploitation, deceit and violence. They talked about their decisions to seek work and willingness to travel with traffickers, who they called 'thikadars' (contractors), to cities where they would find work. Some were open about seeking work in the sex industry. They also said that members of their inner and extended families, friends and relatives were fully aware of their intentions and whom they were travelling with. An overwhelming number of these cases showed that traffickers, law-enforcement agencies and local political functionaries remained closely connected with these processes.

When we begin to talk about the need to hear such voices of women and girls trafficked for open or garbed sex work, we get drawn into the debates about forced prostitution and voluntary sex work. We then also have to get into the economics of sex trade, rights of sex workers and social stigmatization of this most ancient form of human labour. Instead of focusing on that debate over 'legalization of sex work', I have tried to concentrate more sharply on the vagaries and contingencies these women and girls have to endure.

The Method

This was done by asking them to narrate their stories to a person who acted as our interlocutor-cum-data collector. He has in-depth local knowledge and long-standing connections with our informants and is also a well-informed research enthusiast. I began with a thoroughgoing stocktaking of stories of torture, sufferance and exploitation, depending heavily on their abundant availability on the net from various organizational and institutional sources covering cases of trafficking in several regions across the world and also from online postings of independent projects and initiatives.[3] It occurred to me that there was a crucial need to deepen the spectrum of lived experiences in the pre- and post-trafficking periods, taking the exercise far beyond the tropes, protocols and moralizing functions of narrativization (White 1985, 1987) followed and discharged in the combative anti-trafficking discourses that have emanated from various governmental and NGO sources.

The method we have adopted is construction of 'biographically structured narrative fragments' of 'lived experience' of trafficked women in a somewhat sanitized version of their 'words of mouth' expressed mostly in a local tribal dialect-overlaid Bengali our researcher is well conversant with. I should also like to mention here that in this essay, no attempt will be made to deal with an entire range of complex methodological issues relating to considerations of language, memory and identity. Nor shall we look into the vexed epistemological concerns about selective memory, social amnesia and memorial knowledge. By 'lived experience', we shall mean 'the narration of various events and acts by a trafficked woman from her own life and its simultaneous or subsequent noting by our local researcher'.

Let me give one example of how we have noted down the raw words of mouth. Asked to comment on why his daughter is leaving home repeatedly with men having shady personal credentials known to many local people, a father had reacted as follows:

> Don't ask me to talk about what that loose woman does. She is always burning inside as she has worms in her cunt.

The daughter retorted no less violently to accuse the parents:

Do they have any shame? Any guts? How could they have told me to do otherwise? They kept eating to their heart's content in fucking pleasure by allowing their daughter to get fucked by men who brought the food.

It may be instructive to note here that these expressions of crude emotion and pent up furies clearly hint at the fact that both the father and the daughter have their own perceptions of each other's intentions and they use the same to legitimize what they want to pursue as their own designs of what could be called 'abatement to trafficking'. Of course, this is not to suggest that all conversations were replete with such slangs or expletives. It's also true that this language doesn't find expression in any anti-trafficking literature. Our goal has been to capture the nuances of the spoken words as effectively as possible.

As regards the consultation of our documentary sources comprising of court and thana (police station)-level records and other types of written material, which were collected from the families of trafficked women and various institutional sources, the standard method of archival research has been followed in terms of critical reading of the same with the help of corroborative or contradictory oral information procured from the life-stories.

THE DATA

We had begun data collection in the early months of 2014 in an area considered to be one of the major catchment zones of trafficking not only in West Bengal but also in the whole country. At the outset, it must be mentioned clearly that for reasons of confidentiality we will maintain in accordance with the standard social science practices involving human subject research protection, we are not naming the areas, individuals and our local researcher.

There is a high proportion of the SC / ST component in the population of the villages located in the catchment zone under reference, which lies in the close proximity of the Indo-Bangladesh international borders. While the literacy rate is quite low, the unemployment scenario is rather grim. Agriculture, fishery, poultry, dairy, weaving, handicraft and village industry are the main sources of livelihood in general, but most families of the trafficked women we have spoken to don't have much of an access to many of these activities. In small numbers, able-bodied men of these families work mostly as day labourers in agricultural fields or bricklins.

Women go out to work as maid servants in large numbers. Very limited opportunities exist in some home-based trading activities. The sex ration per 1000 males in the SC/ST population category varies between a little over 900 and 950 and 'non-workers' constitute about 70% or more in the overall population profile, indicating a very high rate of unemployment.

Some of these broad demographic and socio-economic characteristics are based on the information from the data generated by the National Rural Employment Guarantee Scheme. According to opinions expressed in interviews taken by our interlocutor, our informants and their family members have been found thoroughly dissatisfied with the ways in which many of the social welfare schemes of the Govt. of India are being implemented through the local panchayats and other administrative machineries. They make serious complaints of non-availability due to corruption and favouritism on the part of the local panchayats and other administrative personnel.[4]

Let me enumerate now the nature and extent of the quantitative and qualitative data we have been collecting for more than two years now. The quantitative component comprises of thematically abstracted and abridged information gathered from 140 three-to-five page-long and hand-written data sheets constructed from responses to 11-point queries on family situations, socio-economic characteristics of the trafficked persons' areas of residence, circumstances leading to the acts of trafficking and their aftermaths, current whereabouts and future plans of the trafficked persons, information about the traffickers and their collaborators/associates, roles of the law-enforcement agencies and local political workers, including panchayat functionaries.

32 extended narratives of lived experiences were constructed by using the method of 'life-writing' to create 'biographically structured narrative fragments' wherein memories have been invoked from the early childhood to the most recent past and then to the present as well. Subsequently, further clarifications were sought in some cases with new queries on health hazards and risks, which couldn't be covered in the first round of interactions because these didn't figure in the normal course of conversation.

We have also collected a number of typed and hand-written documents from the private collections of the families of trafficked women as well as from other local sources, including lawyers involved locally in various anti-trafficking cases. These include the following: (1) photocopies of hand-written letters of complaint submitted by family members to local police stations, which later became texts of general diaries as per the standard practice followed in police stations; (2) photocopies of such letters of complaints submitted to police stations of places where placement agencies had taken women for domestic service; (3) photocopies of FIRs submitted in the official format; (4) photocopies of 'SIKRITI-NAMA[Statement of Acknowledgement of a Trafficker's Obligations]', a document signed, in presence of panchayats functionaries as witnesses, by the family members of the trafficked persons and the alleged traffickers; (5) photocopies of affidavits and counter affidavits by parties involved in court cases against traffickers; (6) photocopies of letters of complaints submitted to the West Bengal Commission for Women and the State Human Rights Commission by the aggrieved family members of trafficked persons; (7) photocopies of letters submitted to higher police officials complaining of 'police inaction' at the local level; (8) photocopies of letters sent from the Women's Commission to higher police officials with aggrieved families' letters of complaint; and (9) photocopies of contracts of domestic service, containing brief details of the terms and conditions agreed upon by the contracting parties.

Many of these submissions contain copies of several enclosures of supporting documents like photo-identity cards of the Election Commission of India, ration cards, certificates and mark sheets of trafficked persons and visiting cards used by the local and outstation representatives of various registered and unregistered 'placement agencies' known to be involved in providing domestic service of all sorts.

In maintaining confidentiality, we haven't compromised on either quality of research or academic freedom to a very large extent and have felt free to dwell upon and utilize the entire bulk of the substantive contents of our findings for this article without disclosing the identities of persons who made it happen. They keep bearing the brunt of discrimination, exploitation and violence of scheming men and women in everyday settings. Yet they have to live with and through all this to survive in an extremely inhospitable world. Social workers who render human services to victims of trafficking have opportunities to witness their struggles for existence from close quarters and in the process, may develop an empathetic understanding of the same. They wonder and try to understand how life goes on in the light and shade of lust, greed and will to resist injustice.

The Stories and Information from Documentary Sources

An interesting starting point in the emplotment of narrativized lived experiences was located in the invoked memories of early childhood and adolescence. It was here that we tried to unearth linkages between neglect, deprivation and deceit in a trafficked woman's life and then to move on to trace what came subsequently. Let's start with how MARIOM MK (25), who was trafficked in 2007 at the age of 16, wanted to look back when she said she had remained 'unhappy and unfortunate' ever since her birth:

> Then hear how I've remained unhappy perhaps since the day I was born. My father had married twice. The first wife expired, leaving one son. He married my mother after that. Mother never ever got along well with my grandmother who used to bring up the son of the step mother. Mother fell ill after my birth. Father was a day laborer and he became physically unfit to work. He was reported to have expired all of a sudden when I was two-year-old. From that time on people used call me 'witch' and the 'unfortunate one'. I've heard all this from mother because I can't obviously have direct memories of such early times, but when I had become able to make out what was happening, I could still remember people calling me 'witch'. I couldn't make out anything on that score.
>
> I used to accompany mother to houses where she was engaged as a domestic help. In many of these houses, I was not allowed to eat anything, but she couldn't tell me the truth because after all she was my mother. She used to ask me to stay at home and I would eat the food she used to bring from those houses after a whole day's work. Pretty often granny used to tell me: 'You've killed my son and my family has been ruined after your birth. You should be driven out of my house. You just leave my house'. Upon her return from daily work and hearing about these allegations, mother used to cry and say that all this was due to faults caused by her fate. After hearing all this, I used to be in a fix and wonder what was my fault in it. Even the boys and girls of our locality used to boycott or avoid me, staring at me all the time and discussing something amongst them whenever they would see me. I was unable to understand much of it then and for that reason, I left home and went with the people of a music and dance troop without informing anyone of the same.

MK is from a low-caste 'molla' Muslim family. She was rescued from men who forced her to perform erotic dances for local audiences, do all kinds of domestic chores for the members of the dance troop and have sex within and outside the troop. Her mother initiated police action with the help of a local NGO functionary and MK was brought home by the police. It may be mentioned here that under the garb of making them join music and dance troops, a good number of minor girls are now being trafficked in the rural and semi-urban areas of UP, Bihar and West Bengal. The recent approval given by the Central Govt. of India to the much discussed 2015 Amendments to the Child Labour (Prohibition and Regulation) Amendment Bill, 2012, allowing children below 14 years of age to work in family-owned enterprises and entertainment industry will only increase the risk of young women like MK falling in the trap of people who are running such 'entertainment troops and outfits' with ulterior motifs of trafficking.

Three interrelated features of the situation facing MK, which isn't atypical at all, emerge from the above excerpt. First, the notion of family as understood in its urban middle-class context doesn't hold in a context where families are often broken through regular or intermittently occurring remarriage, desertion, divorce, elopement or abandonment by their male or female members. Second, the established norms and values of personal and societal attachment or obligation get mutated or destroyed pretty often. Third, as outcomes of these developments and coupled with incidences of sheer neglect and deprivation, young women like MK feel encouraged to trust the promises of contractors for a financially secure future. Joining music and dance troops becomes yet another way of finding work.

But very soon she discovered what the work was all about. Apart from washing clothes and utensils and doing other daily scores, at times she also had to give a whole-body massage to the owner and used to be forced to change clothes in front of men of the troop and sleep with them whenever they would ask her to do so. But sexual favours and abuses didn't stop at all this. MK said:

> Many a day the owner of the party used to have contracts with some men and around 11 pm to 12 o'clock at night we used to be sent to them in such scantily-clad conditions. At first I used to be told to go with a certain man to get my payment and I used to wonder how I would come back all alone. The man would then say that he would escort me back. Then he would take me to a house or a desolate place and would do whatever was expected and most obvious at that hour and in such a situation. Initially, I

used to put up resistance and used to remain reluctant to accompany such men, but used to be left with no alternative. What could I do really? On my disclosing the same to the co-workers, they said: 'Don't pretend like an uninitiated person. As if you don't quite know where have you come to work? We've been brought here to do all this. Singing and dancing is just a cover up to create a garb of decency for people around'. Then I thought I would have to go through whatever is there in my fate. So I stopped resisting and began to oblige whenever they would ask me to do such things.

Acting upon her mother's complaint, the police had ultimately rescued MK from the clutches of the troop and handed her over to the mother who was advised to keep her daughter under strict vigil. But dodging surveillance, she did manage to go to Delhi to work. This is how she had justified her decision:

All girls want to remain at home to have a settled married life and run their husbands' households, but when someone gets stigmatized all the time for going out to work and has a bad name already, you tell me, who would then like to stay back and face accusations coming from all sides? Besides, brothers and sisters-in-law don't look after my mother and so I am left with no other option but to earn. Otherwise who else will look her?

Asked as to why she didn't want to explore livelihood options by remaining at home, she said:

But who will recruit me here? Everyone thinks that I'm a witch and a loose woman. I'll harm everybody and for that reason only I have to take up work in Delhi where no one will accuse me of all this or I'll not bring misfortune to anyone.

In Delhi, it was domestic work involving washing utensils and clothes, providing assistance in cooking, brooming and wiping floors with water and escorting the employer's child to school and bringing him back home at a monthly salary of Rs.2000/- with expenses for food and visiting home incurred by the employer. What about the treatment at the workplace? She had the following to say:

The treatment has been more or less good, but of course they used to scold and abuse me if had delayed something or lacked in cleanliness. Apart from that, I also had to work like a bonded labour. No valid excuses or logical refusals used to be tolerated. I wasn't allowed to go out and would always be confined within the house.

Her concluding statements were clearly indicative of a situation of helplessness as there was no alternative means of livelihood to fall back upon:

> What else could I do? I will either have to go to Delhi or make some other arrangement. I can't remain in empty stomach. If I fail to earn in any other way, I have this body to make use of and will have to do that in the end. Does anyone want to marry a loose and characterless woman? But then I too wanted to marry a boy and I don't quite know where and how he is doing now. I still feel sad for him. Let him be fine always.

This point about the absence of some viable alternative means of livelihood figures almost in all the extended narratives. There are interesting stories from women who made sustained attempts to try out marriage as an alternative option in this situation of overarching helplessness. In disintegrated and disparate family situations with parents remarrying, deserting, appearing or disappearing intermittently, children in general and girl children in particular get attached to ailing or functioning grandparents. SK SARINA is one such woman who left the village with a contractor at the age of 23 and she narrated the attempts made to organize funds to buy items demanded as dowry:

> Mother had found a match for my marriage. He was the son of my elder maternal uncle who agreed to the proposal as soon as mother gave it, but he told her, 'It's fine, but you have to spend for the marriage at the current market rate. Apart from that, her [SK's] father doesn't look after her, what would you do?' After that, mother took my granny into confidence and talked about the demands. We were to give a ring and a bicycle to the boy. It was decided that mother would buy the bicycle and granny was supposed to have bought the ring. Where would granny have got the money for it? She was poor and tried to secure financial assistance from the rich and the party functionaries of our village [but] who would have given such a huge amount? So finding no other way out, I decided to arrange for this amount to buy the ring by going out to work. Accordingly, Granny and I got in touch with a thikadar [contractor] who lived in an adjacent village. That contractor told me, 'If you work with me, you will get Rs.3000/- per month. I will also pay for your meals.' I went to Delhi, accepting these

terms, but got nothing after working for a year and I have no words to describe the sort of treatment I received there.

SK went on to talk about the heavy burden of household work, physical torture, sexual abuse and even forced starvation at her first work place in Delhi. Her marriage remained a distant dream as she and her grandmother had failed to save or raise funds for the dowry the groom's family had demanded. Asked to reflect on her situation at that point in time, she came up with a candid reply:

> I don't care what opinions others hold of me. I ignore what they say. Did they ever care to know how and with what hardship we tried to live our lives and what we had to do to survive? I go to Delhi pretty often for work and also come back at intervals. I move around all sorts of places at night. People say many things about my character, but I don't really bother about all that. To tell the truth, I can't say or I'm not saying that there isn't any repentance, but what will I do? I can't do anything else but this. I have nobody to fall back upon, no one to help or feed me. I have to survive. Granny has grown old, I have to look after her. You know, I cry when I'm alone. Who will listen to what sorrows I nurse in my mind? I have no one in this world. I'm aware that I'm making many mistakes but these is no way out. I have to survive. I'm also a human being

More revealing were SK's observations when asked about her mistakes:

> I won't be able to tell you about all these mistakes, but I'm telling you because I do trust you. I need money obviously, but at the same time there are physical needs as well. I live with men and go places with them for both pleasure and money. There are times when I have to do it for money, although I don't need it physically. Come what may, let me live my life here and now. I feel sad if I start thinking about all this. I cry to feel it within myself. What else can I do? Whatever is going to happen will happen.

It became clear from the stories of SK and several other women that they sought to work as domestic servants ('thikajhi' is the colloquial Bengali word used in middle-class households for female domestics) in Kolkata and other faraway places with the help of men they call 'thikadars' (contractors). Moreover, they were fully aware that such job opportunities might involve demands for minor or major sexual favours. For a huge majority of families living in the area of our research, this has become almost a 'way of life' in the sense that these women themselves and their family members remain used to getting in touch with these thikadars for work in a situation where they may have very limited and immensely uncertain alternatives like working as agricultural or bricklin labourers or in the home-based zari trade for embroidery work.

In this area, there are numerous thikadars and representatives of 'placement agencies', who even show their visiting cards bearing registration numbers and office addresses in many big north and west Indian cities and towns. They form networks of locals, males and females, which pretty often also include members of the inner and extended families of women who do the liaison-building with the outstation people. In fact, these men keep roaming around the villages, searching for and befriending prospective preys not as strangers but as locally acquainted providers of work. Involved family members often receive cash payments informally and in many cases, they even act as local agents. This complex enmeshing of identities and activities of outsiders with insiders makes it highly problematic, if not quite impossible, for administrative and law-enforcement agencies to identify culprits and pinpoint responsibilities of criminal intents of particular acts of trafficking.

Sometime back I had raised the point in a meeting on the 'Draft Trafficking of Persons (Prevention, Protection and Rehabilitation) Bill, 2016, which Govt. of India's Ministry of Women and Child Development has recently circulated for stakeholders' consultations. In Chapter-VIII of the proposed Bill, entitled 'Registration of Placement Agencies', all such agencies have been asked to get registered afresh for the purposes of this Act. I had expressed the view that given the very complicated nature and ever-changing extent of family involvement in processes of trafficking, such re-registration is going to pose immense socio-administrative challenges to concerned governmental authorities.

In many cases, these agencies enter into contracts to spell what is on offer. We do get some episodic information about a few blatant non-fulfilment of contracts from the life-stories. Fairly detailed mention of the same could also be found in letters of complaint, which subsequently become texts of general diaries and FIRs, submitted and filed by trafficked women's parents, relatives and guardians to local police stations when they stop receiving monthly payments from their working daughters or female relatives. Copies of such contracts with facsimiles of the placement agencies' visiting cards and other photo-identity proofs of the victims clipped at their top-left corners have also been found with some of these letters of complaints.

One major complaint is that, despite repeated requests and reminders, thikadars refuse to bring back women unwilling to continue working due to severe maltreatment and abuse. Documents show that these women were in regular communication with their family people through calls made from their own or others' mobile phones. There is written evidence in the form of letters and prayers addressed to higher police officials in the district headquarters or even at the state secretariat for inquiry into cases of inaction on the part of the local police personnel. Interestingly enough, reference is made only of what is there in a contract. There are also cases where trafficked women remain missing for a very long time or their whereabouts remain untraceable even after inquiries made at police stations of faraway places where the traffickers had taken them for work.

In this context, it must also be mentioned that despite the involvement of law-enforcement agencies, traffickers do manage to roam scot-free in broad day light. Life-story information also bears a clear testimony of what the victims and their families call 'wilful non-compliance and immunity' of traffickers due to an alleged nexus of traffickers, local police and panchayat functionaries. We have accessed a number of SIKRITINAMAS, which are acknowledgements of traffickers' responsibilities of bringing back missing victims. The standard practice is that panchayat functionaries bear witness to signing of these acknowledgements in presence of the victims' family people. But for want of any follow-up investigations, the outcomes of these actions remain undocumented.

To what extent such a nexus can frustrate and nullify efforts made by families seeking action against traffickers by exhausting all possible options of police and legal action would become clear from a prayer made by the mother of a victim to the West Bengal State Human Rights Commission. Alleging that her minor daughter named RK was forcibly taken to Kolkata on a false promise of finding a good job without informing the parents, she held that the trafficker was caught by her husband who first pressurized the culprit socially and upon his dillydallying, had lodged a complaint at the local police station. Fed up with police inaction, he had filed a case at the sub-divisional court of the Additional Chief Judicial Magistrate (ACJM). Instead of asking the local policemen to act, the ACJM went on to prolong the case by referring it to the court of the First Additional Judicial Magistrate. Under these circumstances, she maintained:

It won't be possible to get justice for my daughter in the above case and I have come to know that the accused has already sold her for a huge amount of money. Hence, I am seeking the Commission's intervention to get back my trafficked daughter subject to the disposal of the court case.

It would be relevant here to refer to some broad findings from our quantitative data to corroborate the enmeshing of these shortcomings and bottlenecks of anti-trafficking work. Out of the 140 cases we have researched, complex family involvement has been reported in 87 cases. In a good number of them, the victims are found to have been in consultation or dialogue with the parents, brothers or sisters, uncles and aunts, cousins and other close relatives of their inner and/or extended families about the courses of action they had taken before and after getting trafficked. Additionally, in about 20 cases, the victims have been identified as 'sole' negotiators of deals stricken with local thikadars or outstation representatives of placement agencies and/or their local collaborators and associates. The notion of a free-flowing consortium of actors can be relevantly used here to describe the association of individuals, all of whom would remain involved in the processes of trafficking in different capacities. In 8 cases where 're-trafficking' has been reported, elder sisters or aunts or even mothers who were trafficked in the past have been identified as 'agents of action' in league with outstation traffickers.

Wide and intense family involvement helps explain the abysmally low rate of prosecution of traffickers. Even when the law-enforcement agencies take up cases for trial and punishment, it is next to impossible to collect evidence that directly or circumstantially implicates family members. This can have serious bearings on the immunity and impunity traffickers enjoy. But it will be instructive here to note that in our extended narratives, almost no references are made to these facts which come out quite conclusively in the replies to the questionnaire. Such mismatch between the contents of a biographical narrative of a trafficked woman and findings from her replies to the questionnaire is most evident for cases where the person in question had resorted to trafficking in later years. For example, in the extended narrative of one LB who was trafficked at the age 19, no mention was found of the girls she was instrumental in influencing or even cajoling into leaving home for domestic work with physical benefits. Later one of our interviewees, named MNK, made an interesting revelation to that effect by saying that LB was her first cousin and she had even taken a cut from the advance amount paid to her by the placement agency.

Emplotment of narrative fragments constructed from memories of people remains predicated upon several structural constraints. Memorial knowledge and information build on suppression, forgetting and colouring of what happened in the remote and recent past. For example, in our narratives, women haven't quite spoken on issues of health and religion on their own. When asked, they have just mentioned about the use of condoms and have said they are all religiously oriented. But detailed interviews with two experienced female health workers named CB and MM of the area have generated a plethora of information about an entire range of common diseases and serious health hazards these women live with: irregular periods, profuse white discharge, itching and ulceration of female genitalia, varied skin ailments, pain in the lower abdomen and chest and continuing fever with cold and cough infections. They have also talked about multiple abortions done by women who suppress diseases and discomforts as far as possible and difficulties of getting blood tests done for STDs and HIV/AIDS because women generally stop coming to health centres if asked to go for blood examinations. According to them, a certain number of women suffer from severe mental fatigue, depression and trauma due to prolonged sexual assaults of various sorts.

Our local researcher also interviewed two old inhabitants of the area— one male aged nearing eighty and a female in her early seventies. Both of them have very sharp memories. They have said trafficking ('pachar' is the Bengali word they used) began in the area about twenty years back and has picked up a big momentum in the last five-six years. They have sound memories of the communist-led peasant movements of the area and torture and oppression of women at the hands of the landed gentry during those years. In their views, 'pachar' takes place because there is greed and lust and also a genuine attempt at not remaining hungry or starving in bad times such as the one we are living in.

In the words of SKR, a woman in her early thirties and who has moved back and forth between brothels and cities to do, as she put it, work of all sorts:

> I realized that love, marriage and relationships are not my cup of tea and the path I've chosen for survival is the right thing for me to do. A good number of influential and educated men of my area want to have sex with

me. These are men people hold in high regard. While people look down upon me, those people they respect want to get physical with me.

She is now being pressurized to leave even her friend's house by an arbitration council of villagers and many of the arbitrators have had sex with her and some of them are asking her for sexual favours even now. SRK wonders as to how and why they have all become saints now. Indeed, hers is a question that begs on to a crumbling order of things.

Conclusions

Trafficking and sex work can always have a cause and effect relationship, which tends to be almost self-evident. Our data, too, shows it in ample measure. But this essay isn't addressing the very complex issues raised by the advocates of the right to sex work. Nor is it getting into the perennially continuing debate over legalization of sex work. Negating much of the abolitionist and correctional notions of socio-legal engineering about sex work, several UN bodies have recently been suggesting measures favouring substantial deregulation and decontrol of governmental activities that have been regarded as anti-trafficking (UNDP-UNEPA-UNAIDS Report 2012; UNDP 2012).

One UN body has recommended decriminalization of pimping and brothel-keeping to deal with prostitutes suffering from or facing the danger of getting affected with HIV/AIDS (UN Women's Note, October, 2013). Academics, women's rights and civil society activists across India have expressed serious concern over this disease-management thinking about sex work. They have pointed out that vested interests of a large number of multinational marketing agencies and their NGO/INGO collaborators depend on pimps and brothel owners for the success of their condom distribution programmes and hence the bid to decriminalize the latter. The apprehension is that these proposed measures will increase the manoeuvrability of traffickers.

The first pan-India survey of sex workers showed that a significant number of females move quite fluidly between other occupations and sex work. It is not easy to demarcate woman's work into neatly segregated compartments. sex work and other work come together in ways that challenge the differentiation of sex work as an unusual and isolated activity. The survey was based on sufficiently large national-level sample of females divided by geographies, languages, sites of operation, migratory patterns, incomes and cultures. One of its major findings was that rather than reducing these women to clichéd stereotypes, there is a need to bring to the surface their non sex-work histories, either alongside or prior to engaging with sex work. The survey addressed the realities surrounding sex work in the country to demystify some of the polarized and often simplistic narratives, which paint such work in opaquely value-laden terms (Rohini Sahni and Kalyan Shankar 2011).

Our data has uncovered interesting information about trafficked women's sex work done either alongside paid domestic work or as consequences of sham marriages where exceptionally heavy burdens of domestic scores have also been an integral part of women's near-bonded labour. Quite the same situation faces very young adult women and minor girls working for various entertainment outfits. We have spoken to trafficked women who have worked in brothels or have continued mobile sex work from home as singles or after marriage in the forms of going out with buyers of sex for short trips or day outs. Many of these activities relate closely to shady and fraudulent deals traffickers strike directly with the victims or with their families or with both.

The stories in particular locate various events and acts of trafficking in a continuum of neglect, deprivation, deceit, domestic violence and other forms of abuse. In varying proportions and intensity, all this forms part of the life of a victim before and after she is trafficked. Many of the stories show that almost totally uneducated and low-caste young Muslim and Hindu women from large and poor families experience repression and exploitation from an early age and the goal of their coping strategies revolve mostly around efforts to move out for work with the help of the thikadars who exploit them in various ways. Offers of domestic service and sham marriages are the two most commonly followed means of trafficking in these areas.

Survival becomes the prime concern in a situation of acute poverty and helplessness. Their family members take money to sell them. Remaining amenable to offers from the thikadars either wilfully or having got hoodwinked, they are led to severe violence and torture pretty often. Yet the trapping and preying continues perennially as these women have nowhere else to go and nothing else other than their body to make use of for a living. So they could be called 'the last girls' (Gupta 2016): the most marginalized and the haplessly resource-starved ones.

Our data has shown that even in this atmosphere of all-pervading desperation and helplessness, a discernibly strong sense of assertion of those, who have had a certain degree of mobility and establishment through sex work in the post-trafficking period, stand out. They remain fairly nonchalant or even dismissive of the criticisms and disapprovals of men in authority, going at times up to the extent of raising a counterpoint about their hypocrisy and double standards. There is a craving for opportunity to be heard. I would call it 'trafficked women's agency in making'. In many instances, these women have been found active in processes of re-trafficking and have become traffickers themselves, developing and spreading networks of their own in later years. This essay makes an argument about the need to hear many voices. It's never enough to concentrate entirely on 'moments of heightened fissures and ruptures'. Alongside sufferance, violence and exploitation, anti-trafficking sensibilities should also be linked up with a progression of continually flowing desires, ambitions, apprehensions, perceptions and expectations of flesh and blood human agents who get trafficked.

Our research has shed new light on the complex ground realities of various means and aftermaths of trafficking in one of its major catchment areas in India from two angles. On the one hand, we have unearthed important biographic and documentary evidence of extensive and deep-seated family involvement in processes of the pre- and post-trafficking periods. We have shown how family members and traffickers can remain integrally connected with one another and can play different roles interchangeably. So the fact of impunity and immunity enjoyed by traffickers becomes almost self-evident because the main fallout of widespread family involvement is non-availability of reliable evidence for prosecution. On the other, we have collected substantial information about the existence of a nexus between traffickers, local police personnel and panchayat functionaries across political spectra, which always has far-reaching systemic bearings on the nature and extent of traffickers' ability to act and react in playing havoc with victims' vulnerabilities and informed or uninformed choices.

Given these integral connections of stakeholders and adversaries of anti-trafficking activities, much of the stereotype programming for re-integration of victims with families and creation of awareness and sensitization for combating trafficking is bound to remain ineffective or even counterproductive. Development sector professionals and government-run social sector project officials and functionaries with close and continuing exposures to ground realities of anti-trafficking work would know pretty well about these problems. But these complexities don't find sufficient and explicit recognition in their preventive or regulatory service delivery activities. It's here that this article tries to make a point of arrival in terms of research and documentation.

I shall end this article with a longish extract from HN's life-story. Now in her late fifties, HN symbolizes the very complicated enmeshing of personal, social and political considerations involved in the processes of trafficking. This enmeshing takes place in the intermingled and shifting spaces of material culture, systemic inequities, emotional or mental involvement, discernibly violent and exploitative power relationships, and individual motivations and ambitions.

Certain feature stand out in HN's extended narrative. First, she was trafficked at the age of 13 or 14 by neglectful and abusive parents who sold her to an 'agent' (her expression). Later she was involved in an affair with an elderly man who took excellent care of her material and emotional needs. After marriage, she maintained what she called an 'illicit' relationship. After a difficult period, she settled finally into commercial sex work in a brothel. When she was older, in her late 20s and 30s, she came back home and continued serving clients from there. She could earn sufficiently and in fact, started saving from that point in time.

When her two daughters grew older, she involved them in what she calls 'family work' and gave them in marriage to men she calls 'friends with sympathies' meaning men who had support for what she was doing. She approached her retirement from sex work in her late 30s. She said that over time her social status improved and people in her immediate neighbourhood and community sought her 'advice and expert opinion' in what she called 'matters of recruitment of young girls for jobs in different cities of India'. She now travels to meet representatives of recruiting and placement agencies and receives assistance from her daughters. HN said she doesn't have too many regrets, but feels sorry not to have a well-knit family. But, she says 'life goes on' and that she is still developing coping strategies to deal with 'scheming men and thugs of society'.

Does this narrative challenge 'conventional knowledge and wisdom' constructed by official agencies and civil society on 'rescue, rehabilitation and re-integration' of trafficked women and girls? Is it strong enough to subvert our sensibilities born out of thoughts and practices, which have got stereotyped or remained stagnated for various academic, cultural and political reasons? Can it succeed in pricking at the core of our benevolent and vanguardist welfarism overlaid by middle-class moralism that tends to remain tendentiously correct in political terms? Trafficking is unthinkably violent and unbearably soul-diminishing. Our narratives do bear testimonies to all that trafficking poisons and destroys in human life. But they also try to salvage the agencies and voices of those who are violated and diminished. Coupled with findings from other documentary sources generated through activities of protests against trafficking, these life-stories outline multifaceted struggles for survival and settlement in one of the most inhospitable terrains of human endeavour.

NOTES

1. A User's Manual for Anti-Human trafficking, jointly published by the Administrative Training Institute, Government of West Bengal & Bureau of Police Research & Development, Government of India, 2013. The manual was developed as 'study material' for a comprehensive training programme of police officers and other government functionaries; and Ujjawala, a comprehensive scheme for the prevention of trafficking and rescue, rehabilitation and re-integration of victims of trafficking and commercial sexual exploitation, Ministry of Women & Child Development, Government of India, 2007.
2. Compendium of Best Practices on Anti-Human Trafficking by Non-Governmental Organizations, New Delhi: United Nations Office on Drugs and Crime Regional Office for South Asia, 2008).
3. I am providing here two duly activated mother links of numerous sites containing such case studies, stories and life histories: (a) From the URL - https://www.google.co.in/#q=life+histories+of+trafficked+women - Victim profiles from the US State Department's Trafficking in Persons Report, 2005; Victims' stories from the Trafficking in Persons Report, 2013; 'I was sold into sexual slavery' in The Guardian: Human Trafficking – The Observer; 'Sex Trafficking in the UK – One woman's horrific story of kidnap, rape and beatings; & (b) From the URL - https://www.google.co.in/#q=human+trafficking+stories+in+europe - Human trafficking stories – catwinternational.org; Stories from the Nightingale's Children Project; Human trafficking in the Middle East: Manola's story; Human trafficking stories: still searching for slavery?. Red Light Dispatch and Our Stories, Aapne Aap – Women Worldwide: http://apneaap.org/our-stories/red-light-despatch/.

4. It would be interesting to mention in this connection that in some of the life-stories of the victims of trafficking and conversations with their family members that we shall present here, local toughs and men with shady community reputation, who are also known to be close to local panchayat functionaries, have reportedly been distributing these services and favours rather liberally to the families of good-looking young women to earn sexual favours to being with and then to take them out of the villages following sham marriages and sell them to brothel owners or individual male pimps.

References

Gupta, Ruchira. 2016. *The Prostituted Woman in Indian Short Fiction*. New Delhi: Speaking Tiger Publishing Private Limited).
Sahni, Rohini, and V. Kalyan Shankar. (2011): *The First Pan-India Survey of Sex Workers: A Summary of Preliminary Findings*. Sangli: Paulo Longo Research Initiative on New Directions in Sex Work Research. http://www.nswp.org/sites/nswp.org/files/Pan%20India%20Survey%20of%20Sex%20workers%20April%202011.pdf.
UN Women. 2013, October. *Note on Sex Work, Sexual Exploitation and Trafficking*. New York. http://www.nswp.org/sites/nswp.org/files/UN%20Women's%20note%20on%20sex%20work%20sexual%20exploitation%20and%20trafficking.pdf.
UNDP. 2012. *Global Commission on HIV and the Law: Risks, Rights and Health*. New York. http://www.hivlawcommission.org/resources/report/FinalReport-Risks,Rights&Health-EN.pdf.
UNDP-UNFPA-UNAIDS. 2012. Sex Work and the Law in Asia and the Pacific. Bangkok. http://www.undp.org/content/dam/undp/library/hivaids/English/HIV-2012-].
White, Hayden. 1985. *Tropics of Discourse: Essays in Cultural Criticism*. Baltimore: John Hopkins University.
White, Hayden. 1987. The Value of Narrativity in the Representation of Reality. In *The Content of the Form*. London: John Hopkins University.

CHAPTER 9

Multiplying Insecurity: Disempowerment of Women's Agency in the Logistics of Transnational Trafficking Networks of South Asia

Paula Banerjee

INTRODUCTION

The evolution of the discourse on trafficking in the last few decades in the context of South Asia is a muddled history of systematically equating notions of female vulnerability with that of victimhood by the media and migration with criminal activities by the state apparatus. Probably the trend began with Nicholas Kristof's mission to Sonagachi, his rescue of five girls and his assertions that India is in the centre of modern slave trade producing more slaves than any other country. This equation with trafficking and slave trade is not new. The term "trafficking" can be traced

P. Banerjee (✉)
IDRC Endowed Chair, Centre on Gender and Forced Displacement, Asian Institute of Technology, Bangkok, Thailand
e-mail: paula@ait.asia

© The Author(s), under exclusive license to Springer Nature Singapore Pte Ltd. 2024
A. K. Sarkar and S. Das Gupta (eds.), *Understanding Women's Empowerment in South Asia*,
https://doi.org/10.1007/978-981-16-7538-6_9

back to the "white slave trade" of the nineteenth century. Before the great wars the term was used to mean the coercion or transportation of Caucasian women to the colonies to service white-male officers. At that point the term did not include indentured labourers from the colonies to the plantations where often they were sent through coercion and in the way or on arrival they were cheated and abused.

From 1904 there were efforts to stop "white slave trade" leading to the *Convention for the Suppression of the Traffic in Person and the Exploitation of Others* in 1949. By that time trafficking had come to be associated with transportation of women for "immoral purposes" such as prostitution. Social scientists believe that after the wars "women from developing countries and countries which were experiencing civil and political unrest ... were migrating to the developed world in search of a better future." Given the gender inequities in these countries women often entered informal sectors such as prostitution, where labour protection laws are minimal. The international community tried to combat these abuses by humanitarian legislation that addressed concerns of women's vulnerability. The term used to describe the abuse of women in the process of migration was "trafficking." Efforts to stop trafficking in the 1980s and 1990s went hand in hand with efforts to abolish prostitution. Therefore trafficking and prostitution came to be understood as two parts of the same process. In the context of the region under discussion, it is likewise understood and the push factors for women's trafficking even now primarily remain gender inequities in the country of origin, endemic poverty and political persecution. Also the routes through which trafficking takes place are usually the traditional routes of migration and the recruiters are usually the family, friends or someone you know.

In newspaper reports, from the last two decades, it has been stated and restated that, "India was among the seven Asian nations put by US on its 'watch list' of countries involved in human trafficking." This is not isolated news but such statements from the West keep recurring. In the same report it was also stated, "not only India is facing this huge problem but also has become a transit point for prostitution from nearby countries like Bangladesh, Myanmar and Nepal." India was also marked as the destination for sex tourism from Europe and the United States. In the last one decade news of thriving business in organ transplantation in India is becoming common knowledge.

These news portray that according to the Western media, human trafficking is a thriving proposition in this sub-region including Myanmar,

Bangladesh, Nepal and India. It is true that huge groups of people have historically moved in this region and they are moving even now. But whether all of them are trafficked is a different question and even if they are trafficked can we mark all of them as hapless victim is another question. In this paper I contend that in this age of sacred borders, by conflating trafficking with migration the states criminalize all those who are migrating. Also by conflating trafficking with sex work, such criminalization is justified as these people are seen as sexually available and morally reprehensible. Contributing to this phenomena is the tremendous increase in women's migration, particularly that of single women, in this region.

The region has witnessed many different kinds of migration including intra-state and inter-state migration, rural to urban migration, marriage migration, forced migration, migration due to environmental changes, etc. I will portray here how whether it is inter-state or intra-state migration, smuggling or trafficking, the migrant is usually victimized, even if they have been trafficked into the region. The UN Trafficking Protocol to prevent, suppress and punish trafficking against persons, especially women and children (The Palermo Protocol) supplemented the United Nations Convention against Transnational Organized Crime of 2000. The Palermo Protocol was built around the notions of coercion, consent and exploitation. About the Palermo Protocol one observer argues that:

> the definitional ambivalence it embodies, in combination with a global panic around sex work and trafficking, have led to the constant conflation of trafficking with trafficking for sex work, and of trafficking for sex work with sex work. Sex work is then presented not only as exploitative per se but also as the most horrific form of modern-day slavery. Consequently, the implementation of anti-trafficking law is both over-inclusive and under-inclusive. It is over-inclusive because it targets women engaged in voluntary sex work. It is under-inclusive because trafficking for purposes other than sex work is ignored, and rendered less worthy of our attention. Moreover, the preoccupation with migration and border control leads to a truncated understanding of coercion as requiring physical force or deception.

Usual Suspects

Anyone who does not bear physical evidences of coercion, therefore, are looked upon as migrants and likewise forcefully incarcerated. The case of Uttarpara Destitute Home For Women (2012) bears evidence to that. 11 women aged between 20 and 35 escaped from the home on 31 December 2012 without a trace of evidence. Three of these women, Doli Sardar, Nilima Biswas and Ratna Biswas were from Bangladesh. To begin with, earlier 50 women were apprehended in Pune under the Immoral Traffic Prevention Act. 18 of these women were sent to Bengal, to be returned to their families. Instead of doing that first they were Liluah home for destitute women and then 11 of them were sent to the Uttarpara Home on November 2012. The Indian women who were apprehended were from Murshidasbad, Nadia and the 24 Parganas.

These women were clearly trafficked and so the Bangladeshi women were not booked under the Foreigners Act of 1946 or the Section 14 of the Indian Penal Code. But in what way were their situation different? Instead of jails they were taken to homes that have been described by observers to be dirty and filthy. Most importantly, many of their rights were denied including the right to communicate and the right of self-determination. Their only possible way of escape was to get their family members to come and claim them. But for Bangladeshi women that was impossible. If caught under the Foreigners Act of 1946, then there was a real possibility that these women could be pushed back after they have served their time of 2 years and 2 months but as victims of trafficking they might have to be in these homes, where they might be seriously abused for far longer. So running away from these homes could have been a real and for a very long time the only option for many of these women. About the anti-trafficking programmes where women are remanded in destitute homes, Kimberley Walters writes:

> Transnational donors have converged on South and South East Asia in the attempt to return trafficking victims to 'legitimate' labour, but this has amounted to the reinforcement of the labour of relations that pays women too little to support themselves or their families My research indicates that anti-trafficking programmes do violence to the bodies and lives of sex workers...attempts (perhaps unwittingly) to reinsert women into the very kin and labour relations that make it likely for them to enter sex work in the first place. Although the humanitarian violence enacted through anti-trafficking efforts assumes new discursive guises in the language of

'modern-day slavery,' its effect is the damaging of lives and delegitimisation of a potential remedy to abject poverty, while failing to offer adequate alternatives.

Indian rules have also expanded considerably in relation to penalizing all forms of trafficking. The IPS section devoted to it prohibits human trafficking for the purpose of "physical exploitation or any form of sexual exploitation, slavery or practices similar to slavery, servitude and the forced removal of organs." Section 370 offers significant potential to address all forms of slavery in India, especially forced labour—which, prior to the introduction of Section 370 was not treated as a serious offence and carried very weak penalties. About foreign nationals, apprehended in India, who are victims of trafficking the Ministry of Home Affairs (Foreigners Division) 2012 directive says:

> It is seen that in general, the foreign victims of human trafficking are found without valid passport or visa. If, after investigation, the woman or child is found to be a victim, she should not be prosecuted under the Foreigners Act. If the investigation reveals that she did not come to India or did not indulge in crime of her own free will, the State Government / UT Administration may not file a charge sheet against the victim. If the charge sheet has already been filed under the Foreigners Act and other relevant laws of the land, steps may be taken to withdraw the case from prosecution so far as the victim is concerned. Immediate action may be taken to furnish the details of such victims to the Ministry of External Affairs (Consular Division), Patiala House, New Delhi so as to ensure that the person concerned is repatriated to the country of her origin through diplomatic channels.

In case of Bangladeshi citizens such as the three Bangladeshi girls in the Uttarpara Home, this process is not so easy. Bangladesh disagrees that there is any illegal migration into India. Repatriation needs the cooperation of the two countries. Since Bangladesh refuses to agree that there is migration into India, the administration often refuses to comply to such repatriations much to the detriment of their nationals. Another matter of concern is that even with such memorandum's neither the courts and nor the security apparatus is willing to mark people as victims of trafficking. A case in point is that of Rabin Mia.

Rabin Mia, son of Md. Habul Mia of Pakundia, Kishoreganj, Bangladesh, was detained in Balurghat District Correctional Home. The young man was apprehended with six others and put behind bars and no efforts were made to find out whether he was an adult or a minor. He was implicated in a criminal case vide Balurghat Police Station Case No. 98/2013 dated 26 February 2013 under Section 14 (A) (B) of the Foreigners Act of 1946. The police filed cases against them as adults. More importantly, there was no effort made to see whether these boys were victims of trafficking. In a conversation with him it was revealed that they did not come to India unassisted. Since the person was a "juvenile" of a foreign national and who was not involved in any criminal actions, he should not have been prosecuted but immediately repatriated under the abovementioned MHA advisory.

There are cases where people who are brought from Bangladesh to the metropolitan towns in India faced tremendous brutality. One such case in the public domain is that of Hamida, a young Bangladeshi girl, who was brought to India at the tender age of ten. She "suffered a series of brutal rapes at the hands of the man who brought her to New Delhi, along with some of his friends who were Delhi policemen....Only one of the accused men has served jail time." In our research we came across many such Hamida's. One of them is Shanaj Khatun. She used to work as a domestic worker in Bangladesh earning Rs. 300–500 a month. In one of the houses she met a man who frequently travelled to India. He told her that she could earn a lot more in India. So she took leave from her mother and younger brother and sisters and left for India dreaming that one day she will be able to come back with a lot of money.

Her ordeal started once she reached Kolkata. The man (trafficker) who brought her from Bangladesh sold her for Rs 20,000 to a man who brought her to a house where several women stayed, including many from Bangladesh. She was told by another girl that, "bad things go on here" (*kharap kaj hoe ekhane*). Shahnaj cried, begged for freedom, but she was beaten up mercilessly, was forced to change into strange dresses that the other women in the home were wearing and locked up in a room. She stayed there for over two months and for each night notionally she was paid Rs 7000 but she was not given any money. From Kolkata Shahnaj was taken to a brothel in Delhi where she stayed for more than a year. One day, when she was commuting from Delhi to another unknown destination with other women from the Delhi-based brothel, she was caught by the police and taken to custody as she is an illegal migrant from Bangladesh. She was first taken to Durgapore jail, then one year she spent in the Asansole jail and finally in Alipur. She has been booked under the Foreigners Act and her prison term is for three years.

It is clear that girls like Shahnaj and Hamida have been trafficked yet most often they are booked under the Foreigners Act. Sometimes, they even told us that the police often advise them not to tell the judge anything about having been trafficked. On hearing this we immediately assume that the police must be in cohorts with the traffickers but there is another reality and that is the problem of repatriation with Bangladesh. Jail birds are often pushed back but girls from homes have to be repatriated and since that is something that the Bangladeshi government has to officially agree to it becomes a much bigger deal and women languish in homes for years.

Unusual Suspects—Some More Cases of Bangladeshi Migrants

Taslima Khatun, a Bangladeshi inmate of Alipur jail was sentenced for twenty-five days for crossing the border illegally. She was caught under the Passport Act. Although her sentence was for such a short term, she has been languishing in the jail for over one year. This is nothing exceptional and most inmates have said that this is a common procedure. When asked about this delay Taslima philosophically stated that "I will have to eat jail rice as long as the Lord has ordained it for me." Taslima does not fit the usual profile of inmates most of whom are younger and have clearly come for work. She is over fifty years of age. She has only one daughter living in India and the rest are all in Bangladesh. When asked about the short span of her sentence she said her son-in-law, who is a civil engineer, spent a lot of money on her case. This was another perception that the inmates shared and that is without money or someone to champion their case they are doomed. Judicial delay seems to be the least of the abuse that these migrants face or fear. There are many more such abuses and a lot of it is perpetrated by the protection agencies.

In January of 2003 five Bangladeshi nationals, of whom two were minor children crossed the Indo-Bangladesh border and entered India. The Border Security Force (BSF) arrested them from a Baro Bridge across the Ichhamati River. The area in which the incident took place is under the jurisdiction of the Basirhat police station in the North 24 Parganas. The Bangladeshi nationals including one Jayanti Bala Das were all taken to the Soladana BSF camp at around 5 pm. On the same night (10

January 2003) one BSF personnel allegedly raped Jayanti Bala. Thereafter these "infiltrators" were put in a small boat with holes and efforts were made to push them back. Allegedly when the boatman refused to go, he was threatened on the point of gun. The boat capsized in the middle of the river and only Jayanti Bala and her one-year-old son could save themselves. On 13 January the villagers of Bagundi, who had given her shelter, handed Jayanti over to the police of Basirhat. She was charged under Section 14 of the Foreigners Act. On 21 January a dead body was found in the Brick kiln Canal in South Basirhat. The man was identified as Jayanti's husband Basudev. When a case was lodged against five BSF personnel the BSF men were unwilling to hand over their personnel to the Basirhat police. Although the BSF disagreed that Jayanti was raped but the officer in-charge of this case stated that initial examinations proved that she was molested. On 27 January the SDJM of Basirhat issued warrants against five BSF men. In July Jayanti was handed over to the Sromojibi Mahila Samity for safe custody and on 15 September 2003 a writ petition was filed on her behalf.

Jayanti's case reflects the situation of women who are trying to cross the border. Their status of being a foreign-born woman increases their vulnerability. No one is willing to shoulder any responsibility for these women. The state that they leave is glad to get rid of them and the state that they enter finds them unwanted. This has been proved when in February of 2003, 213 gypsy snake charmers who have always led a life of seasonal mobility crossing borders at certain times of the year were stopped in zero point in Satgachi in Cooch Behar. They had to remain there for days as both India and Bangladesh was unwilling to take them back until one night they just disappeared. No one knows what happened to them and even less do people care. From the Indian side we were told that they were pushed inside Bangladesh. No one even asked for evidence of what happened because this is a grey area. In such a situation woman can be exploited by anyone and are therefore particularly vulnerable to traffickers.

The case of the Rohingya women from Myanmar is also interesting. The Myanmar government does not recognize Rohingyas as their nationals. These women faced successive attacks from the Myanmar government who have used GBV so that the Rohingyas leave the Arakan Hills. Until 2009 the Rohingyas went safely to Bangladesh but then the Bangladeshi government became hostile to Rohingyas and started repatriating them. After that they started migrating to wherever they could including Thailand, Malaysia and India. In India there are Rohingya camps in Jammu and sometimes the UNHCR accept them as mandate refugees. When they are accepted as mandate refugees, they are given a document from UNHCR so that they can travel outside of India and come back safely. But often when they try to enter India showing this document, the BSF disposes of that document and book them under Article 14 of the Foreigners Act. Once they are booked under the Foreigners Act, they are treated similar to the Bangladeshi women. But the Bangladeshi women have a singular advantage over them and that is they have a country where they can be pushed back. But for Rohingyas even if their jail term is over, they are left in the prison to languish as they have no country where they can be pushed back.

In case of single Rohingya women coming to India, they inevitably take the help of traffickers. But they are never booked under the ITPA because there is no place for them to be repatriated. When we did our research in 2015, there were 8 Rohingya women officially living in Balurghat Correctional Home. The eight women came in a group of 20 from Fanshi, Quarbil, Bali Bazar, Bugrishaw and Bohbazar areas of Rakhine district, Myanmar. All of them—Noorjahan, Nurkalima, Belma, Mumtaz Begum, Samjhu Nahar, Manohara, Mabia Khatun and Fatema Khatun—said they were compelled to flee for mass violence that was unleashed on them from the nineties. Their children are not allowed to go to the madrassas, they are not allowed to pray, not allowed movement. Some of these women have lost their husbands to brutal torture. They have come through Chittagong in Bangladesh, via a long route to reach India in order to go to Jammu where already some of their relatives have settled in the Rohingya camps. Even the Dumdum Central Home and Behrampur Central Home now have a considerable number of Rohingyas and their fate is even graver than the Bangladeshi nationals since they cannot be repatriated or sent back to their country, the reasons being they are not considered as citizens of Myanmar. So even after a Rohingya becomes Jaan khalash, he/she suffers in jails till a decision is reached.

The ultimate destination for these Rohingya women is often Pakistan because they feel they will be safer in a Muslim country. But, the Government of Pakistan has largely ignored the issue of the trafficking of Rohingya women. Seeking work, Rohingya women sometimes become victims of slavery through debt bondage. "At the same time, their undocumented status leaves them open to arrest and imprisonment" during transit (Ghosal 2000: 15). The prisons of West Bengal house over 100

Rohingya men and women, who are imprisoned indefinitely because the South Asian nations do not know how to deal with stateless people. In Baharampur jail, one finds 70-year-old Manadma Begum who can neither express herself, nor understand why she has been incarcerated for so long. Her language (Rohingya) sets her apart from the other Bangladeshi inmates in this West Bengal prison. Parveen Bibi, a 20-year-old Rohingya woman in Dum Dum jail, claims she is from the CHT and sheds tears saying she should be treated as a Bangladeshi since her husband is a Bangladeshi national. But, the police informed us this was not true as she claimed she was a Rohingya when caught. When we asked Parveen Bibi why she originally called herself a Rohingya, she said she was told that it would fetch a lighter prison term. Nurbahar Bibi, a Rohingya from Cox's Bazar, was despondent. Her Bangladeshi husband had been pushed back to Bangladesh and she had no access to the man who had brought her to India. If released, where would she go?

Trafficked Across Open Borders

When women are trafficked across borders such as from Nepal to India, it makes them even more insecure. After crossing a border these women can become stateless if they are without any papers or proof of citizenship. Often they are coerced to travel without papers and follow agents of trafficking to repay their family loan. It has been stated "about 153,000 Nepali girls were in Indian brothels in 1990 and the number has been steadily increasing at a rate of 5,000 every year." Nepal is considered as the most significant source of girl-child commercial sex workers to India. The average age of Nepali girls entering into Indian brothels ranges from 10 to 14. Economic stress and historical oppression coupled with immense profits which accrue to the trafficker leads to the rapid flow of girl children from Nepal to India. In this era of globalization, tourism has become another occasion for child trafficking from Nepal. Although Nepal has passed the Human Trafficking (Control) Act of 1986, these Acts are hardly ever implemented. Trafficking of Nepali women to India continue unabated. A very disturbing phenomenon within this process is that young Nepali "virgins" are trafficked because people not only prefer their fairer complexion but also there is a ridiculous but common belief among some communities that having intercourse with a young girl can cure many sexually transmitted diseases as well as AIDS. So price for these girl children go up. But the moment they contract the illness, they are thrown out of the brothel and come back to their homes where their family is often loathe in taking them back.

These children are oblivious of the risk they are in. According to one social worker in J.J. Hospital in Bombay, "one 15-bedded women ward was occupied with 13 patients with HIV infection, out of this 11 were Nepali." What people in sex trade do not realize is that trafficking is not merely violence against women but against humanity. These young girls living in brothels are so powerless that they can hardly insist that their clients use safety measures. Once they contract the disease, they inadvertently infect many more and contribute to destabilization and insecurity of the whole region. Once their illness is discovered, they are treated like pariahs. They are punished for something over which they had hardly any control and yet the process continues. Trafficking finds little space in traditional security discourse, yet it is one mode of migration that actually leads to physical insecurity of a region and people inhabiting it.

Equating trafficking with sex slavery has given rise to many unforeseen security hazards. One such hazard is the marking of the female subject as nothing but victim. Indeed as Ratna Kapur writes: "the Third World victim subject has come to represent the more victimized subject; that is, the real or authentic victim subject. Feminist politics in the international human rights arena, as well as in parts of the Third World, have promoted this image of the authentic victim subject." The states have appropriated this image of silent female victim as the true representation of trafficked women. This image has also served the states well because now the state policymakers are able to argue that a police regime has to be imposed on the borders to protect these silent victims. Although, such a regime is imposed for the protection of women but women are the most marginalized. The perception of threat derives from women's sexuality and mobility because mobility ordains women's sexuality as uncontrolled. Since migration and trafficking follows the same routes, the two categories collapse. With the criminalization of trafficking migration is also criminalized. Trafficked women and undocumented migrant women therefore become a threat to the purity of the national borders. So to protect women's sexuality a police regime is imposed that have to protect the women from the consequences of their own uncontrolled sexuality otherwise that will affect national security. This leads to criminalization of any form of undocumented migration across the border.

Conclusions

As I had stated earlier a discussion on transnational logistical networks finds its other in transnational trafficking networks or crime networks. As has been suggested by a renowned social scientist this network however is formed of the subalterns. Probably that is why it is easy for transnational security officials to come together and mark it as aberration. The official coordination of countries (the Bali process) and thus the more legal-administrative connections look upon these connections as illegitimate as these connections escape their gaze and thereby subvert the administrative process that is considered as marker of stability. But these networks continue often with the tacit approval of the other networks who gain by it. These narratives of trafficking can therefore be situated as counterpoint to the official narratives of connections. It is interesting to note that most of the participants of this process know what they are getting into. The abuse of victims might not even be tremendously more than in any other forms of migration such as marriage and migration. But official discourses mark the trafficked as victims, thereby denying agency and their ability to represent themselves thus making it easier to place them under police regimes.

It is interesting to note that transnational police regimes are successful in controlling human trafficking largely by killing the victims as is the case with the Rohingyas travelling on boats to Thailand and Malaysia or the refugees travelling across the Mediterranean. The logistics of control are based on presumptions that the bodies they deal with will be docile bodies but when the regime of control finds it otherwise, their only answer is repression. There is little understanding that when transnational networks are formed, it is presumed that their beneficiaries will be the elite who can harness capital such as big business, MNCs, elite professionals. But in every step the subalterns or women, labouring poor, migrant workers will try to subvert the system for their survival. The elite officialdom may call it trafficking, smuggling or otherwise, to the subaltern it is their logistics of survival.

The states will constantly try to subvert any movements across borders and criminalize anyone that tries to challenge those borders, be it internal or external. Even when people move across borders within a country, the migrants are criminalized and sent back to their places of origin. In Maharashtra and Delhi slums are habitually raided and if young women from different regions are found they are bodily removed and put in a home in that region. The former bar dancers of Mumbai are a case in point. Many of these girls were from poorer regions such as West Bengal, Odisha, Bihar and Jharkhand but the Maharashtra government assumed that all these women were Bangladeshi and so they needed to be pushed back. This is a classic case where migration becomes trafficking and trafficking is marked as a criminal activity. Even if crimes are committed against women as they are the persons who have been trafficked but because of their "unharnessed" sexuality, they are marked as criminals. Their sexuality is considered as polluting so they are criminalized and incarcerated so that they can be locked up and forgotten. Or they are criminalized and sent beyond the borders. The fantastic numbers of 150,000 women from Bangladesh and Nepal entering into India increases this xenophobia and misogynism that symbolize a woman as alien and her body as polluting. It then becomes easy to criminalize her in the name of national security and punish her aberration. But women are not passive victims. They fight the situation and keep coming back so that they can survive and dream of a better future.

Notes

1. Bandana Pattanaik, "Where Do We Go From Here?" in Susanne Thorbek and Bandana Pattanaik eds., Transnational Prostitution: Changing Global Patterns (London/New York, Zed Books, 2002) p. 218.
2. "Human Trafficking Cases in Meghalaya Draw US Attention," Shillong Times, 16 June 2004.
3. Ibid.
4. Prabha Kotiswaran, "Vulnerability in Domestic Discourses on Trafficking: Lessons from the Indian Experience," Feminist Legal Studies (2012), Vol. 20, No. 3, p. 247.
5. These facts were culled out from newspaper reports, A Fact Finding Report by Banglar Manabadhikar Suraksha Mancha (MASUM) on Uttarpara Destitute Home, 15 January 2013 and interview with Priyobroto Bakshi, Officer-in-charge, Uttarpara Police Station, 28 January 2013.
6. Kimberly Walters, "Humanitarian Trafficking: Violence of Rescue and (Mis)calculation of Rehabilitation," Economic and Political Weekly: Review of Women Studies, Vol. 51, Nos. 44 & 45, p. 61.

7. Advisory on preventing and combating human trafficking to India – dealing with foreign nationals," Office Memorandum, Government of India, Ministry of Home Affairs (Foreigners Division) No.14051/14/2011 – F, VI, dated 1st May, 2012.
8. Kirity Roy, Secretary MASUM and National Convener PACT, letter to the Chairman, National Human Rights Commission, New Delhi, 4 July 2013.
9. Upala Devi Banerjee, "Sexual Exploitation and Trafficking of the Girl Child: The Indian Scenario," Migrant Labour and Trafficking of Women: Workshop Report (Nepal, National Network Against Gril Trafficking, 1999) p. 64.
10. Interview with the author in Alipore jail on 14 November 2014.
11. Interview with Taslima Khatun on 14 October 2014, in Women's Correctional Home in Alipur, Kolkata.
12. Ananda Bazar Patrika, 14 January 2003.
13. "News From The Indo-Bangladesh Border," Refugee Watch 19 (August 2003) p. 2.
14. Interview with Manadma Begum in Behrampur Correctional Home on 28 November 2014.
15. Interview with Parveen Bibi in Dum Dum Correctional Home on 28 October 2014.
16. Interview with Nurbahar Bibi in Dum Dum Correctional Home on 28 October 2014.
17. Quoted in Upala Devi Banerjee, "Sexual Exploitation and Trafficking of the Girl Child: The Indian Scenario," Migrant Labour and Trafficking of Women: Workshop Report (Nepal, National Network Against Gril Trafficking, 1999) p. 68.
18. Ibid.
19. Pushpa Bhatt, "Trafficking of Nepali Girls in India and AIDS," Women's Voice (A Report Published by National Network Against Girl Trafficking, Kathmandu, not dated) p. 27.
20. Ibid.
21. Ratna Kapur, "The Tragedy of Victimization Rhetoric: Resurrecting the "Native" Subject in International/Post-Colonial Feminist Legal Politics." Harvard Human Rights Journal Vol. 15. (2002) p. 2.
22. Ranabir Samaddar in his review of the paper in April 2016.

CHAPTER 10

Equalizing Gender Imbalance in a Globalized World—The Issue of Transnational Abandonment of Women

Shamita Das Dasgupta

My involvement with anti-violence against women work began in the early 1970s as I enrolled in a college in the U.S. I had come to the U.S. as a young wife and started school as a young mother in a Midwestern university. My initiation into formal feminism occurred when I joined a consciousness-raising group with other women from the community and fellow students in Ohio. I say 'formal feminism' intentionally to distinguish this awareness from the discomfort I felt when, as a young girl growing up in India, I looked around and recognized the restrictions that girded the lives of girls and women, the 'un-freedoms' they suffered in silence. My own growing up as a daughter was curtailed by marriage, which was considered to be the definitive end-state of women by my family. Contrastingly, at my educational institute, an all-female high

S. Das Dasgupta (✉)
Montville, NJ, United States
e-mail: shamitadas@hotmail.com

© The Author(s), under exclusive license to Springer Nature Singapore Pte Ltd. 2024
A. K. Sarkar and S. Das Gupta (eds.), *Understanding Women's Empowerment in South Asia*,
https://doi.org/10.1007/978-981-16-7538-6_10

school led by a visionary headmistress, I came across teachers who pushed us to achieve more and taught us that our responsibility was to give back to our societies. This early encouragement of engaging with the community developed more in the U.S., and I began my work in organizing the burgeoning immigrant South Asian community as it strove to find its footing in a new country.

Moving to New Jersey in 1985 from the Midwest, along with five other immigrant Indian women, I was fortunate to cofound an organization, Manavi, that focused on violence against women in South Asian immigrant families. Part of our inspiration came from the domestic violence-related murder of a young man that occurred in 1981 in New Jersey. A mother of two had killed her husband. She disclosed in court a story of horrific and long-standing abuse by her intimate partner (Dasgupta 2000). The story jerked us out of our somnolence and Manavi became the first organization in the U.S. to focus on violence against women in the South Asian community.

Our work had no predecessors and we knew no beaten path. Learning from the U.S. mainstream organizations' domestic violence advocacy and founding our knowledge on research and writings of women in the developing world, Manavi began its journey. As we moved forward and began responding to requests of help of individual victims and survivors of violence, the structural obstacles that colluded with culture and erected nearly insurmountable hurdles for women became obvious to us. Consequently, our struggle became not just to help individual women overcome these barriers but to make sure the structural obstructions are dismantled forever (Dasgupta 2010a, b). As we worked tirelessly, another realization loomed large. Regardless of how many barriers are minimized or smoothed out, patriarchal structures would be instrumental in perennially renewing and recreating them. A case in point is abandonment of wives, which, although nearly unknown in the early days of Manavi's work, increased tremendously with the changing socio-economic conditions of the world.

A New Form of Violence Against Women

Harmesh Kaur from Amritsar, a lecturer at Guru Nanak National College in Hoshiarpur married Kamal Pradeep Singh, who taught at Khalsa College. After they had a child, Singh left for the United States as an illegal immigrant. For three years he did not contact her. Then he came up with a scheme for obtaining Canadian citizenship by marrying a Canadian citizen. He asked her for a false divorce, to enable him to acquire citizenship papers and then send for her. Harmesh happily gave him the divorce, only to find that it was a real divorce and she and her son have never heard from him again. (Melwani 2005)

More than a decade ago, I had the opportunity to visit Punjab on a project to share information about domestic violence policies and practices in the U.S. with the state's law enforcement practitioners. I travelled to several districts and met not only with the local police personnel, but also with community members who were interested in voicing their complaints and demands, perhaps emboldened by the presence of a neutral visitor. At nearly every meeting, I was surprised to find throngs of elderly men, mothers, and young women with children. Fathers, who were also grandfathers, came up to me with their daughters and demanded that I do something about their sons-in-law who seemed to have disappeared in the U.S. leaving their wives behind.

Young women, often carrying their children in their laps, explained that their non-resident Indian (NRI) husbands had left them in limbo and at the mercy of in-laws or natal families. How could they compel the husbands/sons-in-law to fulfil their marital and parental duties? How could they bring their NRI husbands back to the country or in lieu, compel them to send sponsorship papers for migration of their wives and children? The one family that has stayed with me over the years consisted of an elderly Sikh grandfather, his beautiful daughter, and a twelve-year-old girl, the elderly gentleman's granddaughter. "She has never met her father," the mother informed me. It seems the young girl's father, the woman's husband, had left for the U.S. when the wife was pregnant and had never contacted them again.

Although each woman's story was unique, they were characterized by one common theme: desertion by a NRI spouse who had married the woman before migration or had returned to the country to marry and subsequently abandon her. I came back to the U.S. with the foreboding realization that we were witnessing a new form of woman-abuse taking shape. With my colleagues of Manavi, I kept an eye open for help sought by transnationally abandoned wives. At that time, we were not quite sure what kind of help the women would seek or need. Within a short period of time, we began to hear from anti-violence against women community-based organizations (CBOs, alternately identified as non-governmental organizations or NGOs in India) about victims who were contacting them to find their absconding NRI husbands. In those early days, we attempted to locate the men through telephone directories, web traces, and the U.S. State Department. However, even when we located the men, what the women truly desired was beyond our capacity to accomplish: reconciliation with the husbands.

MAGNITUDE OF THE PROBLEM

The purpose of this chapter is not to elaborate in details the sufferings of Indian women deserted by their NRI spouses and the circumstances of their abandonment, nor the men's insensitivity to their wives' and children's hardships. I am attempting here to discuss some of the issues that have arisen as community-based organizations (NGOs or CBOs), along with country governments, have struggled to respond to the victims' needs. I have culled my experiences from my work at Manavi, the oldest South Asian culture and language specific anti-violence against women organization in the U.S. Manavi has always been sensitive to the needs women voiced in South Asian communities and the phenomenon of wife-desertion moved us towards a new transnational issue that had hitherto been invisible to us.

Once Manavi opened up to the issue of wife abandonment, we were inundated with requests for help from individuals and NGOs in India. Recognizing that we needed to understand the problem better, we began to survey other South Asian organizations in the U.S. and speaking to mainstream agencies that participated vigorously in policy-making and efforts to bring about institutional change in the country. We found that almost 20% of the workload of nearly all South Asian organizations was made up of advocacy for transnationally abandonment women. Contrastingly, the mainstream agencies did not recognize spousal desertion as a form of violence against women at all. Thus, the mainstream advocacy agencies in the U.S. were reluctant to discuss the creation of new policies that would hold the perpetrators accountable. Yet, we found that the data emerging from India alone showed a growing number of women from various states of the country being deserted. Added to this was similar data from Nepal, Bangladesh, and Pakistan, indicating similar trends.

As we researched the issues more, we found that historically, abandonment of wives and children is certainly not a new phenomenon, but one that was on the rise as a by-product of globalization that began in the

1990s and continued in the new millennium. The success of globalization rests on unfettered movement of finances and labour across national borders. The shifting of money rides on the best of profit making motives, and labour in the form of workers moves in search of better jobs and accompanying benefits. Globalization was welcomed by many as a way of instigating rapid growth in developing countries, but most had not anticipated the human cost it might extract. Although theoretically, the free movement of labour allows women to move around the globe just as much as men, the realities are quite different. Most primary immigrants from India are not women. Women migrants tend to follow their skilled or unskilled husbands or other male sponsors as dependant fiancées, wives, mothers, and daughters. The circumstances of such deep dependency render women vulnerable to abuse due to the power differential integral to the men's residency status, employment, and gender privileges.

Although we focused on the U.S. due to our location, it is not the only country where NRI émigré husbands take refuge after deserting their wives. Any country that boasts of immigrants, must deal with the blemish of transnational wife abandonment. The problem is spread across Australia to Canada, from European countries to Singapore. By a 2004 estimate, approximately 12,000 wives were deserted in Gujarat (NRI Internet 2004), and by a 2007 study, 25,000 women had been left behind in the state of Punjab (Malhotra and Malhotra 2007). In 2008, then India's Minister for Overseas Indian Affairs, Vayalar Ravi, declared that in Punjab alone, there were 20,000 legal cases pending against NRI husbands, who had presumably abandoned their wives and children (Joseph 2008). A Canadian study claims there are at least 10,000 'runaway grooms' in the country (Ward 2005a; b). A 2016 news report mentions that two out of every ten NRI marriages end up in desertion of wives (Chakrabarty 2016). The statistics collected are not necessarily reliable and are mainly gathered from official complaints or from individuals who speak up in other ways. From what we know about the stigma of divorce or abandonment carries with them, we may surmise that many women and their families decide to live life under the radar and suffer in silence (Jabbi 2005; National Institute of Public Cooperation and Child Development 2007).

Contours of the Problem

Before I launch into a description of the responses to deserted women, let me elaborate the definition of abandonment that unambiguously places the problem in the category of violence against women. Abandonment or desertion may be defined as:

> [A]n individual left *without* resources by another on whom s/he is dependent for social and financial survival. In the South Asian context, abandonment would entail the endangering of a woman's welfare, safety, and future prosperity, particularly by her husband's design to thwart her access to legal recourses and by his deliberate attempt to deprive her of her rightful financial (marital) and social assets. (Rudra and Dasgupta 2011, p. 12)

The definition is rooted in Indian cultural contexts and women's status within marriage. The reality that women's social, emotional, and economic lives are shattered by the husbands' desertion and that women are helpless to their husbands' power and control over them, makes abandonment a violence that is similar to any other kind of domestic violence.

Anuradha Chadha writes, "In the Indian context, marriage is considered as a sacrosanct institution that unites not only two individuals but also two families" (Chadha 2016, p. 1). Thus, presumably not to be entered in or ended lightly. Additionally, for women, marriage is considered the most important social institution. Family members try to get a daughter married as soon as possible and at all costs (Anitha et al. 2016; Dasgupta and Warrier 1996). Societal expectations require a natal family to encourage a daughter not only to get married but also to remain married regardless of her situation in the relationship. The high premium paid to marriage and maintaining the "married" status renders women vulnerable to various abuses in the affinal family such as beatings, emotional torture, economic control, repeated dowry demands, day to day mistreatments, silencing, and even death (Waters 1999).

By the same token, to most Indians, divorce is generally an unacceptable option to end an unhappy marriage. Although this attitude may be changing slowly, especially in urban areas, divorce is still far from being common or easily permissible. Generally, an unmarried adult woman has a tenuous position and role in society and women strongly try to avoid the breakup of their marriages. Thus, it is not surprising that when wives are deserted by their NRI husbands, they try to compel them to return and renew the marriage, and excuse the men's behaviour by assuming various unavoidable circumstances that force these men to renege on their wedding vows (Anitha et al. 2016). Additionally, when women are abandoned with their children, they feel the responsibility of protecting the children from a fatherless existence.

In the U.S. family law, desertion is defined as, "[W]ilful abandonment by one spouse in a marriage, without the consent of the other" (Answers.com 2009). In 1896, the Law of Domestic Relations in New York categorized abandonment of wives and children without adequate support as disorderly conduct punishable by imprisonment (Gilbert and Battershall 1902). In case of extreme needs such as physical or mental disabilities and ill health of the abandoned spouse, the charges would be increased to the level of criminal conduct. On the other hand, abandonment is certainly considered adequate justification for divorce, even if it does not affect alimony or other property settlement. Regardless of how morally reprehensible it is, spousal desertion has never been included in the understanding of domestic violence in the U.S.

The modal situation of the abandoned Indian woman is described below:

1. When migrating abroad, many husbands leave behind their wives and children with the promise that they would be reunited at the first opportunity. Most women may have been married for years and lived together with their spouses continually before being deserted;
2. A significant group of Indian women who have been living in the U.S. with their spouses are coercively or deceptively brought back to India and abandoned in the country. Often, their travel papers are destroyed to prevent them from returning to the U.S.;
3. Many of the women's families have given large sums of dowry to the men, paid for their migration-related expenses, and been harassed continuously for more dowry at the threat of withdrawing visa-sponsorship of their daughters;
4. Many of the women are divorced ex-parté in the U.S., without any legal representation; others believe they are still legally married;
5. The majority of women are not aware of their husbands' current addresses, telephone numbers, and employment details. Thus, they have no way of contacting their spouses;

6. Most abandoned women live without any financial support from their émigré husbands. Their children are also deprived of child support from the fathers; and
7. Many women live in virtual servitude with their in-laws as their natal families are reluctant to have them return and refuse to financially support them after marriage (Rudra and Dasgupta 2011).

While most of the South Asian CBOs in the U.S. are engaged in individual advocacy for transnationally abandoned women, there has been no evidence-based best practice to protect the women's social, legal, and economic rights. Culling from my research, I found the most pressing question the transnationally abandoned Indian women want answered is why they have been deserted by their husbands. A question that may never be fully or satisfactorily resolved.

Led by Swayam in Kolkata, India, a network of South Asian organizations around the world has evolved to deal with transnational issues surrounding abandonment of wives. The goal of the network, Aman: Global Voices for Peace in the Home, is to provide, among other services, advocacy to alleviate individual women's sufferings and secure their legal and economic rights in transnational spaces. A noteworthy corollary of this is to instigate policy changes in the international arena to ensure that women do not fall through legal cracks in individual countries. In the U.S., Manavi took on the responsibility of collaborating with other South Asian CBOs and connecting with Aman to facilitate advocacy for abandoned South Asian women. However, as Swayam began to coordinate the work, all of us recognized the difficulty of finding justice in a world where laws and practices differ from country to country and frequently are in opposition of one another.

WHAT DO ABANDONED WOMEN WANT, REALLY?

There is no doubt that transnational abandonment is a deliberate effort on a husband's part to deprive the wife's legal, economic, and social rights. Nonetheless, when abandoned Indian women seek help, their strongest desire is to persuade, or even force, reconciliation with the individual who has hitherto endeavoured to dispossess them of basic human rights. The women's concerns stem from the stigma attached to wives who have been divorced, widowed, or abandoned; that is, being left without a man to determine a woman's identity. Part of the problem arises out of the Hindu philosophy of marriage being regarded literally eternal and considered a wife's responsibility to maintain. The same cultural principles have seeped into the practices of other religious communities, such as the Christian and the Muslim, rendering women in all cultures vulnerable to pressures to sustain their conjugal relationships.

But the most insistent problem that women face after being abandoned is financial. Many young brides curb their own financial security after marriage by resigning from their jobs or ending their studies, either voluntarily or due to coercion, to conform to the traditional role of a 'good' wife. Thus, without any court ordered alimony and maintenance, abandoned women and their children slide into poverty. Dissolution of marriage also brings tremendous economic, social, and emotional hardships to them. In Indian cultures, it is a convention that once a woman is married, she no longer has any rights in her natal family, which, then, shrugs off all responsibilities towards her. Furthermore, the parents of a woman do often give substantial dowry to the groom and/or bear hefty wedding expenses. They may even blame a woman for the failure of her marriage and might refuse to support her. Courts in India are cognizant of the financial and social power differentials in a married couple and consequently, have always attempted to equalize it by responding to the needs of the abandoned woman regardless of the length of marriage and cohabitation.

In the U.S., on the other hand, if a marriage is short lived and/or the couple has not lived together for any significant period of time, the prospect of being awarded substantial or any financial support is slim. The courts in the U.S. typically grant spousal support based on age, length of marriage and cohabitation, and the needs of the parties making such claims. U.S. courts assume that able-bodied individuals under the age of 40, regardless of gender, should be able to earn a living and support themselves. Courts are more likely to provide temporary rehabilitative support rather than permanent maintenance to wives. The assumption that young women should be able to work and provide for herself is not well accepted in Indian cultures and frequently, abandoned women loathe to agree to this 'foreign' ideology.

Since declaring one's needs in court is another way of securing financial maintenance in the U.S., Indian women deserted in their home country are especially disadvantaged, as they might be unable to appear to plead for their needs, thus, losing out on alimony and compensation agreements. Unless courts in the U.S. are fully informed and convinced of the socio-cultural contexts of Indian women's existence and their hardships, it would be impossible to extract economic justice. Even when favourable alimony and child support decisions are handed out in Indian courts, it is almost impossible to execute them in the U.S. even though there is some indication that a foreign divorce and maintenance decree could be implemented if presented in a timely fashion and as a judgement on a parallel issue sub-judice in the U.S. Still, further complications arise because Indian women are not able to hire adequate legal representation to support their interests in the U.S. Women's impoverished conditions continue to compromise their efforts to secure legal rights in courts. Added to this is the Indian attorneys' ignorance of U.S. laws and the mistakes they make in advising their clients in India. For example, many Indian attorneys counsel their clients to ignore the notice for court appearance which generally has a 30-day response deadline. Unfortunately, if there is evidence that the notice has been delivered properly, the 30 days deadline is hard and fast. If the woman does not respond within that time, the case in the U.S. is likely to be decided ex-parté.

Citizenship and Legal Jurisdiction

Recently, historically unprecedented worldwide migration due to globalization has created unexpected problems with citizenship of migrants and their families. Citizenship is generally defined as a nation-state's claim on individuals born or living within its boundaries. In addition, children of a nation-state's citizen can acquire citizenship through his/her parents. For example, an Indian citizen's daughter will be considered an Indian citizen by virtue of her parents' citizenship even if she is not born in the country. Additionally, a nation-state bestows certain privileges and rights equally and legally upon its citizenry which distinguishes it from non-citizens (Hobbs and Chernotsky 2007; Lagos, n.d.). Thus, citizenship marks the "in-group" of citizens and separates them from the "out-group" of non-citizens. A state also has the power to punish and rehabilitate its citizens for contravention of its laws. Actually, state is the only legitimate authority to have the right to punish its citizens.

But what happens when a state's citizens are mobile and are not living within its geographical boundaries? If people reside outside the countries where they are citizens, yet retain their original citizenships, who then have the legitimate power to provide them with rights, and sanction them for transgressions? Even though by one part of the definition of citizenship, the nation-state of one's birth may claim sovereign rights over the individual born within its borders regardless of his/her residency, the second part of the definition confers the same rights, barring a few, upon the state where the person is living. To ensure that the people living on its soil abide by its laws, the independent host country claims this autonomous authority. While this right is quite clear concerning criminal activities, it becomes ambiguous when dealing with family law. For instance, when jurisdiction splits due to separate locations of a married couple, who has the ultimate authority to make legal decisions about their divorce or child custody? A case in point would be divorce lawsuits filed by NRI husbands in U.S. courts when their wives are left back in India. These cases are generally resolved ex-parté and thus, fail to provide justice to the women, as the overwhelming majority cannot appear in court or secure legal representation due to financial insolvency, and/or the inability to secure travel permits (Anitha et al. 2016; Rudra and Dasgupta 2011).

Consequently, when immigrants live in a different country than their country of citizenship, determining as to who has the legal right to control their behaviours becomes a thorny issue (Hernández-Truyol and Hawk 2005; Hernández-Truyol and Rush 2000). The situation becomes clear if we consider the case of an Indian who migrates to the U.S. to work. Let us assume he makes good money in the U.S. but refuses to send money back to his indigent parents, thus endangering his aged parents' well-being. By Indian law, his conduct is punishable, but in his country of residence, this is not a legal infraction that is susceptible to prosecution. So, which country's law will have claims over this person? The same is true for an NRI man in the U.S. who seeks divorce from his wife who is still living in India. Which court system has unequivocal authority to grant the requested divorce—the country of this man's residence or the country of his citizenship where he does not reside? In short, laws and policies are playing catch-up to the rapid changes in migration and are also unable to keep up with the ensuing problems. The emergence of dual or multiple citizenships and overseas citizenship are efforts to accommodate the citizens of a nation-state who live outside its designated territory.

However, nothing works satisfactorily in cases of family law-based complaints: divorce, alimony and maintenance, property allocation, as well as child custody. Additionally, the concurrence of two or more citizenships does not necessarily benefit all individuals equally. Rather, contradictions in various country-laws, often deliberately antagonistic to one another, advantage the person who first files lawsuits in his/her resident country. Briefly, deciding as to which state-laws can claim control over an individual when his/her behaviour has harmed another who does not live in the same country remains an open question.

In most countries, spouses are usually bestowed each other's citizenship (of residence or of origin). So, can an Indian wife left behind by her NRI husband claim the rights of citizenship of both her and her husband's countries of residence? Given the ever-increasing restrictions on entry-permits into different countries, how this claim could be successfully implemented is not clear. This becomes a complicated matter when a lawsuit in one country obstructs the execution of rights of an individual living in a different country. Consider the case of an NRI who has filed for divorce in the U.S. from his wife who lives in India. Due to financial and visa restrictions, she is unable to travel from India to appear in a court in the U.S. and has no representation to protect her legal and financial interests. The husband receives an ex-parté decision where the wife receives no financial settlement or support. Undoubtedly, by the ex-parté decision on divorce wherein this woman could not protect her financial and other interests, the U.S. courts have, in effect, crushed her social, financial, and legal rights. In such a situation, how could the wife's rights be preserved without forcing the man to remain married? We must realize that when abandonment is transnational in nature, it erects multi-layered social, legal, and economic barriers for women to obtain justice. The problems lie in split jurisdiction that is integral to the phenomenon of migration resulting from the globalized condition of today's world.

The splitting of jurisdiction affects abandoned women's rights especially because the laws of the U.S. and India are quite disparate in terms of identifying abandonment as a form of violence against women and providing remedies. This identification is essential to the evocation of laws that protect women and their children from intimate partner violence. In the U.S., because abandonment of adult women is not considered to be abuse, such cases wind down as simple divorce. If the woman is unable to appear in court to testify or ensure legal testimony in court, there are no special efforts expended to discover the circumstances of her absence. Even though there are variations in exigencies of laws by states, divorce is granted to anyone who seeks it; in this case, the husband. On the other hand, unexplained withdrawal from marriage or abandonment would be considered abusive in India and remedied by evoking the law on 'Restitution of Conjugal Rights' (Government of India 1955), and also the 'Protection of Women from Domestic Violence Act, 2005' (PWDVA-2005) (Government of India 2005). The disparate laws of the two countries become apparent when a woman in India may have the courts approve her petition for the restitution of conjugal rights and the husband in the U.S., his country of residency, has been granted an ex-parté divorce. Furthermore, in the U.S., the wife may end up without any monetary awards and maintenance based on her non-participation in the proceedings. In contrast, PWDVA-2005 in India may award a woman maintenance, right of residence, and numerous other financial compensations, an order that may not be implementable in the U.S. at all.

The woman's rights may be further crushed as, given that there are no legal contradictions or split jurisdiction, the Supreme Court of India has decreed that it is willing to accept divorce judgements passed in foreign courts. As a result, depending on the timing of the U.S. divorce decree, the Indian legal system may accept the foreign divorce and reject any lawsuit filed in its own legal system or any decision made after the ex-parté divorce decree in the U.S. In the U.S., under the principle of 'comity,' courts wait for the conclusion of analogous cases in another country. However, it is debatable whether a divorce lawsuit in the U.S. and a case on 'restitution of conjugal rights' in India are similar at all in legal scope and intent.

Uneasy Bedfellows: Official and NGO Responses

The main objective of CBOs and NGOs working to end violence against women is to facilitate women's struggles in achieving their socio-economic rights. Yet, the organizations on their own can hardly accomplish this. They must go through the apparatus of the state-run legal system to ensure that justice is meted out. As said before, states are still playing catch up with the realities that are unfolding in the wake of globalization. We still do not have laws that can unequivocally resolve a case of transnational abandonment. Even when there are laws in the countries to remedy woman-abuse, the consideration as to which country's laws will have jurisdiction over the complainant and the respondent, who are residents of different countries, continues to confuse all concerned. In such a situation, could CBOs and NGOs evoke international laws to protect women's rights?

Private international laws including international family laws have a role to play in dealing with divorce, maintenance, and support of abandoned wives (John 2010; Prabhat 2007; Rudra and Dasgupta 2011). International private laws can be utilized to resolve legal conflicts concerning private individuals that cross national borders and circumvent laws enacted by country governments. These international laws emerge from the United Nation Conventions and The Hague Conferences and serve as the primary reference points for multilateral agreements governing international family law disputes. Unfortunately, these treaties are only as strong as the relevant governments' willingness to abide by the agreements. A summary chart of the treaties that are applicable in situations of transnational abandonment is presented below:

Summary of Treaties Relevant to Transnationally Abandoned Wives

Name of the Convention
Relevant States/Ratification Year
Provisions Relevant to Transnational Abandonment

UN Convention on Recovery Abroad of Maintenance (New York Convention), 1956 (UNHCR 1956)
Pakistan/1959
Sri Lanka/1958

Facilitates recovery of maintenance through agencies and offices set up by the member states as transmitting and receiving agencies when the recipient and the person obligated to pay are in different countries.

Hague Convention Abolishing the Requirement of Legalisation for Foreign Public Documents (the Apostille Convention), 1961 (HccH 1961)
India/2004
U.S./1980
U.K./1964

Facilitates the circulation of public documents across state boundaries by replacing the formalities of authenticating signatures and seal/stamps on public documents such as a degree, divorce decree, and court judgments with the issuance of an Apostille Certificate by Consular or diplomatic agents.

Hague Convention on the Service Abroad of Judicial and Extra Judicial Documents in Civil and Commercial Matters, 1965 (HccH 1965)
Canada/1988
India/2006
Sri Lanka/2000

U.K./1967
U.S./1967
Provides for channels of transmission of legal and other documents from one member state to another and protects a defendant prior to a default judgment by ensuring that if the defendant cannot appear before the court, judgment is not issued unless the service of the document is valid as per the laws of the defendant's country of residence. The Convention protects the defendant after a default judgment is passed by allowing him/her to appeal beyond the permitted period so long as the defendant, (a) appeals within a reasonable time after the default decision is issued; (b) was not notified properly; and/or (c) was not allowed sufficient time to respond to the notice.

Hague Convention on the Recognition of Divorces and Legal Separations, 1970 (HccH 1970)

UK/1974

Provides rules for the recognition of divorces and legal separations obtained in one member state by another. Article 2: A divorce decree/ legal separation obtained in a contracting state will be recognized by another if at the time of the proceedings, it was the respondent or the petitioner's habitual residence. If it was the habitual residence of only the petitioner, such residence must be for more than one year or it must have been the last habitual residence where the spouses had cohabited. Recognition of a divorce may be refused if adequate steps were not taken to duly inform the respondent of the proceedings and if the divorce or legal separation is incompatible with a previous decision determining the matrimonial status of the spouses.

Convention on the Law Applicable to Maintenance Obligations, 1973 (HccH 1973, 1977)

Mostly European states

Provides guidelines to the determination of which country's laws would apply to maintenance obligations arising from a marriage and parentage. Article 4: The internal law of the state where the potential recipient resides will apply when determining maintenance obligations. Article 8: The law of the country where the divorce was granted will govern the maintenance obligations between the divorced spouses and/or modification of such decisions.

Convention on the Recognition and Enforcement of Maintenance Decisions, 1973 (HccH 1973)

U.K./1979 & mainly other European states
Provides for reciprocal recognition and enforcement of maintenance decisions by a judicial or administrative authority in one state by another contracting state. The enforcement of decisions is based on the internal laws of the state where the enforcement is sought. Article 5: A contracting state may refuse to recognize or enforce a maintenance related decision if, (a) it does not agree with its public policy; (b) it was obtained fraudulently; (c) there is a pending legal proceeding for the same purpose but initiated first; (d) the decision is incompatible with a prior decision for the same purpose and between the same persons; and (e) if there are no periodic payments allowed.

Protocol on the Law Applicable to Maintenance Obligations, 2007 (HccH 2007a)

Not ratified

This replaces the 1973 Convention on applicable law and provides rules for applicable of law for recognition, enforcement, and recovery of maintenance arising from parental relationship, marriage, and affinity. It states that the law of the state of habitual residence of the recipient will apply for determining maintenance obligations unless one of the spouses objects. In case of such objection, the law of the state of their last common habitual residence would apply. Article 8: The person who is obliged to pay and the recipient can designate the applicable law, but only through a written and signed agreement.

Convention on the International Recovery of Child Support and Other Forms of Family Maintenance, 2007 (HccH 2007b)

U.S. signed. Ratification and EIF pending

Establishes a system of cooperation between contracting states and provides rules for recognition and enforcement of maintenance obligations arising from parental relationship towards a person under 21 years of age and for spousal support when claimed in conjunction with child support. The internal laws of the state where the person obligated to pay will apply towards enforcement of maintenance decisions. It emphasizes "effective access" to legal procedures including linguistic access, provision of free legal assistance for claiming child support, and possibilities of extending such assistance for claiming other forms of support. Article 20 attempts to safeguard the interest of the recipient by stating that if a state exercises a reservation and recognition is based on the law of the state of habitual residence of the person who is obligated to pay, the contracting state will take appropriate measures to grant a decision for the benefit of the recipient.

(Rudra and Dasgupta 2011) The increasing movement of labour due to globalization and its ensuing problems is an unfolding reality that requires collaborative efforts to appropriately respond to transnational abandonment. Since the extant laws and practices of any country are not adequate to deal with the phenomenon of abandonment of wives, new laws need to be crafted. While states may have the authority to pass laws, they rarely are in touch with the ground realities of women's lives and hardships, which must be culled by CBOs and NGOs to help design gender sensitive policies. In addition, international family laws and multilateral agreements must be sharpened to fill the gaps in legal protection that currently exist. Awareness raising about the problem of abandonment and its possible solutions must also happen so that women find appropriate and competent legal representation befitting their needs.

To respond to the increasing complaints from abandoned spouses of NRIs, the Government of India (GOI) convened several workshops and in 2006, the national Commission for Women released a report on the problem. In an effort to provide material support to women, the GOI empanelled a number of CBOs in the U.S., Manavi being one of them, to provide material, legal, and counselling assistance to NRI wives facing various legal problems in the U.S. (Consulate General of India, n.d.). GOI also recruited women's organizations where most migration of Indians occurs such as UK, Canada, Australia, New Zealand, and the Gulf countries. For this purpose, the GOI allocated some funds for individual victims. The criteria for securing the assistance were:

- The women must hold Indian passports;
- The marriage must have taken place, solemnized, and registered in India;
- The women must have been abandoned in India or within five years of reaching the host country;
- The divorce proceedings had been initiated within five years of marriage;
- Ex-parté divorce had been obtained within ten years of marriage and a case of alimony and maintenance has not been filed; and
- No criminal charges were pending against the woman. (Rudra and Dasgupta 2011)

The concerned NGOs and CBOs immediately felt the eligibility criteria charted above did not fully reflect the realities of NRI wives. For example, many Indian women betrothed to NRIs travel to the U.S. on fiancé visa (K1) and get married in the U.S. The cultural norm of getting married as soon as possible and not to keep a marriage pending, pushes families to send their daughters to complete the "inevitable" union. In such as case, the woman would be ineligible for GOI support as her marriage would be registered in a foreign country and not in India. Furthermore, many women are abandoned not necessarily within five years of marriage. Due to the custom of surrendering all financial control to the husband, even after years of marriage, the wife may have little financial security and assets. Particularly when marriages are rocky or outright abusive (Anitha et al. 2016), as would be expected in one that ends up in abandonment of the wife, husbands may exert complete control over the family's financial resources. Consequently, to deprive women who may have been married or lived in a foreign country longer than five years would defeat the actual intent of the GOI's policy.

The last criterion elaborated above might pose a special problem. Although Indian women who use aggressive violence against an intimate partner are a rarity, it is not an impossibility. In my experience, I have found a significant number of Indian women being arrested and charged with domestic violence in the U.S. Such an arrest is a testimony to the decontextualized focus on only incidents of the U.S. legal system. A single isolated incident certainly does not tell the whole story of a woman's use of violence against intimate partners. From what the women who had been arrested and charged with domestic violence in the U.S. told me, I found that most used violence primarily to escape or end abuse, especially when they believed that they had no access to resources or support of a loved one (Dasgupta 2007). As mentioned before, in Indian cultural contexts, women are socialized to preserve their marriages at all costs. Thus, calling the police and getting an Order of Protection against an intimate partner might have been viewed by most women as tantamount to ending their marriage. The majority of Indian women I have worked with in the U.S., wanted the abuse to end, but not necessarily end the marriage. So, a situation of violence might leave women with no alternatives but to use force to escape more abuse. Moreover, institutional biases in the U.S. also contribute to the arrests of Indian women as perpetrators of domestic violence.

The stereotype of Indian women in the U.S. is that they are compliant; helpless; docile; quiet; seek "appropriate" help (in the U.S., it is law enforcement); protective of children; look pitiful, e.g., crying, dishevelled, hurt, etc. They are not expected to be assertive or resist abuse or take matters in their own hands. Thus, a woman who appears to have used force against the intimate partner is seen as an anomaly, a "bad" woman who very well could be an abuser. In such situations, to invalidate a woman's application for assistance from her government because there are criminal charges levelled against her would be injustice indeed.

In January 2010, the GOI Ministry of Women and Child Development proposed that Indian women who are married to NRIs would be issued two passports, so that in one, the husband's particulars are recorded (Thacker 2010). This copy of the passport would be deposited with the Indian Embassy. This move was in response to the needs of women who have left the country and been deserted in a foreign land. It does not address the needs of women who are abandoned in their home country by NRI husbands and have received ex-parté divorce based on their non-appearance in U.S. courts. Neither does it help women obtain legal representation in a foreign land. The small amount of funds available to each woman is not even close to being adequate for legal representation or counselling, at least in the U.S. Nonetheless, issuing dual passport to women residing abroad to provide them with some protection against their spouses, who might destroy their travel papers to harass them, is a small step in the right direction.

Assuming being forewarned is to be forearmed, anti-violence against women NGOs and CBOs have been collaborating to develop brochures and booklets to raise awareness among wives travelling abroad about adverse situations they might encounter and helpful resources that are available. Print materials such as *Guidebook on Legal Rights for Female Foreign Nationals* (Frevel 2001), *A Little Book of Tips and Tricks* (CREA 2006), *Know Your Rights* (Manavi 2006), and *Marriages to Overseas Indians: A Guidance Booklet* (Ministry of Overseas Indian Affairs 2007) target women who are moving to a foreign country to join their husbands. Most of these booklets are distributed through service providing organizations and by visa issuing consulates. India's National Commission for Women has also published a Dos and Don'ts booklet for women who are joining their NRI husbands abroad. While a worthy effort, the instructions are not only unwieldy but burdensome to the women and brides' families (National Commission for Women, n.d.).

Unfortunately, the CBOs'/NGOs' struggles to ameliorate the problems of abandonment are being counteracted by oppositional efforts. Rakshak, a men's rights organization based in California, petitioned The Ministry of Overseas Indian Affairs of the Government of India to discredit the complaints of women and women's organizations (Rakshak 2007). Its petition notes:

> More and more gullible NRIs are falling prey to the devious designs of resident Indians who marry with specific intent to achieve their own personal objectives even at the cost of jeopardising the life of the NRI. Such malicious intent comes to the fore when the unscrupulous Resident Indian realises failure in achieving the desired objectives. Deliberately masterminded tantrums stretching as far as connivance with one's paramour are resorted to in an attempt to pressurise and bully the NRI. Such instances spark further criminal acts which end up casting far reaching ramifications on the socio-economic, political, regional and policy matters of the involved nations. (Rakshak 2007, p. 7)

Rakshak's main concern is about the gendered nature of Indian laws and the 'privilege' it gives women and the repercussions for men springing from these laws. The petition states, for example, the actions recommended and taken in some states to coerce abandoning spouses to face up to their responsibilities, such as filing an FIR (National Commission for Women, n.d.; National Institute of Public Cooperation and Child Development 2007), are particularly problematic for the well-being of NRI men. Complaints lodged against NRI men through FIRs generate hardships such as revocation of passport, difficulties in renewal of passport, Interpol Red Corner Notice, work visa renewal problem, and problems obtaining permanent residency in a foreign country (Rakshak 2007). Rakshak tends to dismiss the complaints of abandonment as paltry at best and disingenuous at worst.

Concluding Comments

A community's culture, tradition of gender roles, and the intricacies of lived realities shape the types and substance of abuse against its womenfolk. Violence is not a static phenomenon, rather its contents and dynamics change according to current socio-political environments. To include abandonment of wives in the category of violence against women, it must be placed against India's socio-cultural backdrop of marriage, tradition of patrilocality, role of natal family, divorce, and marital responsibilities. On top of all these factors, the current issues of mass migration, economy, and the power differentials between the West and India have to be taken into account. Abandoning women in their home countries or in a foreign land, NRI men deprive them not only of social well-being and viable livelihood but also of legal recourses to receiving financial and social justice. However, in legal and in mainstream anti-violence against women advocacy, abandonment of wives is still considered to be nothing more than an unsuccessful marriage. Yet, "[W]hen a South Asian woman is abandoned by her immigrant husband, structural barriers in both natal and host countries interlock with legal, cultural, and individual difficulties to restrict her access to assistance and justice, often making her life intolerable" (Rudra and Dasgupta 2011, p. 47).

Some policy-makers have blamed the practice of emotionally coercing Indian men to marry brides of their families' choice for abandonment of women. Often, parents persuade their sons to marry before they leave for a foreign land to stop them from choosing partners they would not approve. At times, collecting dowry from the bride's family to facilitate an émigré's passage money or getting a caregiver for elderly parents become incentives for such marriages. Even when men enter these unions in good faith in the beginning, they may change their minds once they migrate and psychologically grow away from the wives, due to long separation forced by visa issuing requirements. An Indian man may correct the mistake of such marriage by divorce or abandonment but a woman who has entered the marriage in good faith and is under tremendous socio-economic pressures to maintain it, may have no other recourse but to continue with it. When an Indian woman is abandoned by her spouse, it is with the intention of curtailing her access to legal and financial rights on his part. This deliberate action makes transnational abandonment an infringement of women's human rights. And, when violation occurs in transnational spaces in a systematic way, it needs to be responded to in a coordinated manner—by country governments, law enforcement agencies, judiciary, international bodies, law and policy-makers, advocates, social change makers, and non-state service providers.

Notes

1. Personal communications with attorneys Anish Joshi, June 29, 2009, and Sheetal Patel, July 6, 2009, New Jersey, USA.
2. See, "Maintenance and Welfare of Parents and Senior Citizens Act, 2007."
3. This is known as the rule of 'coverture,' which is applied more widely for women than men. "Under coverture, the husband and wife were one person (the entirety) and that one person was the husband in the eyes of the common law. Therefore, as to her personal and property rights, the wife's legal existence was suspended during the marriage and merged into that of the husband." See, *Women and the Law*, available at: http://umich.edu/~ece/student_projects/bonifield/rape2.html. Although this rule is no longer fully in effect, some vestiges of the Common Law still exists in practice.see, Pashaura Singh vs. 4. State of Punjab and Anr on November 13, 2009; Bench: Tarun Chatterjee and R. M. Lodha. In this landmark judgment, the SC of India accepted a divorce decree passed in Canada on February 8, 2001, by overturning an earlier High Court decision. Available at: https://indiankanoon.org/doc/174511/.

References

Anitha, S., A. Roy, and H. Yalamarty. 2016. Disposable women: Abuse, violence, and abandonment in transnational marriages—Issues for policy and practice in the UK and India. Lincoln: University of Lincoln.

Answers.com. 2009. *Columbia encyclopedia: Desertion.* http://www.answers.com/topic/desertion.

Chadha, A. 2016. *Plight of abandoned Indian women in non resident Indian marriages: A critical analysis.* May 3. Department of Laws, Guru Nanak Dev University Regional Campus, Ladhewali, Jalandhar, Punjab, India. http://ssrn.com/abstract=2773989.

Chakrabarty, S. 2016. Maneka crusades for wives of NRIs, knocks MEA door. *Indian Express.* July 18. http://www.newindianexpress.com/nation/Maneka-crusades-for-wives-of-NRIs-knocks-MEA-door/2016/07/18/article3534445.ece.

Consulate General of India. n.d. *Scheme for giving legal/financial assistance to women deserted by their overseas Indian spouses.* http://www.indiacgny.org/php/showPressDetails.php?linkid=113&newsid=267.
CREA. 2006. *A little book of tips and tricks: A guide for South Asian immigrant women.* New York: CREA.
Dasgupta, S. D. 2000. Charting the course: An overview of domestic violence in the South Asian community in the United States. *Journal of Social Distress and the Homeless* 9: 173–185.
———. 2007. *Exploring South Asian battered women's use of force in intimate relationships.* Manavi Occasional Paper No. 1. New Brunswick, NJ: Manavi.
———. 2010a. Abandoned and divorced: The NRI pattern. *Infochange.* March. http://infochangeindia.org/women/features/abandoned-and-divorced-the-nri-pattern.html?Itemid=
———. 2010b. An intimate dilemma: Anti-domestic violence activism among Indians in the United States of America. In *Nine degrees of justice: New perspectives on violence against women in India,* ed. B. Datta, 52–82. New Delhi: Zubaan.
Dasgupta, S. D., and S. Warrier. 1996. In the footsteps of 'Arundhati': Asian Indian women's experience of domestic violence in the United States. *Violence Against Women* 2: 238–259.
Frevel, A. 2001. *Guidebook on legal rights for female foreign nationals.* March. http://www.gladbeck.de/frauen.
Gilbert, F. B., and F. W. Battershall. 1902. *The law of domestic relations of the state of New York with forms.* Albany, NY: Mathew Bender.
Government of India. 1955. *The Hindu Marriage Act, 1955.* May 18. http://www.vakilno1.com/bareacts/hindumarriageact/hindumarriageact.html.
———. 2005. *The Protection of Women from Domestic Violence Act, 2005.* September 13. http://www.vakilno1.com/bareacts/domestic-violence/domestic-violence-act-2005.html.
Hague Conference on Private International Law (HccH). 1961. *Convention abolishing the requirement of legalisation for foreign public documents.* October 5. http://hcch.e-vision.nl/index_en.php?act=conventions.text&cid=41
———. 1965. *Convention on the service abroad of judicial and extrajudicial documents in civil or commercial matters.* November 15. http://www.hcch.net/index_en.php?act=conventions.text&cid=17&zoek=serviceabroad
———. 1970. *Convention on the recognition of divorces and legal separations.* June 1. http://www.hcch.net/index_en.php?act=conventions.text&cid=80
———. 1973/1977. *Convention on the law applicable to maintenance obligations.* October 2 and October 1 http://hcch.e-vision.nl/index_en.php?act=conventions.text&cid=86.

———. 2007a. *Protocol on the law applicable to maintenance obligations.* November 23. http://www.hcch.net/index_en.php?act=conventions.text&cid=133

———. 2007b. *Convention on the international recovery of child support and other forms of family maintenance.* November 23. http://www.hcch.net/index_en.php?act=conventions.text&cid=131&zoek=serviceabroad

Hernández-Truyol, B. E., and M. Hawk. 2005. Traveling the boundaries of statelessness: Global passports and citizenship. *Cleveland State Law Review* 52: 97–119.

Hernández-Truyol, B. E., and S. E. Rush. 2000. Culture, nationhood, and the human rights ideal. *Michigan Journal of Race & Law* 5: 817–846.

Hobbs, H. H., and H. I. Chernotsky. 2007. *Preparing students for global citizenship.* American Political Science Association Teaching and Learning Conference. February 9–11, Charlotte, NC. http://www.apsanet.org/tlc2007/TLC07HobbsChernotsky.pdf

Jabbi, M. K. 2005. *A diagnostic study of wives deserted by NRIs.* November. New Delhi: Council for Social Development. http://wcd.nic.in/Schemes/research/diagnostic_study.pdf.

John, T. E. 2010. *A study of fraudulent migratory marriages in Canada and India.* Unpublished Master of Laws Thesis, University of Toronto, Canada.

Joseph, G. 2008. Complaints about NRIs deserting their wives are skyrocketing. *India Abroad*, A47, October 3.

Lagos, T. G. n.d. *Global citizenship-towards a definition.* http://depts.washington.edu/gcp/pdf/globalcitizenship.pdf.

Malhotra, A., and R. Malhotra. 2007. *Report on seminar on "NRIs Abandoned Brides—A Challenge to Meet.* February 14. Organised in association with Faculty of Laws, Panjab University, Chandigarh. http://www.lawasia.asn.au/uploads/images/NRI__s_abandoned_brides_seminar_.pdf.

Manavi. 2006. *Know your rights: A legal guide for South Asian women facing domestic violence.* New Brunswick, NJ: Manavi.

Melwani, L. 2005. Dishonor and abandon: The word is out in India: Marry an NRI at your own peril.... *Little India.* February 5. http://www.littleindia.com/nri/1475-dishonor-and-abandon.html.

Ministry of Overseas Indian Affairs. 2007. *Marriages to Overseas Indians: A guidance booklet.* New Delhi: Government of India. https://www.mea.gov.in/images/pdf/marriages-to-overseas-indians-booklet.pdf

National Institute of Public Cooperation and Child Development. 2007. *A study on desertion of married women by non-resident Indians in Punjab and Andhra Pradesh.* New Delhi: National Institute of Public Cooperation and Child Development.

National Commission for Women. n.d. *Problems relating to NRI marriages: Dos and donts.* http://ncw.nic.in/pdffiles/nridodont.pdf.

NRI Internet. 2004. *12,000 cases in Gujarat of women abandoned by their NRI husbands, a figure higher than Punjab.* November 23. http://www.nriinternet.com/Marriages/Desrted_Wife/2004/3_Gujrat.htm.

Prabhat, D. 2007. Transnational legal issues: Domestic violence complications among South Asian immigrants in the United States. Manavi Occasional Paper No. 4. New Brunswick, NJ: Manavi.

Punjab Police NRI Affairs. 2012–2015. *Do's and dont's* [sic]: *NRI marriages.* NRI Assistance. http://nripunjabpolice.com/dos_dont_nri_marriages.php.

Rakshak. 2007. *NRI marriages and abandoned brides.* Fremont, CA. July 25. http://www.498a.org/contents/pressConference/moiaMemorandum_25July07.pdf

Rudra, U., and S. D. Dasgupta. 2011. *Transnational abandonment of South Asian women: A new face of violence against women.* Manavi Occasional Paper No. 6. New Brunswick, NJ: Manavi.

Thacker, T. 2010. To protect women who marry NRIs, ministry proposes dual passports. *Indian Express.* January 19. http://www.indianexpress.com/news/to-protect-women-who-marry-nris-ministry-pr/569056/.

UNHCR. 1956. *New York convention on the recovery abroad of maintenance.* http://www.unhcr.org/refworld/docid/3dda24184.html.

Ward, O. 2005a. 'Runaway grooms': Documentary points to young Indian expatriates who marry for cash and then desert their wives. *Guelph Mercury* (Ontario, Canada), B13, April 22.

———. 2005b. 'Runaway grooms' leave shame behind. *Toronto Star*, A14. April 23.

Waters, A. B. 1999. Domestic dangers: Approaches to women's suicide in contemporary Maharashtra, India. *Violence Against Women* 2: 525–547.

In essence, mass migration and its concomitant issues of jurisdictional control has rendered modern citizenship trans-national.

CHAPTER 11

Understanding 'Consent' in Rape Laws

Ruchira Goswami and Aratrika Choudhuri

The public discourse on rape that emerged in the 1970s in India was marked by the dissonance between the conceptualization of rape in Indian legal discourses, on the one hand and the emergent feminist movements on the other.[1] As this chapter seeks to show, this dissonance has undergone far-reaching changes, in terms of content, structure and form today, yet one aspect appears immutable: the indubitable existence of the gap and disconnect between these two discourses in spite of the passage of several decades since.

Certain landmark moments mark the evolution of the rape discourse and the anti-rape movements in India. The infamous Mathura rape case marks the inception of rape as a political issue in India. The open letter to the Chief Justice of India in the aftermath of the Supreme Court's verdict in *Tuka Ram v. State of Maharashtra*[2] in 1979 marked the first

---

R. Goswami (✉)
The West Bengal National University of Juridical Sciences, Kolkata, India
e-mail: ruchira@nujs.edu

A. Choudhuri
AZB & Partners, Delhi, India
e-mail: aratrikachoudhuri@gmail.com

© The Author(s), under exclusive license to Springer Nature Singapore Pte Ltd. 2024
A. K. Sarkar and S. Das Gupta (eds.), *Understanding Women's Empowerment in South Asia*,
https://doi.org/10.1007/978-981-16-7538-6_11

225

moment of this publicized contestation.[3] While legal discourses viewed rape through an antiquated lens of shame and loss of honour of the victim, the feminist movement clearly regarded it as an instrument of patriarchal subjugation, institutionalizing hegemonic modes and tools of control over women's bodies and psyche.[4] The law as enacted in S375 of the Indian Penal Code, 1860, conceptualized rape as a gender-specific crime, with a construction of penile penetration into the vagina forming the only legally recognized mode of rape. Thus, a man was said to have committed the offence of rape if he had sexual intercourse with a woman in each of the following circumstances: *"against the victim's will; without the victim's consent; with her consent, when her consent has been obtained by putting her or any person known to her in fear of death or harm; with her consent, when the man knows that he is not her husband; with her consent, when at the time of giving such consent she was intoxicated, or suffering from unsoundness of mind and unable to understand the nature and consequences of that to which she has given consent; with or without her consent when she is under 16 years of age"*. The exception clause stated that having sex with a wife who is not under 15 years of age within the socially sanctified ambit of marriage would not be considered 'rape in legal terms'.

In the Mathura case, the Supreme Court had problematically conflated consent with submission, failing to recognize that submission or the absence of resistance does not necessarily imply consent. Among several points raised in the open letter, a significant one was that the court seemed to have completely ignored the power dynamics of custodial rape, especially prominent in the *Rameeza Bee* rape case, and in line with Justice Krishna Iyer's verdict in the case of *Nandini Satpathy v. P.L. Dani*, censuring the practice of summoning women to police stations in breach of §160(1) of the Criminal Procedure Code, 1973, which states that a woman shall not be required to attend the police investigation at any other place than her place of residence. The constraint placed upon the woman and gross power-imbalance in such a setting, the socio-economic circumstances of the victim, her age, etc., had all gone unnoticed by the Supreme Court.

How had consent been interpreted as a concept, in the context of rape, prior to *Mathura*? In the case of *Idan Singh v. State Of Rajasthan*, the SC clearly defined consent as an "act of reason, accompanied with deliberation", emphasizing on the voluntariness and consciousness of concurring acceptance of the acts undertaken in sexual intercourse. The distinction between consent and submission, as highlighted in the 1979 open letter, had been pointed out long ago in the 1957 case of *Rao Harnarain Singh Sheoji Singh v. The State*, which stated that passive acquiescence, resignation and helpless non-resistance could not be equated with the standards of voluntary participation. While "*every consent involves a submission but the converse does not follow and a mere act of submission does not involve consent*". Unfortunately, this distinction drawn out as early as 1957 was completely ignored in later cases including that of the Mathura judgement two decades later.

In the case of *Jarnail Singh v. State of Rajasthan*, the court stated that "*if the woman consents prior to penetration, no matter how tardily and reluctantly, and no matter how much force had been used, the act is not rape. In the instant case...the prosecution has failed to bring home the use of force to overcome the prosecutrix's will to resist and the resistance to the utmost by her*". Using the semantics of resistance, the legal expectation is that the victim would resist the "utmost" to the act of rape. The statement also demonstrates the lack of cognizance that consent is necessary for all acts of sexual intercourse, not simply at the beginning.

Though honour and shame remained dominant motifs in rape cases, certain judgements moved beyond to acknowledge women's experience of pain instead of narrowly focussing on evidence. In the case of *Bharwada Bhoginbhai Hirjibhai v. State Of Gujarat* (1983), Supreme Court recognized its "colonial hangover" in insisting upon corroborative testimony in rape cases, which only perpetuated further victimization of the rape survivor. The court interestingly held "*....there is no reason to insist on corroboration except from the medical evidence...*". In spite of being a progressive articulation, the power of medico legal discourse in evaluating whether the woman's subjective experience match up to the medico-legal standards of "truth" and "fact" is evident in the judgement.

In *State of Karnataka vs. Krishnappa* (2000), the SC conceptualized sexual violence as not only an act depredating the humanity of the victim, but also infringing her privacy and intimate space. The court also notably held that a consideration of the accused's circumstances such as his illiteracy and lack of education, his membership of a lower economic stratum, his chronic alcoholism and the fact that he had several familial dependents were irrelevant to sentencing the accused and would not justify a lesser sentence than as prescribed in the IPC, S376(2). The court considered "*the conduct of the accused, the state and age of the sexually assaulted female and the gravity of the criminal act*" to be relevant factors but "*the social status of the victim or the accused*" were not deemed legally relevant.

Does a dismissal of the accused's circumstances concomitantly warrant a dismissal of the victim's circumstances, which may in contrast be particularly important to understanding her experiences and testimony, as argued in the 1979 open letter to the Chief Justice?

As Flavia Agnes has argued, if quantum of laws passed is taken as an indicator of realization of women's rights, the 1980s would be a golden decade, owing to the slew of legal reforms undertaken in that period. Demands of the anti-rape campaign by the autonomous women's movement India and recommendations to the Law Commission of India were partially accepted. The 84th Law Commission Report on "*Rape and Allied offences-Some Questions of Substantive Law, Procedure and Evidence*" was released in 1980. The report noted the phenomena of secondary victimization of the rape victim by the legal machinery, as also placed emphasis upon the importance of consent, positing it as the "antithesis of rape". It acknowledged the demands of the anti-rape campaign to shift onus for proving consent from the prosecution to the accused, recommending insertion of a new Section 114-A in the Evidence Act that would read: "*In a prosecution for rape under clause (a) to clause (J) of sub-section (2) of Section 376 of IPC (45 of 1860), where sexual intercourse by the accused is proven and the question is whether it was without the consent of the woman alleged to have been raped and she states in her evidence before the Court that she did not consent, the Court shall presume that she did not consent*". It also expressed the view that women's prior sexual history and general character should not be employed as evidence in a rape trial, by amending Section 155 of the Evidence Act accordingly (the prior sexual history with the accused would continue to be a relevant factor). The commission recommended that women should not be arrested after sunset and before sunrise, that women's statements should be recorded in the presence of a relative/friend/social welfare official and that a police officer's refusal to register a complaint of rape should be treated as an offence.

However, the 1983 Criminal Law (Amendment) Act mediated through the parliamentary joint committee scrutinizing the bill did not accept a majority of these recommendations. It completely ignored the Section 155-related amendment aspect, and the rule of shifting onus for proving consent to the accused was heeded to only in limited cases of custodial rape, i.e., rape by policemen, public servants, managers of public hospitals and remand homes and wardens of jails. As Agnes argues, the central legacy of the 1983 Amendment was the mandatory imposition of minimum punishment for rape for the first time in the Indian penal framework10 years in cases of custodial rape, gang rapes, rape of pregnant women and girls under 12 years of age; and 7 years in all other cases. Moreover, Section 228A of the IPC which proscribed disclosure of identity of victims of rape resulted in censorship of press coverage of rape trials. Responding to the plight of rape victims to secondary victimization during the trial, the amendment accepted the demands of the women's movement to conduct rape trials 'in -camera' and not in an open court. Much later, feminist lawyers and activists pointed out to the limitations of in camera trials. The victim was often the only woman deposing in front of an all-male court—the judge, defence counsel and public prosecutor.

The amendments did not alter the definition of rape, which remained as heterosexual penile penetration into the vagina. This imagery also served to reinforce the premium placed on regulation of women's sexuality by the patriarchal State, society and legal institutions. With stigma and shame attached to rape, it was considered 'worse than death'. Judgements, too, reflected this perspective where punishment was awarded for the loss of honour and chastity of women. Autonomy, bodily integrity, privacy and intimate space were not considerations for recognition of harms and awarding of punishments. The rhetoric espoused by the amendment thus actively propounded and promulgated a retributive and penal form of criminal justice for victims of rape. The ideal woman was conceived as essentially devoid of sexual agency. The madonna-whore binary played out through the construction of the rape laws and the trials. The normalization of sexual violence against women was made possible where she deviated from the ideals of purity and chastity enforced and upheld by the law. Thus, the sexual politics of the Indian legal project entailed "pathologization" of women's individual sexuality, and "normalization" of sexual violence against women. As Veena Das argues, "the State intervention, intrusion and regulation of sexuality, brings to the fore thorny interpretive issues of consent".

From Sakshi to Nirbhaya

The 1990s saw the active entry of two distinct players in the discourse of rape and sexual violence. The child rights groups and activists were drawing attention to incidents of sexual abuse on children—both penetrative and non-penetrative—that could not be covered by the existing rape laws. Provisions of the Indian Penal Code relating to outraging modesty of women, indecent gestures and obscenity clauses could not adequately address children's experience of sexual offence. More importantly, sexual abuse of boys was left completely unaddressed by these gender-specific provisions that constructed only women and girls as victims of sexual violence. The solution was using Section 377 of the IPC that criminalized 'unnatural' sexual intercourse and sodomy, thereby becoming the only provision that can be used to penalize sexual violence perpetrated on boys. This was heavily criticized by the queer rights groups—mainly the gay rights community—the emerging second player in the sexual violence discourse. There were groups which were opposed to the deletion of Section 377, arguing that this was the only legal provision that could be used to penalize child sexual abuse, specifically sodomization of boys. However, queer rights and many women rights and human rights groups opposed the retention of Section 377 on the grounds that this section does not distinguish between consensual and non-consensual sexual intercourse and penalizes same sex relations between consenting adults. Queer, child and women's rights groups recommended that child sexual abuse warrants separate attention and a new law be brought in to protect children, both boys and girls from sexual abuse. Decriminalization of consensual same sex relations snowballed gradually to the creation on a new legal discourse on sexual rights in India. This meant that instead of using Section 377 of IPC, there was need for a comprehensive law on child sexual abuse.

In 1999, Sakshi, a feminist legal advocacy NGO, moved the Supreme Court seeking issuance of a writ for an expanded definition of rape that includes oral and anal sex beyond the heterosexual penile penetration construct, be included in Section 375 IPC. Sakshi contended that Section 377 of IPC was in violation of Articles 14 and 21 of the Constitution of India. The Law Commission delivered its 172nd report on "**REVIEW OF RAPE LAWS, MARCH, 2000**", which recommended replacing rape with a gender-neutral conception of sexual assault, both with reference to the accused and the rape survivor; and recommended that penetration be expanded to include non-penile penetration; proposed the offences of aggravated sexual assault and unlawful sexual contact.

A gender neutral conception of sexual assault meant that women and men could both be held as victims and perpetrators of sexual assault, including rape. The oppositions to gender neutrality came from different quarters. Women's rights groups contended that gender neutrality in rape laws would disadvantage women further where structural, social and sexual power privileged male sexual desire. If gender neutrality is introduced, women could be charged with sexual assault of men! Gender neutrality would do little to redress the historicized and institutionalized oppression perpetuated against the LGBT community so long as the understanding underlying Section 377 would persist. Others argued that it would be more useful to conceptualize most vulnerable transgendered persons in terms of rape, simply as women, under a gender-specific rape provision.

The other suggestion was introducing limited gender neutrality in which the perpetrator would be male and the victim could be of any gender. This recommendation was pushed more vociferously during depositions to the Verma Committee in 2013.

In spite of the of repeal of Section 155(4) of the Evidence Act, 1872 in 2002 regarding the relevance of past sexual history of the rape victim in, generation and use of admissible evidence, sexual history was often invoked by the defence counsel in rape cases. The two finger test done by medical examiners to detect if the victim had been or was habituated to sexual intercourse and medical reports that mentioned whether the victim was habituated to sexual intercourse reeked of patriarchal biases of the medico legal procedures. Yet overall, the movement from the 1980s' understanding of rape to the debates in the 2000s illustrates the trajectory and evolution of the Indian feminist movement in relation to rape. Whereas rape was simplistically viewed as sexual assault in the 1980s, it was now conceptualized as belonging to a spectrum of sexual violence.

The judgement in *Sakshi vs Union of India*, AIR 2004 SC 3566, delivered in 2004 noted the petitioner's argument that "sexual violence besides heterosexual penile penetration has been prosecuted as lesser offence under either Sec 377 or 354 of the IPC". This created an artificial distinction between sexual offences perpetrated by penile/vaginal penetration and other kinds of penetration. Sakshi had petitioned that sexual assault should be construed as a hierarchy of sexual offences depending on the extent and severity of harms caused to the victim. This would decentre penile/vaginal penetration or rape as the 'worst' kind of sexual assault. The idea was to conceptualize rape in a continuum of sexual assault and the punishment should be determined on the basis of harms caused. However Supreme Court held that the "*dictionary meaning of the word "sexual intercourse" is heterosexual intercourse involving penetration of the vagina by the penis*". Here again we see the discursive power of legal systems, and selective appropriation from discourses of medical lexicon, grammar, etc., to endorse distinctive views exerting disciplinary control on women's bodies. The court refused to accept the expanded definition of rape as falling under Section 375. 'Sexual intercourse' in Section 375 was limited to penile-vaginal penetration, thus relegating other forms of sexual intercourse "penile-oral penetration, penile-anal penetration, finger-vagina, finger-anal penetration and object-vaginal penetration" as carnal intercourse against the order of nature under Section 377.

An interesting rationale of the judgement's unmoving insistence on reading Section 375 as heterosexual penile penetration was stated to be the lack of education and incapacity of police personnel to understand the redefinition of rape and the confusion that this radical rehaul of the rape law framework would create among law students, courts and magistrates.

In December of 2012, the gang rape of a young student in a moving bus in Delhi was another high moment in public consciousness and deliberations on rape. Debates re-opened on age-old issues of consent, women's safety and inviolable dignity, stigmatization of rape and the death penalty rhetoric evincing the retributivist bent of law. The legal discourses mobilized yet again to bring about long awaited reforms in rape law. Within days of the incident, a three-member Committee headed by Justice J.S. Verma, former Chief Justice of the Supreme Court, was constituted to recommend amendments to the Criminal Law so as to provide for quicker trial and enhanced punishment for criminals accused of committing sexual assault against women. The 2012 report shifted the discussion from a primarily retributivist and penal sanction for rape, with public calls for chemical castration and death penalty for the accused, to a more nuanced, grounded analysis of the sexuality and power dynamics at play in rape, such as lack of deterrence value of death penalty in curbing serious crimes. Aligning with progressive feminist jurisprudential norms, it recommended criminalizing the entirety of the spectrum of non-consensual sexual acts conceptualized by feminists as sexual violence. The Committee opined that rape should be retained as a separate offence and it should not be limited to penetration of the vagina, mouth or anus, thus expanding the ambit of Section 375. Any non-consensual penetration of sexual nature is rape. The petition by Sakshi made over a decade ago found fruition in the expanded definition of rape. However, unlike Sakshi's petition to replace the term 'rape' with 'sexual assault', Verma Committee recommended that rape be retained as a separate offence. Section 354 of the IPC criminalizes assault or use of criminal force on a woman 'to outrage her modesty'. Section 509 of the IPC criminalizes words and gestures to 'insult a woman's modesty'.

In line with the feminist critique of the victorian notion of modesty, the Committee recommended that all forms of non-penetrative and non-consensual form of sexual contact including touching should be regarded as sexual assault. All forms of gestures, acts and words that are unwelcome threat of a sexual nature will be called 'verbal sexual assault'. Acid attack was to be constituted as a separate offence from that of grievous hurt in the IPC. It recommended that the exception to marital rape should be removed and stated that the institutional sanctity of marriage cannot be a defence to sanction rape and impute irrevocable sexual consent. The committee also considered it an imperative to revisit the Armed Forces (Special Powers) Act (AFSPA) in conflict areas, which prescribes requirement of sanction for prosecuting armed forces personnel in rape cases, and recommended removing this provision in case of all sexual offences. The committee recommended removal of the problematic finger test in medical examination of rape and reiterated that prior sexual history of the victim cannot be used. It also recommended establishment of rape crisis cells to provide assistance to rape victims, police training to deal with sexual offences, online FIRs, etc.

The 2013 Criminal Law (Amendment) Act ("2013 Amendment") that followed the above-mentioned report brought in an express definition of consent as: "an unequivocal unilateral agreement, when a woman by words or gestures or any form of verbal or non-verbal communication conveys willingness to participate in the specific sexual act". A proviso clarifies that absence of physical resistance would not itself amount to consent. Victim's prior sexual history, lack of injuries on her body, etc., should not be used to establish that she was not raped. Furthermore, a clause was inserted stating that a man would be said to commit a rape if a woman "is unable to communicate her consent". In a narrower sense, it includes situations where a woman is unable to articulate and communicate consent due to physical and/or psychological illness or in a state of intoxication or under duress, etc. However, it may also be argued that especially in an age of #MeToo, where the lines of consent are being increasingly blurred and sexual politics increasingly demands accountability and positive sexual rights of a woman, it is especially interesting to note that this provision, coupled with the consent definition involving "unequivocal unilateral agreement", could also be interpreted to include situations of sexual acts performed in callous/reckless disregard of a woman's desire as constituting rape. This gives increasing importance to consent in any sexual interaction as "freely given, enthusiastic, informed, reversible, and specific".

The 2013 Amendment enacted the Verma Committee's recommendation of expanding the ambit of Section 375 to include non-penile penetration acts of rape. It brought in Section 354A to criminalize sexual harassment, and new sections ranging from Sections 354B to 357D to criminalize new offences of voyeurism, stalking, acid attack, etc. Where the victim is left in a vegetative state and where there is a repeat offence, death penalty may be awarded.

However, there were significant limitations of the amended act. Rape remained as a gender-specific offence, where the woman is a victim and a man as the offender. The former debates of full (where women could be both offenders and victims) or partial gender neutrality (where men were offenders but anyone men, women and transgender persons could be victims) were not reflected in the amendment thus leaving same sex violence on men and more importantly, sexual violence on transgenders completely outside the legal protection of the law. In spite of years of struggle of the women's movements to criminalize marital rape and the recommendation of the Verma committee to criminalize marital rape, it was not legislatively enacted leaving open the pathway for continuance of sexual violence in the confines of marriage in India. Evidently, the Indian feminist discourse is itself also divided on the issue of criminalization of marital rape: Flavia Agnes argues that in the presence of the Protection of Women from Domestic Violence Act 2005 and Section 498A of IPC that criminalizes cruelty in marriage which can prosecute marital rape, why should rape as sexual violence be hierarchized over other forms of violence to delete the marital rape exception, seemingly espousing the patriarchal narrative that rape is worse than death? Yet other feminists advocate that this critique is not grounded in the reality of the socio-political context in which the marital rape exception operates, where institutional sanctity of marriage justifies spousal exploitation and sexual violence against women.

Dichotomies exist within the women's movements as to whether marital rape should only be a ground for divorce and seeking civil remedies under PWDVA or should it be criminalized thereby partially destabilizing the immunity embedded in heteropatriarchal institution of marriage to engage in sexual violence. As Nivedita Menon argues, the patriarchal framework of the Indian state and society remained protected through rejection of some significant and far reaching recommendations.

It has been established firmly by women's rights and human rights organizations that rape is used as a political weapon—by the majoritarian forces during communal tensions and by the armed forces in conflict ridden areas of India. The struggles against the impunity offered by the Armed Forces Special Powers Act probably reached its zenith in 2004 when women in Imphal, Manipur, demonstrated in front of the Kangla Fort, the headquarters of the Assam Rifles after the rape and death of Thangjam Manorama by the armed forces personnel. The Verma committee's recommendation to review the AFSPA and to bring armed forces personnel within the purview of the domestic criminal law was rejected in the amended Act. Significantly, the committee also recommended 20 years imprisonment for rape and ruled out death penalty as a deterrent measure. However, the Act had death penalty for rape, further strengthening coercive state power.

How did the case law pan out after the 2013 Amendment? Certain key themes are discussed below: In *V. Mohan vs. the State* (2015), the Madras HC initially ordered that the offender, convicted of raping a minor by the trial court, be given the opportunity to settle the matter with the victim through mediation. Observing that alternative dispute resolution could now be used in criminal cases, Justice Devadass observed that such mediation could lead to a "happy resolution", especially given the alleged uncertainty looming in the victim's future being an unwed mother, and problematically invokes the stigmatization of the child born out the rape as a factor to be considered in favour of finding a peaceful solution. Nowhere, however, does the judgement address how such mediation with the rapist seven long years after the act of violence, could possibly redress the stigmatization, let alone consider the very real possibility of exacerbation of trauma, as articulated by the victim herself.

Furthermore, this judgement goes clearly against legal precedent, as established in *State of M.P. vs. Bala*, where the Supreme Court held that the long pendency and duration of the criminal trial or offer of the rapist to marry the victim are no relevant reasons for exercising the discretionary power under the proviso of Section 376(2) IPC to reduce sentencing. In *Gian Singh vs. State of Punjab*, the Supreme Court held that "heinous and serious offences" like rape cannot be quashed notwithstanding the fact that the dispute may have been settled between the offender and the victim or victim's family. It was clear that a compromise between the parties could not be utilized as a factor in sentencing policy in rape cases. This was reiterated in *Shimbhu vs. State of Haryana*, where the court explicated that *"since the Court cannot always be assured that the consent given by the victim in compromising the case is a genuine consent, there is every chance that she might have been pressurized by the convicts or the trauma undergone by her all the years might have compelled her to opt for a compromise"*. The court in fact recognized that accepting this proposition might well prove more burdensome for the victim, and the accused could exert substantial influence to effectuate her assent to a compromise. It is strange that the Madras HC completely ignored the well-established legal position that mediation and alternative dispute resolution could not be adopted in rape cases.

In the very same year, the SC, while delivering its judgement in *State of M.P. vs. Madanlal*, reiterated its stance that in rape cases, there can be no import of mediation or compromise. It cautioned against the "subterfuge" of an offer to marry the victim as an unmistakable breach of the victim's dignity. Although the language and semantics employed by Justice Misra in this judgement evinced a distinct paternalistic bias, the invocation of legal precedent appeared to have percolated effectively to the Madras HC, such that it promptly withdrew its order in the *V. Mohan* judgement.

In an interesting judgement, Justices Sikri and Nazeer recently held in *Dr. Dhruvaram Sonar vs. State of Maharashtra* (2018) that if a person had not made the promise to marry with the sole intention to seduce a woman to indulge in sexual acts, such an act would not constitute rape. The court in this case recognized women's sexual agency and initiative, often ignored in rape cases. The court drew from the observations in *Deelip Singh vs. State of Bihar*, (2005) 1 SCC 88, where it had framed a two-fold question relating to consent:—"*(1)Is it a case of passive submission in the face of psychological pressure exerted or allurements made by the accused or was it a conscious decision on the part of the prosecutrix, knowing fully the nature and consequences of the act she was asked to indulge in? (2) Whether the tacit consent given by the prosecutrix was the result of a misconception created in her mind as to the intention of the accused to marry her?*" The court thus emphasized that it is imperative to distinguish rape from consensual sex. However, the argument that women from less privileged backgrounds have no other legal mechanisms other than the rape laws to establish their sexual rights in patriarchy has not completely dissipated.

Factors such as "*whether the complainant had actually wanted to marry the victim or had mala fide motives and had made a false promise to this effect only to satisfy his lust*" must be evaluated, since the later would tantamount to cheating or deception. The court also held that there is need to distinguish between mere breach of a promise to marry, and non-fulfilment of false promise to marry, which the offender knows to be false from the very inception. Thus, where the "*prosecutrix agrees to have sexual intercourse on account of her love and passion for the accused and not solely on account of the misconception created by accused, or where an accused, on account of circumstances which he could not have foreseen or which were beyond his control, was unable to marry her despite having every intention to do*"—it is at best only a breach of the promise to marry. In this case, the acknowledged consensual sexual affair for a prolonged duration, the widowed prosecutrix's admitted desire for companionship and consequent entry into the relationship, her conscious choice to pursue a relationship after "*active application of mind*" and lack of any probative evidence to evince exertion of pressure or force on her, thus made it clear that such consensual sex could thus not fall within the ambit of Section 376 of the IPC.

Yet, in both higher and lower courts, challenges remain. Thus, in *Rohit Tiwari vs. State* (2016), the Delhi High Court, while refusing to make a finding of rape, observed: "*If a fully grown up lady consents to the act of sexual intercourse on a promise to marry and continues to indulge in such activity for long, it is an act of promiscuity on her part and not an act induced by misconception of fact*". The choice of the word promiscuity, instead of sexual agency/autonomy/consent in this context, is especially troubling for the implications of victim-shaming. In *Anant vs. State of Maharashtra*, the Bombay HC was unable to make a finding of rape for lack of forensic evidence, pointing to the very real possibility of dearth of evidence and thorough investigation as continuing to be immense hindrances to the criminal system's mode of addressing rape.

Similarly, in *Raja &Ors vs State Of Karnataka*, the SC, in 2016, set aside a Karnataka High Court judgement, reversing the acquittal by a trial court in a gang rape case, and sentencing the accused to life imprisonment. The judgement invokes an ideal victim of forcible rape and cites the victim's "somewhat submissive and consensual disposition" as departing from this normative ideal. The sexist rhetoric that the victim was not "*unwilling, terrified and anguished victim of forcible intercourse, if judged by the normal human conduct*" without engaging with the lack of legal sanction for these norms of sexual conduct, clearly demonstrates that the implementation of rape law in India is still fraught with highly patriarchal attitudes toward regulating sexuality and conceiving consent and resistance in rape.

In the Jindal University rape case, the Punjab and Haryana High Court, in its order pronounced on 13 September 2017, released on bail the three students accused of having committed rape. The judgement goes back to sexist invocations of victim-shaming and attacking the victim's character, credibility and past sexual history as factors relevant for obviating a finding of rape. Despite the survivor's account detailing the harrowing nature of sexual coercion exercised on her, the court appeared to give leeway to the perpetrators as reflective of voyeuristic youth bogged by "casual sexual escapades, drugs, alcohol etc.". Despite the deletion of Section 155(4) of the Evidence Act, the victim's testimony was directly cited to show her prior sexual history of casual affairs with friends, and as a manifestation of "hook-up culture", was habituated to such "adventurism in sex".

Even more troublingly, the lack of "gut-wrenching" brutalization as conceived in classical cases of rape was invoked by the HC to impute that no finding of rape could be made a trend we shall also see in the *Aziz Ansari and Farooqui* cases discussed below. The court seems to ignore the violence of the accused's threats and blackmail that they would release nude photos of the victim and allows sexual permissiveness to the point of violence in case of the accused. On the other hand it denies positive sexuality of the victim herself and instead deploys it against her as "promiscuity", all clearly show the enduring hold victorian colonial morality still has on legal and judicial institutions. A temporary reprieve has been granted by the SC in staying the HC's order.

Further instances of highlighting the lack of brute force as imputing absence of rape can be found in *Mahendra Subhashbhai Vankhede vs. The State of Gujarat and Ors.* (08.08.2017—SC): MANU/SC/0999/2017. In *State of M.P. vs. Munna*, MANU/SC/1033/2015, the SC held that a woman had consented to the act of sex and therefore refused to convict the accused for rape. Arguably, the pattern revealed in this case demonstrates the arguments made by Flavia Agnes and Prabha Kotiswaran on the effects of increased criminalization in the domain of law-making, as also creating several loopholes in interpretation even after the 2013 Act. Age-determination of the victim was central to the case at hand, owing to the sixth clause of Section 375 that imputes finding of rape irrespective of consent when the victim is less than 16 years of age. From the X-ray report of the ossification test, the doctor opined that the age of the prosecutrix could not be more than 14 years. However, since the doctor was never examined, the X-ray report was not regarded adequate to prove the age of the prosecutrix.

Further lack of compelling forensic evidence in the eyes of the court, and the fact that prosecutrix was found with the accused hiding for nearly two hours, led to the inference of consent, thus led to the accused being acquitted of all rape charges. Moreover, the death penalty rhetoric upsurge after the *Nirbhaya* case reached yet another crescendo following the outcry over the rape and murder of a minor girl in Kathua in Jammu and Kashmir and the rape of another woman at Unnao in Uttar Pradesh. The 2018 Criminal Law (Amendment) Act now prescribes a minimum jail term of 20 years which may go up to life in prison or death sentence, for the rape of a girl under 12 years, while perpetrators involved in the gangrape of a girl below 12 years of age will be awarded life imprisonment or death. The retributivist penal ideal is thus re-introduced yet again in the discourse, as also gradation of punishment for rape based on the age of the victim.

How many rapes were reported in India in 1979, the year of the judgement in the *Mathura* rape case? As per the official NCRB statistics, a measly total of 4300 cases were reported, with Maharashtra, Madhya Pradesh and Uttar Pradesh securing the top three positions in terms of numbers reported a trend that appears to have continued well into 2016. In 2004, the year when the SC delivered the *Sakshi* judgement, a total of 18,233 rapes were reported nationwide. By the time the *Nirbhaya* rape occurred in 2013, the numbers shot up to 33,707 rapes reported across India. As the 2016 NCRB statistics demonstrate, a total of nearly 85,000 cases were reported nationally pertaining to assault on woman with intent to outrage her modesty (S354 of the IPC), while nearly 39,000 cases were reported pertaining to rape (including offences related to not only S376 of the IPC, but also gang rape under S376D and custodial rape under S376C, 376(2)A, 376(2)D IPC), with the aforementioned three states yet again occupying the top of the list.[45]

SEXUAL HARASSMENT AND RAPE
IN WORKSPACES: *VISHAKA* TO #METOO

Despite the shifting of onus of proving consent to the accused in custodial rape situations post the 1983 amendment, and the widespread public mobilization of Indian feminist discourses on women's sexuality and bodily autonomy, the change in the judicial discourse in regulating workplace sexuality and gradually moving away from emphasis on the complainant's character, were slow. In the 1992 *Bhanwari Devi* rape incident, Bhanwari Devi, a social worker belonging to the Kumhar caste, working to address issues of rampant child marriage in rural areas in Rajasthan, was raped by several upper-caste men, who had been angered by her campaigning and advocacy. Despite having registered a FIR with the police, commentators noted that her case was treated with condemnation. More than 50 hours passed after the rape that the mandatory medical examination was conducted. Reiterating rhetoric of stigmatization, despite Justice Tibrewal's initial findings "*I am convinced that Bhanwari Devi was gang-raped in revenge for attempting to stop the marriage of [one of the accused] Ramkaran's daughter, a minor*" the sudden and unexplained change in judges over five times in the case led to acquittal of the accused of rape, in November 1995. While they were convicted of lesser offences like assault and conspiracy, they were all given just nine months in jail, and the implication was clear. The legal system and discourse had miserably failed the victim through a complex congeries of socio-legal biases adopted by the patriarchal State machinery sanctioning the acts of the accused, and allowing them to go scot-free. From the intersectional perspective, the court's observation that the higher caste people cannot rape lower caste women was particularly egregious, perpetuating a plethora of oppressions.

The public furore pursuant to this judgement led to a filing of a Public Interest Litigation petition in the SC, demanding that "workplaces must be made safe for women and that it should be the responsibility of the employer to protect women employee at every step". Thus was born the landmark 1997 judgement of *Vishaka v. Union of India*, where guidelines were evolved to regulate sexual harassment at workplace. This case can be viewed as one of the landmark epochs of feminist constitutionalism the feminist project to inscribe constitutional recognition of women's rights to redress women's social subjugation and enforce both formal and substantive notions of constitutional equality. The feminist constitutionalist approach endorsed by the SC thus conceived of sexual violence in the context of a lexicon of *constitutional rights.*

This reconceptualization of sexual harassment of women in workplaces underlines the agency of women and enshrined a legal standard of consent and sexuality rather than social norms of virtue, modesty or victimhood. It is especially remarkable that rape was conceptualized in a construct of not merely criminal *statutory* rights, but in the far more entrenched, fundamental and pervasive *constitutional* rights. In a modern constitutional democracy such as India, with vibrant constitutional interpretive dynamism legacies, this judgement thus marked a much-needed recognition of expanding notions of equality under Article 14, the Right to Practise any Profession, trade or business under Art. 19 and dignity under Article 21 the famous "Golden Triangle" of the coda of the Basic Structure underlying the constitutional edifice to effectuate elimination of sexual harassment and violence at the workplace.

The 2013 Act has been lauded for several of its progressive reforms ensconcing civil remedies in case of violation of women's right to safe work environments free of sexual harassment; placing of onus on employer to maintain such work environments; expansion of definition of "workplace" to include the sphere of paid domestic work; broad definition of "employee" including the workers in the informal/unorganized sector, etc. However, patriarchal biases and issues remain: what is the rationale for conferring powers of a civil court on "Internal Complaints Committees" with sketchy compositions oft-biased against the victim, as attested by empirical evidence? Who shall take responsibility for improper composition of "Local Complaints Committees"? Where S211 of the IPC already contains a provision to protect citizens from false complaints, why was it considered necessary to incorporate the rhetoric of Section 14 seeking to penalize women for making "false and malicious complaints"?

Is such rhetoric apposite in an age where the dynamics of harassment have mutated beyond legal conservatism and found new ways to undermine women's autonomy, as evinced from #MeToo? As the Report of the Justice Verma Committee observes: "*We think that such a provision is a completely abusive provision and is intended to nullify the objective of the law. We think that these 'red-rag' provisions ought not to be permitted to be introduced and they show very little thought*". The requirement of women members and those "familiar with issues related to sexual harassment" is appreciable, yet it is to be seen if the intermingling of power and sexuality as brought forward by #MeToo can actually be addressed by this Act.

The challenges are appreciable when analysing the two recent incidents of acquittal of *Peepli Live* filmmaker Mahmood Farooqi by the Delhi HC of all charges of rape brought against him in *Mahmood Farooqui vs State (Govt Of Nct Of Delhi)* (2017), and the allegations made against Aziz Ansari, comedian and actor who has also been a vociferous supporter of the #MeToo and "Time's Up" movements (demanding accountability of sexual harassers and abusers at the workplace, particularly the film industry in the latter case).

Certain common elements run through the factual background of both cases: both men accused exercise significant influence in the respective entertainment industries of Bollywood and Hollywood; the complainants in both cases are well-educated, sophisticated urbane young women (an American Ph.D. student in the Farooqi case); both incidents occurred at the residences of the accused men which were hitherto unfamiliar spaces to the women; both incidents demonstrated a significant power dynamic at play, though its form and manifestation was relatively understated and does not fit into the conservative notion of rape as brutal penetrative sexuality perpetrated by "uneducated monsters", but rather evinced unrelenting persistence on oral sex (in Farooqui's case) or insertion of fingers into the complainant's vagina (in Ansari's case), i.e., insistence on sexual intercourse despite discomfort/resistance of complainants in each cases. The central age-old question newly problematized by both incidents is: what constitutes sexual consent in today's age? The reactions to both incidents demonstrate that even today the boundaries and contours of consensual and non-consensual sexual activity continue to be transgressed by patriarchal rape culture norm agents in new ways.

Both Ansari and Farooqui defended themselves, stating that the women had acquiesced to the sexual acts perpetrated. As per the complainant's account in Ansari's case, she made repeated gestures to move her hand away from his penis, displayed reluctance to undertaking the sexual acts and stated she did not want to feel forced: yet these verbal and non-verbal cues did not sufficiently alert Ansari to her lack of consent to his sudden and strong infringement of her intimate space. Similarly, the boundaries of assent and resistance and their relevance to consent in rape cases gain traction because of the Farooqui case, despite the legal discourses such as the 2013 Amendment advocating unequivocal unilateral agreement as the standard for consent. Both incidents highlight the need for deliberating upon the need for a pure affirmation model of explicit sexual consent in "yes means yes", away from tacit consent as recognized by the extant model of "no means no".

In the Farooqui case, the complainant visibly tried to pull her underwear up as an intoxicated Farooqui kept pulling it down to forcibly perform oral sex on her. He subsequently forcefully pinned down as she made attempts to leave. As the complainant stated in her later email to Farooqui, despite her repeated verbal and non-verbal resistance, he continued to perpetrate sexual assault and rape. Her fears of escalation in case of protests and the clear power dynamics exerting tremendous psychological pressure on her were however completely ignored by the Delhi HC. In light of the 2013 amendment, a finding of rape should have been relatively straightforward, as her lack of consent was obvious and any ceding of resistance in fear constitutes consent obtained through fear of hurt, although even the employment of this assent vs resistance rhetoric is unnecessary and problematic in light of the clear sanction of Section 375 as amended in 2013.

Yet the Delhi HC endorsed inexplicably regressive patriarchal sexual mores of consent stating: "*instances of a woman's behaviour are not unknown that a feeble 'No' may mean 'Yes'*". Quite troublingly, the court then arbitrarily distinguishes between "conservative" women and those involving "intellectually/academically proficient" women "of letters" for whom "equality is a buzzword" with no rational nexus with the matter at hand. An additional burden is imposed on women of the latter category, in that they must vociferously render their "unwillingness known" to the accused. Thus, the burden of communicating consent is placed on the woman, where a woman's silence or hesitation would not meet the standard of explicit unambiguous "*No*" required for imputing lack of consent. In complete disregard of the evidence, therefore, the complainant's resistance was characterized as so "feeble" as to find a *positive* importation of consent. In Farooqui's case, the email sent by the victim to him was construed as acquiescence. Besides the court, such mistrust was also expressed in discussions and reports about the case. Would any rape victim send an email to her harasser that 'merely' expressed that she was hurt in a tone that did not sound shocked and angry as an ideal rape victim should. The generous benefit of doubt bestowed upon the accused, the emphasis on the victim's socio-economic circumstances inviting different standards of evaluating rape, despite the 1980s judgements holding otherwise as discussed above, all evince the law-sanctioned patriarchal norms at play.

The clear space to invoke rape and sexual harassment provisions for punishing "digital rape"/"digital penetration" has been highlighted in recent cases of *Tarun Tejpal* and *R K Pachauri*. The narrative of the non-consensual sexual encounter between Tarun Tejpal and the intern, as well as the circulation of the 'mushy' persuasive SMSs sent by Pachauri to a women employee, have brought out the nature of sexual harassment in virtual space.

From December 2018 to February 2019, the GarimaYatra or 65-day Dignity March initiated by Rashtriya Garima Abhiyan in Mumbai, covered over 24 states and over 200 districts. Mobilizing over 5000 survivors of sexual violence to share their experiences and articulate their journeys of negotiating with the legal system, the March brought to the forefront the stories of women from the underrepresented SC/ST categories, issues of caste-based commercial sexual exploitation and victim-blaming in the Indian hinterland. Such movements also demonstrate the need for intersectionality of the #MeToo movement. The movement has been critiqued as operating among urban, middle class elite with digital access with little visibility or representation of women from disempowered communities who lack access to the internet, let alone the linguistic-technocratic skills/power to engage effectively in these spaces. It thus becomes imperative that the feminist movement against sexual violence reach its critical mass in terms of intersectionality and participation of women from all sections of the society.

Notes and References

1. 1979 SCR 1 810.
2. Gangoli, Geetanjali. 2011. Controlling Women's Sexuality: Rape Law in India. In *International Approaches to Rape*, eds. Nicole Westmarland and Geetanjali Gangoli, 101.
3. Id.
4. Despite the Muktadar Inquiry Commission finding Rameeza Bee to be an innocent victim of rape at Nallakunta Police Station, Hyderabad, and the eight policemen guilty of rape and/or murder, the policemen were acquitted by the Supreme Court here as well. http://shodhganga.inflibnet.ac.in/bitstream/10603/108969/8/08_chapter%202.pdf.
5. (1978) 2 SCC 424.

6. Das, V. 1996. Sexual Violence, Discursive Formations and the State. *Economic and Political Weekly* 31 (35–7): 2411–23.
7. 1977 CriLJ 556 5 1958 CriLJ 563 6 1971 (4) WLN 651.
8. 51958 CriLJ 563.
9. 1971 (4) WLN 651.
10. 1983 SCR (3) 280.
11. 2000 CriLJ 1793.
12. Agnes, Flavia. 1992. Protecting Women Against Violence? Review of a Decade of Legislation, 1980–89. *Economic and Political Weekly*.
13. http://lawcommissionofindia.nic.in/51-100/Report84.pdf.
14. Agnes, Flavia. 1992. Protecting Women Against Violence? Review of a Decade of Legislation, 1980–89. *Economic and Political Weekly*.
15. Baxi, Pratiksha. 2000. Rape, Retribution, State: On Whose Bodies? *EPW* 35 (14): 1196–1200.
16. Das, V. 1996. Sexual Violence, Discursive Formations and the State. *Economic and Political Weekly* 31 (35–7): 2411–23.
17. Id.
18. Kotiswaran, Prabha. 2017. A Bittersweet Moment: Indian Governance Feminism and the 2013 Rape Law Reforms. *EPW*.
19. Mitra, Durba, and Mrinal Satish. Testing Chastity, Evidencing Rape Impact of Medical Jurisprudence on Rape Adjudication in India, EPW Special Article. https://nludelhi.ac.in/UploadedImages/96d63f5d-9c23-4cb7-aeb6-43774da81992.pdf.
20. https://indconlawphil.wordpress.com/2018/09/10/guest-post-navtej-johar-v-union-of-india-what-remains-ofsection-377/.
21. Prabha Kotiswaran 2017.
22. https://www.prsindia.org/report-summaries/justice-verma-committee-report-summary.
23. https://www.researchgate.net/profile/Bula_Bhadra/publication/315812565_Rape_Law_Reforms_in_India_Catalyst_to_Gender_Justice_or_Modernization_in_Legal_Reforms/links/5a66f17e0f7e9b6b8fdf2727/Rape-LawReforms-in-India-Catalyst-to-Gender-Justice-or-Modernization-in-Legal-Reforms.pdf#page=369.
24. Agnes, Flavia. 2015. Section 498A, Marital Rape and Adverse Propaganda. *EPW* 50 (23).
25. http://nujslawreview.org/wp-content/uploads/2017/12/10-4-Editorial-Note-1.pdf.

26. Menon, N. 2019. The Gap Between the Feminist Understanding of Sexual Violence and the Law. *The Wire*, February 24, last accessed 21 February 2021.
27. https://www.livelaw.in/madras-hc-passes-order-permitting-person-convicted-of-rape-of-a-minor-to-settle-thematter-through-mediation/.
28. https://www.livelaw.in/madras-hc-passes-order-permitting-person-convicted-of-rape-of-a-minor-to-settle-thematter-through-mediation/.
29. (2005) 8 SCC 1.
30. (2012) 10 SCC 303.
31. 2013 (10) SCALE595.
32. https://www.livelaw.in/under-no-circumstances-a-rape-case-can-be-compromised-supreme-court/.
33. https://www.indiatoday.in/india/story/madras-high-court-controversial-order-on-rape-compromise-281872-2015-07-11.
34. https://www.sci.gov.in/supremecourt/2018/26627/26627_2018_Judgement_22-Nov-2018.pdf.
35. https://indiankanoon.org/doc/173826538/CrApp. 928/2015 Delhi High Court
36. Cri Appeal 449 of 2013 Bombay High Court.
37. https://www.livelaw.in/sc-acquits-men-accused-gang-rape/.
38. VikasGarg v. State of Haryana (Cr.M.No.23962 of 2017 in Cr.A.No.S-2396-SB of 2017), Karan v. State of Haryana (Cr.M.No.26910–11 of 2017 in Cr.A.No.D-653-DB of 2017), Hardik v. State of Haryana (Cr.M.No.26930 of 2017 in Cr.A.No.D-662 of 2017), 13.9.2017 (P&H HC).
39. Nigam, Shalu. From Mathura to Farooqui Rape Case: The Regressive Patriarchy Found Its Way Back. https://papers.ssrn.com/sol3/papers.cfm?abstract_id=3049756.
40. https://www.livelaw.in/jgls-gangrape-sc-slams-punjab-haryana-hc-order-suspending-sentence-accused/.
41. https://www.scconline.com/blog/post/2018/09/06/criminal-law-amendment-act-2018-salient-features/.
42. NCRB, Crime in India—1979, Chapter 10—Victims of Rape (1980). http://ncrb.gov.in/StatPublications/CII/CII1979/cii-1979/CHAPTER-10%20VICTIMS%20OF%20RAPE.pdf.
43. http://ncrb.gov.in/StatPublications/CII/CII2004/cii-2004/CHAP5.pdf.

44. http://ncrb.gov.in/StatPublications/CII/CII2013/Chapters/5-Crime%20against%20Women.pdf.
45. NCRB, Crime in India—2016 (2017).
46. https://www.bbc.com/news/world-asia-india-39265653.
47. Murthy, Laxmi. 2013, June 8. From Mathura to Bhanwari. *EPW* 48 (23).
48. https://www.epw.in/engage/article/aziz-ansari-mohammad-farooqui-and-the-dangerous-myth-of-a-right-wayto-resist.
49. http://ohrh.law.ox.ac.uk/farooqui-v-state-government-of-delhi-confusing-consent/.
50. https://blogs.dw.com/womentalkonline/2016/06/07/shrouded-under-a-veil-of-shame-sexual-harassment-atwork/.
51. https://thewire.in/women/jaipur-dignity-march-sexual-assault.
52. https://www.news18.com/news/india/how-the-online-boom-is-helping-dalits-reclaim-and-reassert-theiridentity-1643819.html.

INDEX

A
Abandonment, 200, 202–206, 210–212, 215, 216, 218, 219
Accredited professionalised NGOs, 41
ADB, 126
Agency, 50, 52, 53, 63, 65–67
Agion, 131
Agriculture, 141
All Bengal Women's Union (ABWU), 25, 27–30
Ariyawardana, 137
Arulrajah, J.A., 137
Autonomous groups, 37
Autonomous women's movements, 37
Autonomy, 229, 237, 240, 241
Ayadurai, S., 136

B
Bangladesh, 75–78, 83, 86, 90
Bangladeshi women, 188, 193
Barton, L., 135
Bharathamma, 135

Biographic narrative, 164
Boender, C., 128
Bombay Hindu Women's Rescue Home Society (BHRHS), 27, 30

C
Canadian International Development Agency, 126
Capabilities, 100, 103, 104, 116, 117, 119, 120
Capacity-building, 42
Census Report, 138
Child custody, 209
Child sexual abuse, 230
Chowdhury, M.J.A., 153
Chulangani, 137
Citizenship, 201, 208–210
City Corporation, 78
Civil society, 36, 51, 53, 55, 61, 66, 69
Civil society functionary, 3
Collateral, 128, 129, 137

250 INDEX

Colonial India, 18, 29, 30
Community-based organizations, 9, 120
Consent, 226–229, 232–234, 236–243
Constitution, 76–78
Credit scheme, 134
Criminalization of migrants, 195
Criminal Law Amendment Act, 2013, 233
Critical questioning, 36

D
Dahej Virodhi Chetna Manch, 37
Dependency, 44
Desert/ed, 202–207, 217
Development, 49–57, 59–61, 64, 66, 69
Development discourse, 1
Development-welfare-empowerment continuum, 3
Disempowerment, 45
District Council, 78
Divorce, 201, 203–205, 208–213, 217, 219, 220
Domestic affairs
  male involvement in, 2
Domestic violence, 200, 201, 204, 205, 216
  four accounts of, 4
Durga Vahini, 38

E
Economic empowerment, 153
Edgecomb, E., 135
Empowerment, 1
  definition of
    de-politicized, 2
    individualist, 2
    instrumental, 2
    vertical, 2

politics of, 39
Equity and Human Rights, 101
Ethnic groups, 110, 111, 113, 116, 117, 120

F
Family-community-society continuum, 4
Family involvement, 174, 176, 180
Feminism, 199
Feminist movement, 18, 225
Feminization of poverty, 2
Financial needs, 57
Financial services, 125, 126, 130, 131
Forced prostitution, 164
The Foreigners Act, 1946, 188, 190

G
Gaiha, R., 135
Gainful work, 3
Galappattige, A., 137
Gender, 49–51, 53, 56, 59, 61, 63–65, 67–69
  politics of, 37
Gender discrimination, 81, 88, 89
Gender inequities, 186
Gender neutrality, 230, 231, 234
Gender regimes
  five contexts of, 3
Global/Globalization, 202, 203, 208, 211, 215
Government intervention, 36

H
Hague Conference, 212
Haley, 136
Hasan, 134
Hashemi, 128
Hazardous contraceptives, 46
Home, 2

mental abuse, 2
physical abuse, 2
violence, 2
Hulme, 136
Human development, 99–101, 103, 104, 116, 118
Human services, 42

I
ICDS, 46
Immigrant/Émigré, 200, 203, 206, 209, 219
Indian legal discourses, 225
Indian women's organisations, 22, 24, 30
Insurance, 126, 130, 154
Intersectionality, 244
Ismailov, N., 152

J
Justice, 50, 51, 53, 63, 68

K
Kabeer, Naila, 4
Kennedy, F.B., 137
Khachatryan, K., 134
Khan, M.A., 131

L
Law-Enforcement/Police, 201
League of Nations, 23–26
Ledgerwood, J., 126
Left women's groups, 38
legal amendments, 242
Legalization of sex work, 164, 178
Legislative reforms, 75, 88
Liberalisation, 49
Littlefield, 128
Lived experiences, 165, 167, 169

Lived realities, 2
Local governance, 76–79, 81, 86–88

M
Maheswaranathan, S., 137
Malhotra, A., 128
Manavi, 200–202, 206, 215, 217
Market, 49–52, 60, 68, 69
Marriage with NRI Men, 219
Mathura, 225–227
Mental entitlement, 2
#MeToo, 233, 241, 242, 244
Michael, S., 126
Microcredit, 135, 139, 144, 153
Micro enterprise, 126
Micro finance, 55–58, 60, 61, 69, 136, 137, 139–144, 146–151, 153, 154
Microfinance institutions (MFIs), 44, 128, 130, 131, 134, 136, 137, 141, 142, 154
Ministry of Women and Child Development, 217
Morduch, 128, 131
Mosley, 136
Muslim Women's Act, 37
Mustafa, Z., 152

N
Naoko, I., 132
National Commission for Women, 40, 215, 217, 218
National Rural Employment Guarantee Scheme (NREGS), 46
National security, 195, 197
Neocolonial development model, 2
Neoliberal development model, 2
Nepali women/"Nepali virgins", 194
NGOisation, 50, 65, 66, 68
Nirbhaya, 239

Non-governmental organisations (NGOs), 17, 18, 29, 30, 49–55, 57, 59, 60, 62–70
non-resident Indian (NRI), 201–203, 205, 209, 210, 215–219
Noreen, S., 129

O
Organ transplantation, 186

P
The Palermo Protocol, 187
Passive beneficiary, 36
Patriarchal development model, 2
Patriarchy/Patriarchal, 200
  politics of, 47
  primacy of, 37
Perera, R., 168, 174, 176, 181
Philip, P.G., 137
Placement agencies, 168, 174, 176, 181
Platforms, 37
Policies, 90
Policy and Practical challenges, 97
Political empowerment, 54
Political establishment, 36
Politics of empowerment, 39
Politics of gender, 37
Politics of patriarchy, 47
Poor, 50, 53, 55–59, 61, 69
Poverty, 56–58, 60
Power imbalance, 81, 86, 88
Power relation
  five contexts of, 3
Pre and post-natal care, 103, 110
Premaratne, S.P., 136
Prostitution, 25–27, 186
Pushpakumara, W.P.N., 134
PWDVA-2005, 211

Q
Queer rights, 230

R
Rahaman, M.A., 131
Rahman, 152
Rape, 225–244
Rathiranee, Y., 153
Rehabilitative Support, 207
Repatriation, 189, 191
Reproductive health, 97–108, 110, 115–120
Rescue, rehabilitation and re-integration narrative, 164, 181
Reserved seats, 76, 78–89
Rohingya women, 192, 193
Role of NGOs, 102
Rural development, 136

S
Safe migration, 42
Sahay, 133
Schuler, S.R., 128
Secular women's movement, 38
Self-employment, 127, 128, 139, 140
Self-help group (SHG), 55–60, 63, 69, 70, 135
Self-reflexivity, 36
Sex-selective abortion, 46
Sexual assault, 230–233, 243
Sexual harassment, 84, 90
Sex work, 164, 178–181
SIKRITINAMA, 168, 175
Slave trade/White slave trade, 185, 186
Social empowerment, 153
Social engineering, 42
Socio-cultural taboos, 97
South Asia, 185
Standing Committees, 79, 81, 82, 89
State, 49–53, 55, 62, 64, 66–68

INDEX 253

Suppression of Immoral Traffic, 25
Suttee, 37
Swider, Paul, 135

T
Third sector, 49, 53, 67
Third world victim subject/silent female victim, 195
Tilakaratna, G., 137
Trafficked women, 164–167, 175, 179
Trafficked women's agency, 164, 180
Traffickers/Thikadars /Contractors, 164, 173
Trafficking, 24–26
Transnational logistical networks, 196
Transnational trafficking, 196

U
Undocumented migration, 195
UNFPA report, 127
Unpaid work, 3
Unusual suspects, 191

V
Verma Committee, 231, 232, 234, 235, 241
Village Courts (VC), 83, 93
Visaka Guidelines, 43
Voices of victims of trafficking, 164, 168, 183
Voluntary organisation, 37
Vulnerability, 52

W
Western and Indian feminist academics, 3
Women, 3, 17–30
  community managers, 3
  producers, 3
  reproducers, 3
Women's Action Network, 127
Women's development, 3
  hierarchy of five criteria, 3
  access, 3
  conscientization, 3
  control, 3
  participation, 3
  welfare, 3
Women's empowerment, 1, 49, 51, 52, 54, 55, 57, 59–61, 65, 66, 69, 125, 126, 128, 129, 132, 134, 143, 150, 151
  national policy on, 36
  three-dimensional model of
    macro-level, 2
    meso-level, 2
    micro-level, 2
Women's Leadership, 75
Women's lives
  multifaceted existential encounters of, 4
Women's material well-being, 2
Women's movement, 35
Women's vulnerability, 186
Workplace, 2
  mental abuse, 2
  physical abuse, 2
  violence, 2
Writings, 4

Printed in the United States
by Baker & Taylor Publisher Services